FINANCIAL REPRESSION AND ECONOMIC REFORM IN CHINA

FINANCIAL REPRESSION AND ECONOMIC REFORM IN CHINA

Kui-Wai Li

PRAEGER

Westport, Connecticut
London

Library of Congress Cataloging-in-Publication Data

Li, Kui-Wai.
    Financial repression and economic reform in China / Kui-Wai Li.
        p.   cm.
    Includes bibliographical references and index.
    ISBN 0-275-94801-3
    1. Finance—China. 2. China—Economic policy—1976-   I. Title.
    HG187.C6L44   1994
    332'.0951—dc20   93-50074

British Library Cataloguing in Publication Data is available.

Library of Congress Catalog Card Number: 93-50074
ISBN: 0-275-94801-3

First published in 1994

Praeger Publishers, 88 Post Road West, Westport, CT 06881
An imprint of Greenwood Publishing Group, Inc.

Printed in the United States of America

∞™

The paper used in this book complies with the
Permanent Paper Standard issued by the National
Information Standards Organization (Z39.48—1984).

10 9 8 7 6 5 4 3 2 1

Contents

Tables and Figures

TABLES

FIGURES

Preface

By 1989, the People's Republic of China had gone through her first decade of economic reform. There is no doubt that a considerable degree of economic achievement has been made; but equally there are various economic problems, such as inflation, shortages and huge imports, that have emerged. China was the first socialist country which had chosen the path of economic reform, and her experience will be a treasure not only to other socialist countries that are rapidly liberalizing their economies but also to China herself if she wants to further deepen her own reform achievements.

This book attempts to use a macroeconomic and financial framework in general and the financial development and repression theories in particular to examine China's performance in her first decade of reform. By reviewing China's statistical performance on income and consumption, money and banking, state budget and fiscal expenditures, savings and investment, foreign trade and investment, and prices and inflation, five components of financial repression can be identified. Various simple linear regressions are formulated and empirical results show that China is a financially repressed economy and that inflation is negatively correlated to consumption, while expectation and large money supply are the major causes of inflation. Among the various financial resources, foreign-direct investment, bank loans, and self-raised funds performed better in general, but budget expenditures performed most inefficiently.

There are two channels which can improve China's financial productivity. One is to relax the real interest rate ceiling so that unproductive investments are discouraged and at the same time free the financial resources for more productive investments. By doing this, output expands and the shortage problem can be eased; money growth decreases as state banks exercise a more prudent credit policy; and inflation and expectation fall, thereby making money a more attractive asset to hold. The other aspect is to fasten the development of the equity market. In the 1980s, equity market development in China had been slow and made very little impact on the economy. With the establishment of the Shanghai and Shenzhen stock markets in the early 1990s, equity trading is expected to play a more significant and leading role in financial liberalization. The advantage of a well-functioning equity market is that funds raised are managed by nonstate enterprises. Improvements in both the institutional mechanism and the equity market would surely exert positive impacts on each other.

Acknowledgments

This book is based on a doctoral thesis submitted to the Department of Banking and Finance, City University Business School, London. I would like to thank my thesis supervisor, Professor Zannis Res; the two external examiners, Professor John R. Presley and Dr. Kate Phylaktis; the State Information Centre in Beijing for releasing some of the Chinese quarterly data; the City Polytechnic of Hong Kong for providing me with the computing facilities; Mr. Winson S. C. Leung for his computing assistance; and most of all, my wife, Cecilia Kau Wah, for her constant and patient support. The views expressed in this book are entirely my responsibility.

FINANCIAL REPRESSION
AND ECONOMIC REFORM
IN CHINA

Introduction

The objective of this book is to examine, model, and estimate some of the important financial and macroeconomic relationships in China's first decade of economic reform (1978-1989). China is the first socialist country which opted for economic reform and liberalization. Its success or failure will have great impact on other liberalizing socialist countries. The Chinese experience offers an interesting case study in that it is characterized by rapid economic growth for a few years followed by economic overheating in the later years. The increase in economic growth in the early part of the 1980s resulted in rising income, standard of living, and consumption. The Chinese economy, however, reached full capacity and bottlenecks appeared in the mid-1980s. Inflation rose rapidly in 1984 and 1988, and gave rise to other problems such as speculation and hoarding of raw materials and consumer goods. Political unrest in 1989 temporarily cooled off the economy. By 1991, however, most developed countries resumed to provide loans and other financial assistance to China again. Economic reform speeded up again following Deng's visit to southern China in early 1992. Economic overheating in 1993 has led the Beijing authority to look for new solutions.

Various studies have been conducted on the Chinese economic reform, such as the introduction of the market mechanism, transaction cost and property rights, sectoral studies, trade and foreign investment, income and consumption changes, and price reform. To study the first decade of reform in China from a financial viewpoint offers a new dimension to existing literature. There are several advantages in using the financial approach. One is that financial developments have further implications on other aspects of the economy. Ultimately, it is the provision of financial resources that activate various sectors of the economy. Economic problems such as inflation and the supply of money are financial in nature, and a good use of financial resources can solve other economic problems. Second, given that China has recently completed her first decade of economic reform, data availability is limited. Analysis has to be kept simple on the one hand but has far-reaching implications on the other so that directions of future research work can be identified.

There are three theories in financial development. One advocates that capital market development is the major instrument of financial development. Financial resources can be exploited most efficiently under the ownership of free enterprises, and the market mechanism will regulate the allocation of financial resources. The issue of equities by private enterprises can improve financial efficiency. In China, although enterprises and the state started to issue bonds in 1984–1985, the development of an equity market was slow. It was not until 1990–1991, with the opening of the Shanghai and Shenzhen stock markets, that China's capital market became active.

The structural theory argues that financial development is associated with development in other aspects such as income distribution and wage increase. Structural models must cater to development in other sectors. These model constructions, however, soon become complicated and require much detailed data. Since structural models relate to so many aspects, problems cannot be easily identified and solutions may not be precise. In the case of the Chinese reform, the application of this theory is particularly difficult when data availability is limited.

The financial repression theory argues that money complements capital in the initial period of financial development. A positive real interest rate makes money an attractive asset to hold, while a negative real interest distorts the utilization of financial resources. The financial repression theory can suitably be applied to China. First, China has a long history of institutional setup, the only difference is whether these institutions and their practice are conducive to efficient allocation of financial resources. Second, given the short history of reform and the limited availability of data, the financial repression theory provides a framework to examine the productivity and efficiency of various financial resources.

The focus of this study is to look at both the development of the financial market and financial repression theories. Financial development in China can become efficient if recommendations from the two theories are taken up. A sound development in the private financial market helps to quicken the process of financial deepening. Due to data constraint, however, the empirical work employs extensively the financial repression theory. Quarterly data are used in the regression, though some are proxy quarterly data. This study is composed of six chapters. Chapter 1 is a review of the three theories in financial development. Chapter 2 is a statistical review, analyzing all the major macroeconomic, monetary, and financial performances in China's first decade of economic reform.

Statistical analysis is classified under income and consumption, money and banking, state budget and fiscal reform, savings and investment, foreign trade and investment, and prices and inflation. Between 1978 and 1989, the Chinese economy experienced three cycles of increase in income and consumption. Banking reform started in 1979 after a series of meetings of national bank leaders, but monetary growth was high in the 1980s. The fiscal budget has been in deficit constantly, and extrabudgetary figures are high. Together with state borrowing, China's budget is very "soft." High savings may be due to shortage in consumables, especially in the rural areas. Despite the inflow of foreign resources in the form of borrowing, investment, and export, China's import since 1985 has far exceeded its export ability, resulting in a nominal outflow of resources. Price reform applied to the final products was unable to curb inflation, and the official inflation figures are much lower than both "repressed" and "true" price inflation. The chapter concludes that China is a financially repressed economy. Growth in monetary and financial resources far exceed the growth in output, implying inefficiencies and distortion in the utilization of capital resources.

Chapter 3 looks at the development of the equity market and examines its applicability in the Chinese context. Despite the lack of development before 1989, the equity market offers a promising solution to efficient financial development in China. Equity market development and privatization of production enterprises permit a greater amount of financial capital raised in the private sector. Chapter 4 examines the financial repression theory and explains how the economy relates to the Chinese situation. An analytical framework with simple linear relationships is set up on financial repression, inflation and consumption, and financial productivity. The empirical results shown in Chapter 5 confirm that China is financially repressed. Inflation is caused mainly by expectation and is inversely related to real consumption. Efficiency differs among different types of financial resources. China has kept a low interest rate ceiling for many years, and it has detrimental impacts. Typically, it encourages inefficient investment and distorts financial efficiency. Institutionally, the Chinese authority should relax the interest rate and increase it gradually so that unproductive investments are discouraged on the one hand and more resources are redirected to productive investments on the other. The overall effect is an increase in output, which has other linkage effects such as a reduction in inflation and an improvement in fiscal deficits.

Development in the equity market and institutional revision on the interest rate form the basis of financial development in China. An efficient financial sector has positive linkage effects on other aspects of the economy. Major economic problems such as inflation and shortages can be controlled gradually. Price reform should start at the resource end, not the output end, which is what happened in the 1980s.

1

Financial Development Theories

FINANCIAL RESOURCES
AND ECONOMIC DEVELOPMENT

In economic development, financial resources mobilize all other resources. Expansion of industrial and agricultural output, for example, depends on the availability of financial funding or investment; and the size of investment depends not only on the availability of funds but also on the mechanism in which investment resources are raised. The mechanism and effectiveness of fund transfer from surplus-holding households to deficit-spending investors determine how funds are generated and used. The foreign sector is involved when there is not enough surplus generated domestically. Generation and transfer of financial resources determine the speed of economic development in the real sector. The efficient use of financial resources could provide insight into the development of other sectors in the economy.

Financial development, according to Drake (1980, p. 27), is defined as "the expansion and elaboration over time of the financial structure (institutions, instruments and activities)." Tobin (1969, 1974, 1978), and Tobin and Brainard (1977) have discussed the importance of the q ratio in the asset market and capital accumulation. The numerator of the q ratio is the market valuation of the physical asset (i.e., the going price in the market for exchanging existing assets), while the denominator is the replacement or reproduction cost of the same asset (i.e., the price in the market for newly produced commodities). Tobin (1969, p. 16) argues that the financial and real sides of the economy must be consistent because "the financial inputs to the real side must reproduce the assumed values of the real inputs to the financial side." For the economy as a whole, a normal equilibrium value for q is 1; namely, the market value of an asset is the same as its reproducible cost. Tobin and Brainard (1977, p. 238) argue that the value of q above 1 should stimulate investment – namely, market value is in excess of requirements for replacement – and a value of q below 1 discourages investment. In the case of an individual firm, Tobin and Brainard (1977, p. 243) reason that what matters in investment is the marginal value of q (the ratio of the increment of market valuation to the cost of the associated investment). The average value of q may be different from 1, but the crucial value of the marginal q is 1. A monopolistic firm will have an average q ratio higher than its marginal value. The difference is just the market's valuation of its monopoly profit.

Tobin (1978, p. 423) claims that the q ratio represents theoretically the comparison between the marginal efficiency of capital and the financial cost of capital. Inflationary expectations may not have any impact on q because expected inflation is fully reflected in nominal interest rate and discount factors, though it is equally likely that increase in expected inflation lowers the real interest rate on money and possibly raises q. The more crucial point is the comparison of earnings prospects and interest rates. Earnings prospects depend largely on the efficiency of the financial system. Tobin (1984) illustrates the four definitions of financial efficiency. The first is "information-arbitrage" efficiency. A market is considered to be efficient if it is impossible to gain from trading, except the insiders, because all the available information has been "discounted." The second definition which relates to an asset is "fundamental-valuation" efficiency. A financial asset is efficient if all future payments are reflected in the current valuation. "Full-insurance" efficiency concerns a system of financial markets in which all agents are insured against all future contingencies. The fourth definition, known as "functional" efficiency, relates to the economic functions of the financial industries such as the pooling of risks and the mobilization of saving for investments.

Financial efficiencies can be achieved by the efficient functioning of a capital market and bank intermediation. Typically, capital markets and financial intermediaries facilitate the transfer of funds from surplus companies and households to deficit companies and households. In the case of financial intermediaries, deregulations can remove many shortcomings and exert more competition into the financial system.

Goldsmith (1969, p. 44) examines the role and impact of the private equity market in economic development and believes that a country's financial superstructure grows more rapidly than the infrastructure of national product and wealth and that financial development is change in financial structure. Goldsmith (1969, p. 38) constructs the financial interrelations ratio (FIR) to reflect the basic feature in financial development. The FIR, defined as the quotient of the aggregate market value of all financial instruments in existence in a country at a given date to the value of its tangible net national wealth, has a tendency to increase in the course of economic development. A higher value of FIR implies that the net of financial interrelations in comparison to the size of national wealth or national product is high. The FIR can provide a good measure on the level of financial development reached. Goldsmith (1969, p. 45) argues that when FIR reaches between 1 and 1.5, the ratio tends to level off; but developing countries have a much lower FIR. The level and movement of the FIR reflects the extent to which investors need to resort to external finance through borrowing or through issuance of equity securities. In essence, the FIR shows the issue of debt and equity securities by the nonfinancial sectors of the economy to national product. The higher this ratio, the higher is the extent of separation between saving and capital formation. The FIR, therefore, is the broadest measure of the relative size of the financial superstructure and is strongly influenced at any given time by the path which the country has reached its current position relating to the price level, the rate of growth, and the size of new equity issues.

The degree of financial institutionalization is measured by the ratio of financial assets held by financial institutions to total financial assets. The higher this ratio, the greater is the extent of indirect finance. Goldsmith (1969) has identified three types of financial structures. Type A is recognized by a FIR below one half, by a predominance of fixed claims (loans, debentures, etc.) over equity assets, and by a small share of financial assets accounted for by financial institutions. Goldsmith (1969, p. 33) gave the example of Europe from the early eighteenth to the mid-nineteenth century. Type B resembles type A, but the additional feature is the existence of government financial institutions and activities. Most developing countries belong to this category. Type C is the example of industrialized countries in which both government and corporate enterprises are the major players in the financial market. Type C is characterized by a high FIR, a markedly high ratio of equities to claims, a higher share of financial institutions in total financial assets than are found in types A and B, and by diversified and specialized financial institutions other than banks. Goldsmith concludes that there is a common path of financial progress marked by uniform behavior of FIR, of the share of financial assets controlled by financial institutions, and of the importance of the banking system.

Drake (1980) argues that the positive correlation between levels of economic development and financial development can be explained in terms of the division of labor in three aspects. First, monetarization and the use of money have permitted the division of labor in production. Second, division of labor between saving and investment yields benefits in that investment can be based on borrowed funds. The introduction of financial instruments provides a bridge between surplus savers and deficit investors. The third aspect is the beneficial division of labor in the process of financial intermediation by institutions. The provision of better intermediary facilities promote increases in aggregate saving and investment. Drake (1980, p. 34) concludes that specialization and division of labor in production, savings, and investment and in intermediation go a long way to explain the association between financial development and real growth.

STRUCTURAL APPROACH

The structural approach states that the role of finance is important in economic development, but analysis has to go beyond financial variables to look at structural constraints. FitzGerald and Vos (1989, p. 27) point out that although "the structuralist approach is not easy to define because it is not given to 'pure' or 'high' theory," the structural approach contains three basic premises: (1) analysis has to go beyond the operation of economic agents and look into their behavior, which depends on the particular context of the institutions and production organization in which they operate; (2) analysis has to take into account market rigidities for reasons of different institutional behavior, market power, transaction costs such as imperfect information, and conflicts of interest (agency problems); and (3) endogenous structural rigidities and the process that drive institutional change should be analyzed simultaneously.

The "two-gap" analysis proposed by Chenery and Bruno (1962) and Chenery and Strout (1966) provides a simple version of the structural model. The two-gap analysis basically considers the inadequacy of foreign exchange and domestic savings as the two financial constraints in economic growth and states that economic growth proceeds at a rate permitted by the more limiting factor. Investment and saving tend to be the initial limit, but they are replaced by the trade gap as the binding constraint at a later stage of economic development. Gersovitz (1982) raises the time factor and argues that different constraints are binding at different times and that it is difficult to realize which constraint prevails. Thirlwall (1978, p. 295) summarizes the two-gap analysis by pointing out that growth can be self-sustaining if two conditions are satisfied: a rising marginal savings rate and a marginal rate of export rising faster than the marginal rate of imports, or export increasing at a faster rate than national income.

In the two-gap approach, foreign capital is assumed to complement domestic savings so that capital transfers increase investment and growth in developing countries. Numerous scholars have constructed macroeconomic models using the Chenery–Bruno–Strout two-gap analysis, including Diwan (1967), Fukuchi (1971), Cochrane (1972), Michalopoulos (1975), Blomqvist (1976), and Gunning (1983). Studies in relation to the various constraints on economic growth as discussed in the two-gap analysis include the works of Yamashita (1968), Griffin and Enos (1969), Weisskopf (1972), Aho (1973), Dacy (1975), Feder (1979), and Marquez (1985). The two-gap analysis was once popular in the 1960s when most developing countries were lacking import capacity and export earning was considered as supplement to domestic savings.

More recently, neostructuralists (van Wijnbergen 1982, 1983a, 1983b, 1985; Buffie 1984; Taylor 1983; FitzGerald and Vos 1989) have constructed more complicated frameworks. Van Wijnbergen (1982, 1983a, 1983b, 1985) studied Korea and observes that financial structure can influence the extent of financial repression and outcome of financial liberalization. In particular, the existence and operation of "curb markets" can make a crucial distinction in the outcome of any financial policy. Van Wijnbergen (1982) argues that the short-run effect of a higher time deposit rate is important in Korea. Time deposits are shown to be a closer substitute to curb market loans than to cash; and a higher time deposit rate may, in fact, lead to "financial shallowing" – namely, a decline in the ratio of the monetary base over the capital stock. An increase in time deposit rate raises the real curb market rate and slows down the growth rate. Van Wijnbergen's (1982) empirical results show a strong influence of the real curb market rate on savings: a strong positive impact of the curb market rate on saving reflects the dominance of substitution effect over income effect. With the existence of the curb market, firms will first try to get whatever bank financing they can. This makes rationing necessary and quantity the more relevant variable. Changes in the bank-lending rate under a system of rationed bank credit have no allocation impact. All they do is change a firm's cash flow position and the "scarcity premium" earned by those who managed to obtain rationed loans.

Taylor (1983) constructs an economy-wide structural model and incorporates other important behavior relationships such as income distribution and output levels. Taylor (1983) states two accounting balances which must be satisfied: the trade deficit (foreign savings) must equal investment minus national savings, and must equal the sum of imports (capital, intermediate, and consumer imports) and net investment payments on debt minus exports and other net current foreign exchange receipts. Three adjustment mechanisms (expansion of output, price changes, and demand variation) can be exercised when saving is not equal to the value of investment. By extending his analysis to a two-sector model, with price clearing in the agricultural and infrastructural sector and a quantity clearing in the industrial sector, Taylor (1983) considers the absorption problem in the real side of the economy. Financial markets are introduced into the model at a later stage. Contrary to the monetarists' view, Taylor (1983, p. 10) argues that monetary contraction can be inflationary in the short run because it raises the interest rate and cuts loans available for output expansion. In the long run, a slower money growth can lead to faster inflation, a lower growth rate of output, and a more unequal income distribution.

FitzGerald and Vos (1989, p. 33) criticize the two-gap approach. First, foreign capital is used to finance consumption, and second, changes in the sectoral balances of the economy as a result of capital inflows lead to changes in domestic relative prices. However, FitzGerald and Vos (1989, p. 28) defend the lack of market force in the structural approach by arguing that "markets work in structured ways quite different from that which neoclassical theory suggests and that state intervention of some kind is required for any market to function at all." A major problem with the structural approach is its complexity. For example, by using the Indian economy, Taylor (1983, pp. 66–67) has constructed five sectors, twenty-three endogenous and thirty-six exogenous variables, fifteen parameters, and three initial values. One has to be critical regarding the amount and availability of accurate information. The degree and extent of complexity makes the analysis difficult, if not impossible. Furthermore, the analysis becomes country-specific rather than providing a comprehensive body of knowledge applicable to different economies.

FINANCIAL REPRESSION THEORY

Financial repression advocates examine the institutional impact of financial development and believe that financial resources are the single most powerful form of resource that can mobilize activities of all sectors. Activities in the financial sector are most crucial in giving indications on how other aspects of the economy develop. The financial approach arises largely due to the inadequacy of the Keynesian economics in explaining economic situations in developing countries. Gurley and Shaw (1955, p. 524) specify that the Keynesian model is inappropriate to financial aspects of growth for three reasons: it does not permit direct debt to accumulate; it admits only two kinds of financial assets; and it has overlooked the development of financial intermediaries other than commercial banking. Gurley and Shaw (1955, 1960) propose a theory of interest and income which allows for debt accumulation and for the growth of nonmonetary financial intermediaries. Financial intermediaries create a shifting pattern of deficits and surpluses in the growth process.

In a neoclassical economy, an increase in demand for real stock of money reduces investment. McKinnon (1973) argues that money and real capital are complementary in developing countries: a rise in the average rate of return to real capital increases desired real cash balance holdings because the rise is associated with an increase in the investment/ income ratio. Money is seen as a conduit through which accumulation takes place. The demand for money rises with the increased productivity of real capital. The "conduit" effect dominates in the initial period of development beyond which the neoclassical substitution effect has a greater influence on the investment function. McKinnon (1973) observes that less developed countries suffer from "financial repression," a situation in which investment opportunities are lost and economic development could not take place as a result of a weak and inefficient financial sector.

Shaw (1973) postulates a situation of "shallow" finance, defined as a situation in which the distortion of financial prices, commonly through a government-imposed interest ceiling below the market equilibrium rate, would reduce real growth and size of the financial system. Shaw (1973, p. 5) summarizes his argument as follows: "Where finance is shallow, in relation to national income or non-financial wealth, one finds that it bears low, often negative real rates of return, and holders of financial assets including money are not rewarded for real growth in their portfolios." With "shallow" finance, a country must depend heavily on its government fiscal budget and on its international capital account for savings to finance capital growth.

Financial repression is defined to entail artificially low deposit and loan rates that give rise to excess demand for loans and to nonprice credit rationing (McKinnon 1973, Chap. 7; Shaw 1973, Chap. 4). McKinnon and Mathieson (1981, pp. 3–7) describe four characteristics of a financially repressed economy as follows: (1) the domestic financial system is usually insulated by exchange controls on the capital account of the balance of payments; (2) open markets for primary securities are usually insignificant, and the monetary system plays an important role as an intermediary between savers and investors; (3) governments feel constrained in the amount of revenue they can raise from conventional sources to support desired levels of expenditure on both current and capital accounts; and (4) under a low-interest-rate regime, authorities are allowed to give credit subsidies to preferred claimants, and if sufficient resources cannot be mobilized at a stable price level to cover these explicit and implicit deficits in the public finances, inflation develops and interacts with reserve requirements. Two unfavorable con-

12 *Financial Repression and Economic Reform in China*

sequences can be isolated: one is the reduction in the monetary base and the flow of loanable funds in the economy, and the other is that investors favored by the official agencies may borrow at negative real rates that often promote investment projects of a poor quality, whereas other potential borrowers with high-yield projects are severely rationed.

The complementarity hypothesis between money and physical capital in the McKinnon (1973) framework can be seen from his construction of the demand for money and investment functions:

$$(M/P) = f_1(Y/P, I/Y, d-i^*)$$

$$I/Y = f_2(c, d-i^*)$$

where M is the money stock, P is the price level, M/P is the real money stock, Y is the GNP and Y/P is the real GNP, I/Y is the ratio of gross investment to GNP, d is the deposit rate, i^* is the inflation rate, $d-i^*$ is the real deposit rate of interest, and c is the average return to physical capital. The complementarity hypothesis is shown by two partial derivatives:

$$\delta(M/P)/\delta(I/Y) > 0; \ \delta(I/Y)/\delta(d-i^*) > 0$$

McKinnon's (1973) conduit effect emphasizes the *indirect* link with the real interest rate $(d-i^*)$ influencing the stock of money (M/P), and the latter in turn affects the investment/output ratio (I/Y). The desire to hold money depends on the real return: a positive real return can raise investment-saving propensities because of the importance of money as a store of value. If the attractiveness of holding money is high, the partial derivative of the real return variable $(d-i^*)$ should be large and positive, namely

$$\delta(M/P)/\delta(d-i^*) > 0$$

If domestic saving (S) is assumed to equal domestically financed investment, McKinnon's (1973) demand-for-money function can be modified by replacing I/Y with S/Y. Shaw (1973) proposes the Debt Intermediation View (DIV) which looks at the income effect of money and real capital generated from a reduction in transaction and information costs. His demand for money function is

$$(M/P) = f_3(Y/P, v, d-i^*)$$

where v is a vector of opportunity cost of holding money in real terms. Shaw (1973) expects real yields on all forms of wealth, including money, to have a positive effect on the domestic savings ratio. On the contrary, financial intermediation is repressed when interest rates are fixed administratively below equilibrium levels.

Both McKinnon (1973) and Shaw (1973) recognize the crucial significance of real balances. The idea is that in order to induce the public to hold more real balances, the real return on money $(d-i*)$ must remain positive. This can be done by raising the nominal deposit rate, d, or keeping a low inflation rate, $i*$. The McKinnon–Shaw solution is financial liberalization and deepening, which will enable real saving to increase and the rate of income growth to rise because savings are being transformed into productive investment. Specifically, McKinnon's (1973) remedy considers the quality rather than the quantity of investment and includes (1) the relaxation of internal financial constraints; (2) the exercise of an effective fiscal policy; (3) the exploitation of the complementarity between the real money value and investment; and (4) a radical restructuring of tariff, quota, and licensing restraints on foreign trade. Shaw (1973) gives a similar solution which consists of (1) an accelerated growth in "real" assets and an increase in the real size of the monetary system so that it generates opportunities for the profitable operation of other institutions as well; (2) the specialization in financial functions and institutions; and (3) a high interest rate which reflects more accurately the available investment opportunities.

Numerous scholars have employed the McKinnon–Shaw financial repression hypothesis to analyze financial development in developing countries. Viksnins (1980, p. 10) defines five types of financial repression and argues that financial repression usually arises as a result of inflationary monetary and fiscal policies being carried out by government in the form of direct manipulation of credit flows to various sectors and regions; control over interest rates and foreign exchange flows, price ceilings, and floors; and so on. Harris (1979) attempts to incorporate financial repression with the two-gap analysis and finds that credit is the binding constraint on capital formulation. Schworm (1980) uses the theory of intertemporal optimization to analyze financial constraints and the accumulation of capital. McKinnon (1984) extends his own analysis to include the international capital markets. Moore (1986) investigates the effect of inflation on the degree of financial deepening which a country tries to attain. Jao (1976, 1980, 1985) tests and confirms the hypothesis that growth in real balance is positively related to growth in real output, sets out ten indicators of financial repression, summarizes many of the empirical estimations over the 1970s and early 1980s, and concludes that there seems to be considerable evidence in favor of the McKinnon–Shaw hypothesis. However, he points out that there are limitations; for example, most studies concentrate on the effects of financial deepening on saving propensity and investment ratio. The links between the saving-investment and real economic growth are assumed, though, and most studies use relatively small samples. Fry (1988) elaborates the works contributed by other scholars and analyzes the econometric testings on financial development.

The financial market approach can be incorporated into the discussion of the financial repression model. Private funds raised in the financial market can help to deepen the economy, as compared to state funds, for example. The financial repression theory basically suggests that given the various sources of financial capital, real money balances – the most likely form of investment return – increase as investment return rises. Capital market can be studied along with other financial resources stated in the financial repression theory.

FINANCIAL REPRESSION MODELS

Table 1.1 shows the major features of the six models, all of which are based on the McKinnon–Shaw financial repression framework.

Galbis (1979a, 1979b, 1982) considers interest rate policies in developing countries and shows that financial intermediation produces an efficiency effect that increases per capita income. By choosing a two-sector (advanced and backward) model, Galbis (1979a, 1979b, 1982) argues that reallocation of financial resources raises the overall rate of economic growth. Two consequences will occur if circumstances prevent the real rate of interest to rise to its equilibrium level. First, a low rate will discourage transfer of resources from the backward to the advanced sector, and second, disequilibrium between supply and demand for investable resources will result in financial instability. The solution recommended by Galbis (1982, p. 151) is that "interest rate should be raised to the level of the expected rate of inflation to attract enough financial savings in real terms to eliminate the initial excess demand for funds, so that the growth of outside financed investment can be sustained."

By using simple regression analysis on money and interest, inflation and depreciation, savings, and demand for money, Fry (1978a, 1978b, 1982) examines the experience of the Economic and Social Commission for Asia and the Pacific (ESCAP) countries and finds that excess demand for funds leading to nonprice rationing results in economic distortion. Relaxing interest rate ceilings would increase the average efficiency of investment and the level of income. Fry (1978a, p. 94) points out various contradictions of a selective credit policy: (1) it encourages low-yielding investment through interest rate subsidies; (2) it involves an upside-down term structure of interest rates for loans; (3) it frequently inverts deposit and loan rates; (4) interest rate subsidies distort factor prices resulting in labor relatively more expensive to capital; and (5) it provides precisely the wrong signals to institutional

Table 1.1
Summary of Six Financial Repression Models

Author(s)	Model	Features and Findings
Galbis (1979a, 1979b, 1982)	Resource Transfer	Sectoral transfer of financial resources raises the overall rate of economic growth. Increased financial intermediation produces an efficiency effect on income.
Fry (1978a, 1978b, 1982)	Investment Efficiency	Interest rate ceilings discourage risk taking by financial institutions. Relaxation of nonprice rationing of investable funds raises investment efficiency.
Mathieson (1979, 1980)	Two-Phase	Integrate financial reform with stabilization policy consisting of two phases and specify four key relationships in a stabilization program.
Newlyn and Avramides (Newlyn, ed. 1977, pp. 146-206)	Simulation	Financial intermediation undergoes three separate stages, along with the development of financial markets.
Gupta (1984)	Finance and Growth	Causality tests show that economic growth is the result of financial development.
Molho (1986)	Life-Cycle	A three-period model with multiple assets shows that any theory of saving behavior in financially repressed economies should also take into account the investment motive.

Sources: Galbis, Vincente. 1979a. Inflation and Interest Rate Policies in Latin America 1967-76, *IMF Staff Papers* 26(2):334-336; Galbis, Vincente. 1979b. Money Investment, and Growth in Latin America, 1961-1973, *Economic Development and Cultural Change* 27(3):423-443; Galbis, Vincente. 1982. Analytical Aspects of Interest Rate Policies in Less Developed Countries, *Savings and Development* 6(2):111-165; Fry, Maxwell J. 1978a. Monetary Policy and Domestic Saving in Developing ESCAP Countries, *Economic Bulletin for Asia and the Pacific* 29(1):79-99; Fry, Maxwell J. 1978b. Money and Capital or Financial Deepening in Economic Development, *Journal of Money, Credit and Banking* 10(4):464-475; Fry, Maxwell J. 1982. Models of Financially Repressed Developing Economies, *World Development* 10(9):731-750; Mathieson, Donald J. 1979. Financial Reform and Capital Flows in a Developing Economy, *IMF Staff Papers* 26:450-489; Mathieson, Donald J. 1980. Financial Reform and Stabilization Policy in a Developing Economy, *Journal of Development Economics* 7:359-395; Newlyn, Walter T., ed. 1977. *The Financing of Economic Development,* Oxford: Claredon Press; Gupta, Kanhaya L. 1984. *Financial and Economic Growth,* London: Croom Helm; Molho, Lazaros E. 1986. Life Cycle, Individual Thrift, and the Wealth of Nations, *American Economic Review* 76(3):297-313.

lenders and institutional finance becomes even less accessible. Fry (1978a) recommends a process of interest rate reform. The abolition of both deposit and loan rate ceilings increases real domestic credit and the average efficiency of investment because the higher rate reduces the demand for investable funds by those with the lower-yielding investment projects. The consequence is a rise in the output/capital ratio. Three impacts can be identified: (1) the currency/deposit ratio falls as substitution takes place from currency whose return remains unchanged into deposits whose return has increased, the result being a larger money multiplier and money stock; (2) a change in the composition of saving occurs because deposits have become more attractive, increasing the supply of goods, including investment goods; (3) increases in saving rate leads to a fall in demand. These latter two impacts can be contractionary but must be weighted against the expansionary effect of a fall in the currency/deposit ratio.

Mathieson (1979, 1980) assumes a labor-surplus economy and considers problems arising from the removal of nominal interest rate ceilings. He highlights the linkage between economic performance and financial markets distortions and then sets out to focus on specifying the relationship between the financial system, capital formation, and price expectations as they impinge on the inflation and growth process. A two-phase model is used. The initial phase is characterized by an increase in the deposit and loan rate and a rate of monetary expansion consistent with long-run desired rate of inflation. The second phase involves changes in three policy instruments: (1) the deposit rate moves in line with the expected rate of inflation; (2) the lending rate must change more rapidly than the expected rate of inflation; and (3) the rate of monetary expansion must be increased in line with the long-run desired rate of inflation. Mathieson (1980) raises the possibility where complete interest decontrol leads to widespread bankruptcies in the financial system and recommends that a program of interest decontrol should ultimately allow the authorities to eliminate financial market distortions that will remove the threat of financial bankruptcies.

Mathematical models have been constructed to explain financial repression. Kapur (1986a) constructs a ten-equation model to show financial dualism and repression. However, simulation models offer a simple and more applied approach. Newlyn and Avramides (Newlyn, ed. 1977, pp. 146–206) develop an economy-wide simulation model to study the effects of domestic credit expansion, fiscal transfers, and external resource flow. Based on the experience of fifteen developing countries, a set of nine financial equations and eighteen identities are constructed. The equations specify financial relationships while the identities show the interrelated indirect effects. In addition, monetary parameters such as the money multiplier, income velocity, and international reserves are employed to examine the extent of financial intermediation. Newlyn and Avramides (Newlyn, ed. 1977) classify their regression results under three headings: external factors, fiscal effects, and monetary effects. Export multiplier finances export growth and raises reserves. Increases in export can activate private investment. In the case of fiscal effects, there is no adverse direct effect of the tax rate on private investment, and government expenditure on infrastructure is complementary to private investment. Two conclusions are derived from the monetary effects: financial intermediaries in the formal sector determine the supply of finance at the administered rates, and the supply of money is determined by external and domestic transactions and the money multiplier.

In Gupta's (1984) finance and growth model in which causality tests show that economic growth is the result of financial development, he identifies the effects of financial liberalization on financial deepening, savings, saving structure, and capital formation. Nine financial equations and six identities grouped into three blocks are constructed. The empirical tests are based on twenty-five Asian and Latin American countries. Three simulation experiments are conducted to look at the implication of financial liberalization. The results show that households in developing countries prefer real to financial assets. Gupta (1984, p. 208) concludes that the long-term equlibrium effects of financial liberalization are sensitive to the inflationary environment of an economy and to the particular policy adopted.

A three-period life-cycle model of consumption and saving is constructed by Molho (1986). The model allows the study of the effects of deposit rate changes under various circumstances, such as self-finance and external finance, and features multiple assets so that the study of the complementarity hypothesis can be made. The impacts of substitution and income effects are compared within the complementarity framework. Molho's findings highlighted three important aspects of the saving–investment process in financially repressed economies: (1) interest rates affect individual asset holders' decision with lags; (2) external financial possibilities at the aggregate level are closely related to saving flows and are affected by interest rates as a result; (3) savings and investment decisions are intimately related and can be viewed as different stages of the same process.

Each of the six models has helped to strengthen the financial repression paradigm. One consensus is that financial deepening can facilitate economic growth considerably. The major elements in financial deepening are a positive real interest rate, the emphasis on qualitative investment activities, monetary expansion in line with the expected rate of inflation, a financial structure inducive to promote development, and above all, a freer hand given to the private sector in conducting financial matters. In many ways, these financial repression models have specified various conditions under which financial deepening can be achieved. Different models, however, suggest different paths to achieve financial deepening.

RECENT DEVELOPMENTS
AND RELEVANCE TO CHINA

The financial repression theory is not free from criticisms. Jansen (1989b) criticizes it from the structural viewpoint, raises some interesting questions between financial development and the structure of economic growth, and argues that activities of self-employed households in the agricultural sector have links with the unregulated money market and that the pursuit of social efficiency imposes severe constraint on financial liberalization. Jansen concludes that with the expansion of the official financial system, the overall impact on resource allocation is uncertain and that it is likely that financial development shifts resources from the sector of small household firms to the sector of large-scale corporations.

Diaz-Alejandro (1985) shows from his study of Latin American countries that financial liberalization often results in financial crash and distress. Snowden (1987) criticizes the incidence of an interest rate rising toward market-clearing levels and raises the question of who must pay for the higher financial cost. Dornbusch and Reynoso (1989) remark that "the financial repression paradigm in some ways seems like supply side economics — a kernel of truth and a vast exaggeration." They comment and criticize each of the five key elements in the paradigm. First, the positive real deposit rates that promote saving is ambiguous when both the income and substitution effects are considered. Second, the correlation of growth and financial deepening is not tight when a cross section of eighty-four developing countries are considered. Third, the argument that a higher real deposit rate raises investment is difficult to pin down. (McKinnon's [1973] complementarity effect is not different from the direct effect of real interest rate on saving.) Fourth, there are two additional channels that can be considered in case the increased real deposit rates promote growth. One is the availability of external resources, and the other is the quality of investment. Last, Dornbusch and Reynoso question the impact of increased real interest rates on the efficiency of investment and support instead a different proposition that deficit finance is a hazardous means for promoting growth.

McKinnon (1973) and Shaw (1973) specify the problems of financial repression and recommend various financial policies, but their success depends largely on the process itself. Despite the few criticisms of the financial repression paradigm, the work of various scholars clearly illustrates the point that the decision of any government to liberalize their financial sector could only be regarded as the beginning. The process of financial liberalization has several dimensions: the effective use of financial variables, complementarity between financial and economic variables, the time frame, and the existing financial structure. Complications arising from any of these dimensions will impose constraints on the process and lead to unwanted results.

The financial repression paradigm continues to provide a useful framework. Both the Asian Development Bank (ADB) reports (1984, 1985) and the World Bank's *World Development Report 1989* deal with the importance of domestic resource mobilization and financial development. The ADB reports reiterate the importance of expanding the size and efficient use of domestic financial resources, while the *World Development Report 1989* applies financial development concepts to a range of developing economies and asserts that finance is the key to investment and hence to growth and that a financial system's contribution to the economy depends on the quantity and quality of its services and the efficiency with which it provides them.

Indeed, the outcome of financial development concepts as specified by the McKinnon–Shaw hypothesis depends largely on the process of implementation. Fry (1989a) argues that the two prerequisites for successful financial liberalization are macroeconomic stability and adequate prudential supervision of the banking sector. Fry (1991) further specifies four policy conclusions of domestic resource mobilization: (1) measures to reduce government deficits, (2) reduction in population growth, (3) remove institutional interest rate ceilings, and (4) encourage foreign-direct investment as an alternative source of foreign capital to government guaranteed foreign debt.

Recently, the financial repression paradigm has been extended to the analysis of financial and economic reforms in socialist countries. The role of the fiscal expenditure, the banking structure, the saving–investment relationships, the use of foreign resources, and enterprise profits are a few major financial problems in the process of financial liberalization and economic decentralization. McKinnon (1991b) points out that economic liberalization involving the dismantling of central planning, decontrol of prices, privatization of property, and free foreign trade requires a proper sequence of fiscal, monetary, and foreign exchange measures. Furthermore, financial sector reform studies have been conducted by Blejer and Sagari (1991) in the case of Hungary, and Byrd (1983) and Tam (1986, 1987, 1988) in the case of the People's Republic of China (PRC). Byrd (1983, p. 76) argues that the most common features of financial repression have been absent in China, while Tam (1988, p. 60) observes that financial repression in the McKinnon–Shaw sense was "untenable" under China's prereform conditions and ideology, but since economic levers have been applied to the management of the economy since 1979, Tam (1987, p. 99) argues that "the condition for a process of financial deepening in the McKinnon–Shaw sense are being created."

Both Byrd (1983) and Tam (1987, 1988), however, have come to a wrong conclusion. By using a two-equation model, incorporating both the financial conditions of the two-gap model and McKinnon's (1973) idea of complementarity between money and capital, this author (Li 1992b) concludes that the Chinese economy since the early 1950s has experienced financial repression. Conditions of financial repression specified in other empirical works can equally be found in China. The difference is a matter of degree. For example, interest rate ceilings can also be extended to other price ceilings. Private investment in McKinnon's (1973) assumption can be extended to investment carried out by public enterprises in China, since they are the largest group of institutions in China conducting investment activities. Another major difference in the case of China is not so much the question of financial resource constraint. Its efficient use has been ignored. Components of financial repression in China elaborated in the following chapters include a low marginal productivity of loans, large monetary growth, a "soft" budget policy, foreign resource "outflow," and high inflation.

Although the capital market has not developed before 1989, rapid development since 1990 shows that the potential benefits of capital market development in the future can help China to deepen her reform considerably. The financial repression model is the most suitable framework for studying China's economic reform. There are advantages of using the financial repression paradigm to analyze China's reform. First, it requires less data as fewer economic variables are involved. The availability of Chinese data has been a heated issue in academic cycles. Lee Travers (1982) points out that the "typical example investigation" survey technique in China can generate substantial bias in statistics and that it is impossible to make probabilistic assertions about the accuracy of the sample. Second, the financial repression paradigm is simple, and financial resources are the most important factor of production that can mobilize all other factors. A good understanding of China's financial performance can help to clarify activities in other sectors. In addition, finanical liberalization and deepening requires institutional deregulations.

In China's first decade of economic reform, one can identify various sources of financial capital. The state budget still plays an important role in the supply of investment funds. Bank loans are another major domestic source of capital. Self-raised funds, composed mainly of bonds issued by enterprises, began to grow in the mid-1980s. Foreign-direct investment, together with foreign borrowing and foreign loans, form the external source of capital. The data of these various sources of financial capital suggest that China is not short of funds for reform and economic development. The more relevant question is the productivity of these financial resources. There is a link between the availability of financial resources and investment productivity and between investment productivity and output growth.

The financial repression theory is relevant in providing conditions upon which financial resources are geared to productive investment. In China, like other developing countries, money is the most popular form of nonphysical assets people hold. Investment returns are measured in monetary forms. The complementarity of money and capital implies that investment return is reflected in the holding of monetary asset. Financial liberalization provides a solution to ensure that financial resources will not be given to unproductive investment. Among the various conditions suggested in financial repression models, the positive interest rate seems to be the most useful mechanism. Typically, it is thought that a low interest rate would reduce the cost of investment and that a rise in investment leads to higher output. A distinction needs to be made between productive and unproductive investment. If public enterprises need not account for financial losses, however, a low level of interest rate can increase unproductive investment at the expense of productive investment.

The argument should be reversed. A positive and high interest rate implies a high opportunity cost to invest. This will not deter productive investment as long as the rate of return exceeds the interest cost but will discourage unproductive investment. A positive and high interest rate can reverse the situation by screening out only the productive investment. Output will rise as more resources are devoted to productive investment activities. The relationship between financial resources and output can be shown as follows:

Financial resources $\rightarrow$ Positive interest rate $\rightarrow$ Productive investment $\rightarrow$ Output expansion

The experience of China's first decade of reform shows that there was not a shortage of financial resources but that the efficiency and productivity of financial resources seem to be the limiting factor.

CONCLUSION

Studies in financial development are well established. The structural approach suffers from its complexity, while the financial repression approach gains from its ability in concentrating on financial variables which helps to understand economic development in other areas. Recommendations in the structural approach are less clear-cut; the two conditions specified in Chenery and Strout's (1966) two-gap analysis are financial in nature. The basic message of the two financial theories is clear: that a sound financial framework is a prerequisite for any genuine financial development and growth and that the development of the capital market can free more financial resources in the hands of private individuals, while severe government intervention in financial development will only lead to a destructive effect on economic growth.

Policy recommendations have been proposed by many scholars. Financial repression advocates, represented by Galbis (1982) and Fry (1978a, 1978b, 1982), recommend the use of a positive real interest rate in eliminating unproductive investments, while Mathieson (1979, 1980) proposes a two-phase model. Recent changes in socialist economies have opened up new horizons for researchers to study financial development in relation to their economic reforms. The experience of economic reform in China offers a good case of financial development in promoting growth. The injection of additional resources in the economy may not lead to output growth if the financial resources are used up by unproductive investment activities. A crucial factor is the role of the interest rate. The belief that a low interest rate could stimulate investment has to be qualified with the consideration of investment productivity.

The decision of any government to liberalize their financial sector should only be regarded as the first step. To see to the success of it has to depend crucially on the process in which liberalization is conducted. There are several dimensions to the process of liberalization, and distortion in any dimension can lead to unwanted results. The special characteristics of any economy may also call for different processes. With her financial rigidities on the one hand and vague policy instruments on the other, China's first decade of economic reform has exhibited features which are typical in a financially repressed economy.

2

Macroeconomic and
Financial Performances

THE SETTING OF ECONOMIC REFORM

Economic reform in China began with Deng Xiaoping's famous remark in 1978 that "It does not matter if the cat is white or black, so long as it catches mice." Deng considers economic development as a parallel to politics, and the aim of political work is to guarantee the success of economic achievements. A process of economic reform was initiated at the party's third plenary session in late 1978 within the framework of "readjustment, restructuring, consolidation and improvement." Readjustment refers to the removal of imbalances between heavy and light industries, agriculture and industry, current production and basic construction, and investment and consumption. Restructuring aims to reform the economy from a centralized, bureaucratic planning system to a decentralized and market-oriented system.

There are various economic imbalances in China at the time of the reform (see Dong 1982, 1990; Xue 1982). They include (1) an excessive accumulation of national income at the expense of consumption; (2) an excessive emphasis on industry at the expense of agriculture; (3) an excessive emphasis on heavy industry and the neglect of light industry; (4) an overemphasis on secondary sector investment at the expense of tertiary sector investment; and finally (5) within the category of secondary sector investment, a lack of investment in energy and infrastructure. The World Bank Country Study (1983 Vol. I, p. 81) reports that for 1977–1979 about 20 percent of total fixed investment has gone into agriculture and about 55 percent into industry, of which 80 percent has been earmarked for heavy industry. Furthermore, the average return to investment has always been lower in industry than in agriculture. Excessive inventory investment and the misallocation and inefficient use of fixed investment within broad sectors are the causes of low efficiency in investment in China.[1]

The structure of five-year plans requires detailed planning at lower administrative levels. There are several problems resulting from the planned system. First, regional and sectoral self-sufficiency reduces the chance of trade and specialization opportunities. Second, enterprises tend to understate their true productive potentials and overstate input needs to make planned targets easier to attain. Third, the number of decisions required is huge, and it is impossible to determine all the decisions centrally. Shortages and surpluses of commodities and resources exist simultaneously. Hoarding of inputs due to uncertain supplies exacerbates shortages further. Nolan and Dong (1990, p. 4) report that by the late 1970s, approximately 26 percent of industrial output production in China was concentrated in a few large plants; 18 percent was produced by medium-sized plants; and 56 percent was produced in small-scale, mainly urban and state-run plants. Liu (1979) and Liu and Zhao (1982) have correctly summarized the defects of the central planning system as a structure which puts the national economy in a straitjacket; discourages initiatives in all sectors; causes serious waste of manpower, materials, and capital; and greatly hampers the productivity of the economy.

This chapter examines the macroeconomic and financial performance in the first decade of economic reform in China. The following sections show in detail China's performances in income and consumption, money and banking, state budget and fiscal reform, savings and investment, foreign investment, and price and inflation. The chapter concludes that there was a large supply of financial resources in the first decade of reform but that output growth did not experience the same magnitude, probably because of various inefficient practices and financial distortions. China is a financially repressed economy. Solutions should be focused in the promotion of financial instruments, system, and practice. The development of an equity market can help to channel investments to the nonstate sector, while the relaxation of the low-interest-rate ceiling can promote output and help China to overcome other financial and economic difficulties.

INCOME AND CONSUMPTION

The Third Plenary Session of the 11th Central Committee that met in 1978 agreed to begin economic reform initially in the rural sector. The various forms of "responsibility systems" introduced in 1978–1979 were geared to promote rural prosperity.[2] The growth of income began to accelerate in the rural sector. In the early 1980s, the average real annual growth rate of agricultural output was close to 10 percent.[3] The essence of the responsibility system is that peasant households have the sole responsibility for agricultural production given certain contractual obligations to the collective or to the individuals from whom peasant households have subcontracted the land, and earnings are based on the production raised on the land. The responsibility system has also been experimented by some state farms in the early 1980s, and reports of "wanyuan hu" (rural households with earnings up to Rmb 10,000) soon spread to different parts of the country, especially the coastal region.[4]

In the industrial sector, emphasis in the prereform years is given to investment in heavy industries at the expense of light and consumer industries. Premier Zhao Ziyang's speech on the "Ten Principles" in 1981 had called for a shift in the pattern of resource allocation from investment to consumption and from producer goods to consumer goods. This effectively meant slashing heavy industrial output targets. The average annual growth rate of heavy industry has declined from 13 percent in 1953–1978 to 10 percent in 1978–1987, while the corresponding figures for light industry in the same periods have increased from 8.7 percent to 14.1 percent.[5] The overall impact is significant on both demand and supply. On the demand side, the income elasticity of demand for light industrial output is definitely higher, and the expansion of income has enlarged the purchasing power. Both income and consumption have grown as a result. On the supply side, the production of light industrial inputs from agriculture has grown rapidly. Furthermore, capacity shift from heavy to light industries has led to an expansion of capital productivity. Nolan and Dong (1990, p. 18) point out that the main contributions to improved capital productivity include (1) an acceleration in real agricultural output growth; (2) the rapid expansion of output and employment in labor-intensive nonfarm activities; and (3) the rapid shift of employment toward the tertiary sector, improving the efficient use of resources.

Table 2.1 shows the major national data in the first decade of economic reform in China, while Figure 2.1 gives the growth rates of GNP, consumption, and total output. In nominal terms, China has experienced three distinctive periods of income growth between 1978 and 1989. The first period is short and lasted until 1980, when the growth rate reached 11.8 percent. Between 1981 and 1985, nominal income growth rate accelerated from 6.8 percent to 22.9 percent. Despite an economic setback in 1986—due mainly to large fiscal deficits, supply bottlenecks, and rapid inflation—nominal income grew from 13.3 percent in 1986 to 22.7 percent in 1988, then fell to only 12.9 percent in 1989.

Table 2.1
China's Performance of Income and Consumption (Rmb 100 Millions)

	(1) Retail Price Index (1977 = 100)	(2) Gross National Product	(3) Real Gross National Product
1977	100.0		
1978	100.7	3588	3535
1979	102.7	3988	3883
		(11.4)	(9.8)
1980	108.9	4470	4105
		(11.8)	(5.7)
1981	111.5	4773	4281
		(6.8)	(4.3)
1982	113.6	5193	4571
		(8.8)	(6.8)
1983	115.3	5809	5038
		(11.9)	(10.2)
1984	118.5	6962	5875
		(19.8)	(16.6)
1985	129.0	8558	6634
		(22.9)	(12.9)
1986	136.7	9696	7093
		(13.3)	(6.9)
1987	146.7	11301	7703
		(16.5)	(8.6)
1988	173.8	14018	8066
		(24.0)	(4.7)
1989	204.8	15916	7771
		(13.5)	(-3.7)
1990	209.1	17686	8458
		(11.1)	(8.8)

Source: Statistical Yearbook of China, Beijing, 1984, 1988, 1991.
Note: Figures in parentheses are yearly growth rates. Real figures are expressed in
  1977 constant price.

Komiya (1989) argues that China has experienced a period of high
economic growth between 1978 and 1983. Major characteristics include a remarkable growth in agriculture and a steady development of
industrial and nonagricultural production in rural areas, while both
trade and fiscal expenditures in the early 1980s did not impose any
burden on the economy. Early economic optimism has led the 12th National Congress in 1982 to decide that in the twenty years from 1981,
the general goals for China's economic construction are a steady improvement of economic results and a quadruple increase in output

Table 2.1 (continued)

(4) Real Consumption	(5) Real Output Value (Agri. + Ind.)	(6) Differences in Growth Rate (4) - (5)	(7) Proportion of Accumulation in National Income
1741	5005		32.3
1875	5599		36.5
(7.7)	(11.9)	-4.2	
2137	6211		34.6
(14.0)	(10.9)	3.1	
2324	6498		31.5
(8.8)	(4.6)	4.2	
2510	6799		28.3
(8.0)	(4.6)	3.4	
2688	7301		28.8
(7.1)	(7.4)	-0.3	
2912	7989		29.7
(8.3)	(9.4)	-1.1	
3298	9140		31.5
(13.3)	(14.4)	-1.1	
3782	10337		35.0
(14.7)	(13.1)	1.6	
4061	11124		34.7
(7.3)	(7.6)	-0.3	
4353	12603		34.1
(7.2)	(13.3)	-6.1	
4625	13860		34.5
(6.2)	(10.0)	-3.8	
4374	13941		34.3
(-5.4)	(0.5)	-4.9	
4516	15101		34.1
(3.2)	(9.3)	-6.1	

from Rmb 710 billion in 1980 to Rmb 2800 billion in the year 2000.[6] The Third Plenary Session of the 12th Central Committee in 1984 reinforces the path of economic reform.

By 1985, however, the Chinese economy was overheated. The twin evils of price inflation and trade deficits had reached unprecedented levels.[7] Malpractices, corruption, speculative activities, and a general lack of discipline on the part of party officials began to emerge. Rapid inflation and speculative activities have led to commodity hoarding by households and industrial inputs by enterprises.[8] The misuse of funds for "official" trips overseas by party members have also been frequently reported in the press.[9] A bold step to correct malpractices by party

Figure 2.1
China's Growth Rates (Percentage)

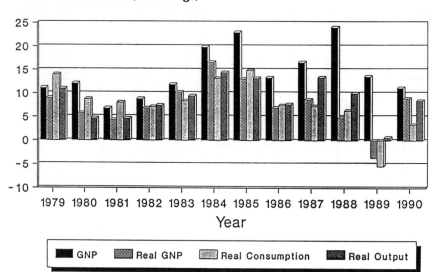

members was taken up in the 13th Party Congress on October 25, 1987. The then-Premier Zhao Ziyang proposed the separation of the party and government and the creation of a civil service to replace the much-criticized bureaucracy under the cadre system. The primary intention was to reduce the influence of the party members particularly in industrial management and to introduce a neutral civil service system.[10]

Since the 13th Party Congress in 1987, nominal income growth reached a new peak in 1988, but fell sharply in 1989. There are several observations one can make from the first decade of economic reform in China. First, the proportion of accumulation (consumption) in national income as shown in the last column of Table 2.1 had declined (improved) in the first half of the 1980s, but by 1985, the trend had reversed. By 1989, the proportion of accumulation in national income was not too different from that of 1977, implying that the intention of resource diversion from heavy to consumer industries has been successful only in the early 1980s. The rigidity of the industrial structure imposes constraints on its expansion. One possible explanation is that heavy industries are mostly state enterprises which supply industrial inputs to consumer light industries. State enterprises can exercise a monopolistic power on the price and supply of inputs to consumer industries. Furthermore, rapid inflation and speculative activities which have become popular in the second half of the 1980s have led to severe bottlenecks in industrial inputs, and consumer industries are hurt significantly.

Second, there is a considerable difference between nominal and real GNP as shown in Table 2.1. The growth rate of real GNP peaks one year before that of nominal GNP in 1980, 1985, and 1988. One can argue that nominal income growth in 1979–1980, 1984–1985, and 1987–1988 was purely inflation driven. Third, as far as the growth rates of real consumption and real output values are concerned, their movements are close to each other except in 1980, 1981, 1987, and 1989, as shown in column 6 of Table 2.1. A large positive difference in 1980 and 1981 indicates a position of excess demand, namely, the growth of real consumption exceeds the growth of real output. A large negative difference in 1987 and 1989, on the contrary, indicates a situation of falling real output growth rather than a fall in consumption. For the period 1982–1986, the differences are small, and real output growth rates match closely to real consumption growth rates. Nonetheless the level of consumption in the first decade of reform has definitely been improved. For example, reports on the possession of consumer goods shown in various issues of the *Statistical Yearbook of China* disclose that between 1978 and 1989, all the principal durable consumer goods have expanded by over 200 percent, while the possession of television sets and tape recorders have risen by more than 4,000 times.

The real consumption/real GNP ratios shown in Table 2.2 remain al-

Table 2.2
Average and Marginal Consumption Propensities

	(1) Real Consumption/ GNP Ratio	(2) Change in Real Consumption (Rmb 100 million)	(3) Changes in Real GNP (Rmb 100 million)	(4) Marginal Propensity (2)/(3)
1978	0.5262	133.9		
1979	0.5504	262.1	347.7	0.75
1980	0.5662	187.6	257.3	0.73
1981	0.5862	185.9	253.7	0.73
1982	0.5881	177.6	379.5	0.47
1983	0.5781	223.9	562.4	0.40
1984	0.5609	382.1	926.3	0.41
1985	0.5701	488.8	806.0	0.61
1986	0.5726	278.1	542.2	0.51
1987	0.5651	292.2	735.7	0.40
1988	0.5734	270.7	502.3	0.54
1989	0.5628	-249.9	-109.8	2.28
1990	0.5340	143.0	842.4	0.17

Source: Statistical Yearbook of China, Beijing, 1984, 1988, 1991.

most unchanged in the entire period. The marginal propensity to consume shown in column 4 of Table 2.2 falls from 0.75 in 1979 to 0.40 in 1984 but rises again to 0.54 in 1988 before exceeding unity in 1989. Looking at the growth rates of real GNP, both the years 1981 and 1988 experienced the lowest growth, and in 1989, there was a negative growth rate. The explanation to the marginal propensity to consume exceeding unity in 1988 was possible due to the large spending used to hedge against deteriorating inflation.

Lorenzen (1989) argues that the "propensity" to consume figures actually indicates the "possibility" to consume. By looking at the differences between urban and rural areas, the increase in income and consumption is considered as "real" in urban areas because additional goods and services can be bought. The same is not true in rural areas, since consumption possibilities are rather limited in the countryside. Nevertheless, despite inequalities and political uncertainty generated in the process of economic reform, both income and consumption have expanded and the general standard of living has improved.

MONEY AND BANKING

Banking reforms introduced by the Chinese authorities since 1978 came earlier than reforms applied to other sectors. Reformists consider the two roles played by the banking system in China. One is the supportive role: the banking system should not hinder enterprises from exercising their legitimate decision making powers. The other role is to influence macrolevel economic activities. The "Four Transformations and Eight Reforms," as summarized in Table 2.3, promulgated in 1979 after a nationwide meeting of bank branch directors laid the foundation for banking reform. The reform of banking and financial institutions, as listed in Table 2.4, consists of (1) establishment of the central bank, (2) reform of the specialized banks, (3) reform and development of urban and rural cooperatives, (4) reform of nonbank financial institutions and the financial market, and (5) reform of the interest rate structure.[11] Table 2.5 shows the total number of domestic banks. Between 1981 and 1988, the growth of domestic banking institutions was 61.2 percent. By the end of 1988, there were almost 100 foreign banks represented in China, of whom about 30 are Japanese. Foreign banks operate approximately 176 representative offices, of which 102 are in Beijing, and 30 branches, almost all of which are in the Special Economic Zones—with the exception of Shanghai, where a small group of foreign banks have maintained a long-term presence.[12]

Banking reforms have obviously revitalized the monetarization process. Table 2.6 shows the various items of bank credit receipts and payments. Between 1979 and 1989, bank credit payments and receipts

Table 2.3
The Four Transformations and Eight Reforms

Four Transformations
1. Use economic means to manage the banks.
2. Concentrating on expanding and using the source of funds.
3. Loans will be based on economic contracts.
4. Implement entreprise-type management at all levels with strict economic accounting.

Eight Reforms
1. An appropriate rise in interest rates on savings deposits and an increase in the variety of accounts available.
2. Loan policy should give "differential treatment, selection and fostering of the best enterprises."
3. Restoration of various specialized banks and corporations, as well as insurance companies.
4. Banks should be allowed to make short- and medium-term loans for equipment purchases.
5. Change the system from credit planning to the method of "unified planning, management at different levels, with control over the difference."
6. Banks should implement enterprise-type management with strict economic accounting.
7. Financial research organizations should be restored.
8. Management of bank cadres and personnel matters should be under the dual leadership of the main office of the People's Bank and local government.

Source: Byrd, William. 1983. *China's Financial System,* Boulder, Colo.: Westview Press, pp. 558–560.

have grown in nominal terms by 529.7 percent. As Table 2.7 shows, the growth rate of total domestic deposits for the period of 1979–1989 is 572.7 percent, while the growth rate of Urban and Rural Savings are 1743.4 percent and 251.7 percent, respectively. The total domestic deposit to GNP ratio has also increased from 0.3352 in 1979 to 0.4864 in 1984 and to 0.5750 in 1989. Looking at the composition of bank loans given in Table 2.8, with the exception of the fixed asset loans which have increased dramatically, loans to industrial production enterprises and loans to collective and individual industrial and commercial units in urban areas have increased, in nominal terms, by 650 percent and 1132 percent, respectively.

Economic reform has also called for a new approach to monetary policy in China. New developments in China's monetary policy include (1) the revised role of the central bank, (2) changes in banking operations, (3) reestablishing financial and capital markets, and (4) development of new financial instruments. In September 1983, the State Council decided that the People's Bank of China (PBC) assumes the

Table 2.4
Reform of Bank and Non-Bank Institutions

Year	Name of Bank	Features
1978	People's Bank of China (PBC)	Separated from the Ministry of Finance, the PBC was raised to the ministerial rank in terms of status and functional organization, and became the country's central bank in September 1983.
1979	Agricultural Bank of China (ABC)	Together with rural credit cooperatives, the ABC is the major source of financing the rural sector. The bank's role is to mobilize and direct financial resources from within the rural sector, as well as industrial enterprises in rural township.
1979	Bank of China (BOC)	Separated from PBC and became an economic organization responsible to the executive arm of the State Council, deals in foreign exchange business and settles the international account of China. Its designated functions include organizing and supplying foreign-exchange funds for investment in China's economic development and handling local-currency loans and deposits related to foreign-exchange operations.
1979	People's Construction Bank of China (PCBC)	Previously, the PCBC was a branch of Ministry of Finance. As from 1981, budgetary grants dispensed through the PCBC to enterprises for fixed capital investment are gradually being changed to repayable bank loans with interest. PCBC can also start to build up its own assets by expanding deposits to strengthen its lending capacity.
1979 1982	China International Trust & Investment Corporation (CITIC)	Concentrates on attracting foreign capital and technology, acts as an intermediary in organizing various forms of joint ventures between Chinese and foreign partners, works closely with BOC. Authority expanded in 1982 to include setting up of financial institutions abroad.
	China's Investment Bank (CIB)	Manages the use of long and medium term loans from the World Bank and other international financial institutions and to attract other sources of foreign funds for lending to domestic projects.

Sources: Huang Hsiao, Katharine H. Y. 1984. *Money and Banking in the Chinese Mainland,* Taipei: Chung-Hua Institution for Economic Research; Tam, On Kit. 1986. Reform of China's Banking, *The World Economy* 9(4):427–440; Jao, Yu C. 1990. Financial Reform in China 1978–89: Retrospect and Reappraisal, *Journal of Economics and International Relations* 3(4):279–309; Wang, Yan. 1988. Financial Reform: Decentralization and Liberalization, in *Planning and Finance in China's Economic Reform,* Thomas P. Lyons and Yan Wang. Cornell University East Asia Papers.

function of the central bank. Its role is to oversee the overall development and activities of the monetary sector, maintaining economic and currency stability. When the economy was overheated and credit was out of control in 1984–1985, the central bank enforced quarterly credit

Table 2.4 (continued)

Year	Name of Bank	Features
1983	People's Insurance Company of China (PICC)	Separated from PBC. Specializes in insurance business.
1984	Rural Credit Cooperatives (RCC)	Sprung up all over the country during 1984/5, mostly in the hands of individuals with different degrees of involvement by the local government. Started to issue shares and short term loans to members.
1984	Industrial and Commercial Bank of China (ICBC)	The ICBC is to take over from the PBC the entire commercial operation in providing bank credits to, and taking deposits from, enterprises. It specializes in the provision of short and medium term credits to enterprises for their working capital requirements and loans for technical transformation, and to self-employed people and township enterprises.
1985-1988	Guangdong Dev. Bank, Xiamen Int. Bank, Fujian Industrial Bank, Shenzhen Dev. Bank	Finance the provinces of Guangdong and Fujian and the special economic zones of Xiamen and Shenzhen.
	CITIC Industrial Bank, China Merchants Bank	Banking arm of CITIC and China Merchants Holdings Co. Ltd. respectively.
	Bengbu Housing Savings Bank, Yantai Housing Savings Bank	Specialize in housing mortages.
1987	Bank of Communications	Reactivated on a joint stock basis, handles both domestic and foreign currency denominated banking business, finances economic development in the eastern coastal provinces with the aim to revive Shanghai's former status as a financial centre. Total asset was Rmb 2 billion with 50% owned by the state and 25% by the Shanghai municipal government. Handles reminbi and foreign currencies in both short- and long-term lendings and is given flexibility to determine interest rate.

limits on its branches and on the specialized banks, such as the Agricultural Bank. Many of the administrative controls employed in 1985 include the order to stop offering loans to inefficient enterprises and to firms that produce poor-quality products for which there is little demand.[13] Since 1986, the central bank has tried to exercise both direct and indirect control measures, such as setting quotas for fixed asset

Table 2.5
Total Number of Banking Institutions (In Thousands)

Year	Total	State Banks	Insurance Co.	Rural Credit Cooperatives	Urban Credit Cooperatives	Fin. & Trust Invest. Organ.
1981	102.9	47.3	0.6	55.0		
1982	105.2	48.9	1.1	55.2		
1983	107.0	49.7	1.3	56.0		
1984	114.3	53.9	2.1	58.3		
1985	119.4	58.4	2.4	58.6		
1986	129.5	67.6	2.7	59.2		
1987	145.4	79.6	2.7	60.9	1.6	0.6
1988	165.9	98.1	2.9	60.9	3.3	0.7

Source: China Report: Social and Economic Development 1952–1989. 1990. Hong Kong: Zie Yonder Company, p. 424.

loans. The central bank indirectly controls credit, mainly by its credits to the various specialized banks.[14]

Huang Hsiao (1982) points out the three aspects of banking operation changes. First is the institution of medium- and short-term equipment loans which are intended to help light industries in order to raise production quickly. The second aspect is the granting of loans to urban cooperatives and individuals. These loans are extended for small-scale equipment purchases by collectively owned urban units or by individuals. The intentions are (1) to encourage production by small and decentralized units of the economy and (2) to alleviate urban unemployment. The third aspect is the availability of commercial credit and trust accounts. Commercial credits are various forms of interenterprise indebtedness, such as advance payments, down payments, installment payments, and deferred payments. Formerly, all transactions had to be paid immediately and credit could only be extended by the PBC. It was then possible for a state enterprise to be indebted directly to another state enterprise. Trust accounts are really time deposit accounts for the state enterprises. In addition, the PBC serves as a custodian and invests the trust depositor's funds in an area or in an enterprise specified by the depositor. In effect, this means that the PBC has begun to act as an investment agent which helps the enterprises to manage their idle balances.

The objective of monetary policy in China can be simplified to two main aims: the maintenance of price stability and the limiting of the amount of currency in circulation to an amount consistent with price stability. Peebles (1991, p. 122) argues that these two aims may conflict each other at times. One can identify two separate spheres of monetary flows in the economy. One is the "passive" noncash sphere, which requires cashless transfers through the banking system. The other is

Table 2.6
Credit Receipts and Payments of National Banks (End of Year, Rmb 100 Millions)

				Payments			
Year	Total	Loans	Gold	Foreign Ex-change	Balance with IMF	Claims on Govt.	Other
1979	2162.60	2039.63	12.16	20.58		90.23	
1980	2624.26	2414.30	12.16	-8.47	36.07	170.23	
1981	3075.25	2764.67	12.04	89.57	38.74	180.23	
1982	3490.14	3052.27	12.04	217.69	37.91	170.23	
1983	3966.04	3431.05	12.04	266.07	57.31	199.57	
1984	5079.51	4419.57	12.04	263.56	67.84	260.78	55.72
1985	6430.87	5905.51	12.04	93.10	88.69	275.05	56.48
1986	8205.97	7590.40	12.04	77.12	100.43	370.05	55.93
1987	9976.17	9032.35	12.04	182.08	178.81	514.96	55.93
1988	11541.25	10551.33	12.04	158.44	187.05	576.46	55.93
1989	13617.90	12409.27	12.04	264.54	191.56	684.56	55.93
1990	16837.88	15166.36	12.04	599.46	258.96	801.06	55.92

				Receipts			
Year	Total	Domestic Deposits	Funds of Banks	Current Balance of Profit & Loss Account	Liab. to IMF	Cur-rency in Circul.	Other
1979	2162.60	1340.04	427.88	49.45		267.71	77.52
1980	2624.26	1661.07	477.12	19.78	31.84	346.20	88.25
1981	3075.25	2035.40	496.90	21.24	51.62	396.34	73.75
1982	3490.14	2366.22	518.14	35.14	52.41	439.12	79.11
1983	3966.04	2761.59	553.28	46.17	53.73	529.78	21.49
1984	5079.51	3386.13	599.45	39.43	62.23	792.11	200.16
1985	6430.87	4273.03	777.82	70.30	78.18	987.83	243.71
1986	8205.97	5381.87	861.65	78.37	124.23	1218.36	540.49
1987	9976.17	6572.05	940.02	121.56	185.63	1454.48	702.43
1988	11541.25	7501.17	1073.81	123.12	148.63	2134.03	560.49
1989	13617.90	9013.90	1196.93	118.90	138.70	2344.00	735.60
1990	16837.88	11644.83	1315.83	165.87	185.71	2644.37	789.28

Source: Statistical Yearbook of China, Beijing, 1984, 1988, 1991.
Note: Since 1985, the Construction Bank is included.

the "active" sphere, where cash is used in all transactions. Peebles (1991, p. 124) points out that Chinese planners did consider the simple ratio of currency to retail sales when formulating policy. When this ratio rises above the critical currency level, there will be policy reaction. Monetary policy tools are simple. If the authority controls the growth of currency, purchasing power and retail sales can be controlled. The main determinant of purchasing power is wage.

Table 2.7
Composition of Domestic Deposits (Rmb 100 Millions)

Year	Total	Enter-prise	Budgetary	Capital Con-struction	Govt. Agencies and Organiz.	Urban Savings	Rural Savings
1979	1340.00	468.90	148.70	131.30	184.90	202.60	203.70
1980	1658.60	573.10	162.00	171.80	229.50	282.50	239.80
1981	2005.60	674.10	194.90	229.20	274.90	354.10	278.40
1982	2287.10	717.90	175.80	284.80	331.40	447.30	329.94
1983	2676.40	840.70	193.70	299.80	378.40	572.60	391.27
1984	3305.60	1333.80	165.90	333.40	323.50	776.60	372.43
1985	3936.50	1495.40	326.40	281.50	325.80	1057.80	449.56
1986	5381.87	2643.36	311.45		395.97	1471.45	559.64
1987	6572.05	3125.55	306.98		449.20	2064.02	626.30
1988	7425.62	2936.58	270.88		392.67	2659.16	669.55
1989	9013.85	3084.85	437.99		483.97	4734.80	716.32
1990	11644.83	3997.68	380.40		614.78	5192.58	850.26

Source: Statistical Yearbook of China, Beijing, 1984, 1988, 1991.

Table 2.8
Composition of Bank Loans (End of Year, Rmb 100 Millions)

Year	(1)	(2)	(3)	(4)	(5)	(6)	(7)
1979	363.09	242.12	1232.25		57.51	136.74	7.92
1980	431.58	236.03	1437.02		78.29	175.88	55.50
1981	487.35	241.24	1641.74		121.25	189.72	83.37
1982	526.72	239.85	1788.21		133.06	212.45	151.89
1983	597.09	268.75	1978.84		159.28	231.19	195.93
1984	883.83	310.03	2272.80		295.17	368.08	289.66
1985	1165.08	380.83	2649.30	267.07	321.28	416.63	705.32
1986	1649.85	477.05	3092.42	369.41	425.54	570.37	1005.76
1987	2043.61	493.47	3506.14	466.52	550.03	685.83	1286.75
1988	2085.09	520.96	4100.61	494.71	656.21	814.21	1559.23
1989	2724.63	582.25	4775.07	601.26	708.55	895.05	1775.96
1990	3559.43	652.95	5768.48	671.45	831.26	1038.08	2245.75

Source: Statistical Yearbook of China, Beijing, 1984, 1988, 1991.
Notes: (1) Loans to industrial production enterprises. (2) Loans to industrial supply and marketing enterprises and materials supply departments. (3) Commercial loans. (4) Construction loans. (5) Loans to collective and individual industrial and commercial units in urban areas. (6) Agricultural loans. (7) Fixed asset loans.

Peebles (1991, p. 107) discusses money supply in China. In the prereform years, the narrowest measure of money (currency) is

$$CURR = W_G + W_E - C_H - S_H$$

where $CURR$ = currency, W_G = wage payment by the government, W_E = wage payments by enterprises, C_H = sales of retail goods and services by the state sector to households, and S_H = changes in saving and other household deposits at banks. In the reform system, money supply is defined as

$$CURR = (B_E - D_E) + (B_G - D_G) - S_H$$

where B = borrowing from the banking system (loans), D = increases in balances at the banks (deposits), and E and G indicate the enterprise and government sectors, respectively. Because the main determinant of money supply is wage, Peebles (1991, p. 124) argues that the PBC has to be a passive reactor to changes in wages. Monetary policy tends to be one-sided if it aims at the contraction of the money supply. Statistical figures do not support Peebles's (1991) observation. The increase of both currency and bank loans has been high. In the case of bank loans, the negative real interest rate is largely responsible for the increase.

Peebles (1991, p. 127) has rightly pointed out that, although the banking reforms of 1984 and 1986 altered the structure and nature of the banking system, these changes did not in principle alter the process of money supply. The day-to-day business is being handled by specialized banks, but they are required to deposit a certain proportion of their deposits with the Central Bank. Thus, the ability to extend loans by the specialized banks is controlled by the Central Bank.

Four factors are used to support the conclusion that monetary reforms have not changed the nature of the money supply process and the extent to which monetary growth could be controlled. First, reserve requirements are seen as the way the Central Bank gets hold of the specialized banks' funds for itself. Second, indirect levers in the early years of reform did not exist. The supply of money process is still dominated by the expansion of bonuses and wage payments and loan extension to local investment projects. Third, interest rate controls were hardly used. They were increased twice in 1985 and in September 1988 in view of rapid inflation. The interest rate was increased in May 1993 in response to rapid growth rate and inflation rate by an average of 1.19 percentage points, bringing the average saving rate to just 9.07 percent, and the loan rate to 9.82 percent, while inflation in major cities was 15.7 percent for the first quarter of 1993.[15] In an attempt to curb runaway economic growth, China's Central Bank raised the interest rate for the second time in early July 1993. The state bank raised the rate for private and institutional fixed-term bank savings by an average of 1.72 percent, bringing the average interest for fixed deposits to 10.42 percent. The average rise of the demand deposits will be 0.99 percent, bringing the rate to 3.15 percent.[16] The exchange rate crisis in early 1993 led the Chinese officials to believe that adjustment in interest rate could be the main tool for guiding China's monetary policy.[17]

Last, administered quantitative limits on bank loans were applied when it was decided to restrain the rate of money growth.

Financial instruments and markets began to emerge in the mid-1980s. The interbank market was approved in principle in 1984 by the PBC. In 1984–1985, credit squeeze in the banking industry stimulated the issue of corporate shares and bank debentures as enterprises and specialized banks short of funds tried to raise capital directly from its own employees and from the public.[18] Secondary markets in stocks and bonds reopened in 1986. The first stock market in China opened at Shenyang, Liaoning, in August 1986. It started with the trading of bonds issued by enterprises. The exchange takes 2 percent on transactions when bonds are traded according to publicized prices, 1 percent when sellers propose prices, and 0.4 percent when bondholders buy and sell freely.[19] Chen Muhua, governor of China's Central Bank, reaffirmed the important development of the money market in 1988.[20]

There are three types of bond issues in China. The state issues treasury bonds domestically and in foreign markets, and enterprises issue bonds for their investment purposes. The state began to issue treasury bonds in 1981 as an effort to combat inflation and fiscal deficits. An amount equal to 4.5 billion yuan of state treasury bonds were sold to state-owned and collective enterprises through departments in charge of enterprises and institutions and local governments. With a repayment period of five years, the bonds had an annual interest rate of 4 percent, which was raised to 5 percent in 1985 and to 6 percent in 1986. The interest rate for bonds bought by individuals was higher at 8 percent in 1981, 9 percent in 1985, and 10 percent in 1986. In 1987, 5.5 billion yuan of bonds were issued for key construction projects in addition to the state treasury bonds of 8 billion to be repaid in two years at an interest rate of 9.5 percent. Repayment of both principal and interest began in 1986. In 1988, the PBC decided to set up on a trial basis state treasury bond transfer markets in Shenzhen.[21] The Chinese authority raised funds from the international money market in the form of government bonds. Between January 1982 and April 1987, for example, China floated twenty-five bond issues in Tokyo, Frankfurt, Hong Kong, and Singapore with a total value of $2.799 billion. The Tokyo market is by far the biggest taker, with 68 percent of the total number of bonds and 74.4 percent of the total value.[22] Table 2.9 shows the values of state debts and borrowings.

Bond issues by enterprises were accused of adopting capitalist ideas, Tam (1991) and Jao (1990) have noted that the turning point was in 1984–1985 when enterprises and specialized banks were short of funds and tried to raise capital from their employees and the public. The nature of corporate bonds in China, as Jao (1990) observes, is similar to the kind of "non-voting, redeemable, participating preferred stock" in

Table 2.9
Incomings and Outgoings of State Debts and Borrowings (Rmb 100 Millions)

Year	Incomings			Outgoings		
	Total	Domestic bonds and treasury	Foreign borrowing	Total	Repayment with interest Bonds	Foreign borrowing
1979	35.31		35.31			
1980	43.01		43.01	28.58		24.40
1981	73.08	48.66	73.08	62.89		57.89
1982	83.86	43.83	40.03	55.52		49.62
1983	79.41	41.58	37.83	42.47		36.56
1984	77.34	42.53	34.81	28.91		22.74
1985	89.85	60.61	29.24	39.56		32.59
1986	138.25	62.51	75.74	50.16	7.98	34.49
1987	169.55	63.07	106.48	79.83	23.18	51.96
1988	270.78	132.17	138.61	76.75	28.44	42.58
1989	282.97	138.91	144.06	72.36	19.30	45.83
1990	375.45	197.24	178.21	190.40	113.75	68.21

Source: Statistical Yearbook of China, Beijing, 1984, 1988, 1991.

developed market economies. Informal financial markets are originated from rural borrowing and lending activities. Tam (1991) observes that China's informal credit activities have a high positive real rate of interest and that most of the loans supplied by private lenders are used for income-producing activities. He concludes that the provision of informal credit played a dominant role as a source of loans to rural households.

The rates of growth of money, measured in percentage of change (shown in Table 2.10), are very high in the 1979–1990 decade, averaging almost 24 percent for M0, 30 percent for M2, 24 percent for M3, and 21 percent for M*, which includes deposits of government agencies. The growth rates peaked in 1984 and have remained high since then. The money M2/income ratio, popularly known as the financial deepening ratio, has increased from 0.1179 in 1978 to 0.5472 in 1990. These ratios are acceptable for a developing socialist economy. They are higher than some Asian countries such as Indonesia and the Philippines but lower than Hong Kong, Singapore, and Malaysia.[23]

Credit creation is another form of money supply. Newlyn and Avramides (Newlyn, ed. 1977) use some monetary parameters to check the role and extent of intermediation and credit creation. One is the velocity of circulation (v), which is the ratio of GNP to M2 $(v = GNP/M2)$. The other is the money multiplier (e), defined as the ratio of M2 to reserve money $(Q + IR$, where Q is the monetary authority's claim on

Table 2.10
Monetary Growth and Performance

Year	Rate of Growth				Money/Income Ratios			
	M0	M2	M3	M*	M0/GNP	M2/GNP	M3/GNP	M*/GNP
1978	26.12				0.0592	0.1179		0.4151
1979	29.32	29.76		12.94	0.0671	0.1376	0.3421	0.4032
1980	14.48	35.90	26.54	24.69	0.0774	0.1668	0.3670	0.4485
1981	10.79	23.38	19.72	19.81	0.0830	0.1928	0.4115	0.5032
1982	20.65	21.14	18.78	13.51	0.0846	0.2146	0.4492	0.5250
1983	49.52	27.61	18.47	17.60	0.0912	0.2448	0.4758	0.5519
1984	24.71	41.10	35.73	27.81	0.1138	0.2883	0.5388	0.5886
1985	23.34	30.08	23.65	20.17	0.1154	0.3050	0.5421	0.5754
1986	19.38	32.39	29.11	34.03	0.1257	0.3564	0.6177	0.6807
1987	46.72	31.01	23.44	21.61	0.1287	0.4007	0.6542	0.7102
1988	9.84	31.09	22.23	19.10	0.1522	0.4234	0.6462	0.6819
1989	12.81	26.20	17.34	18.81	0.1473	0.4706	0.6715	0.7136
1990		29.20			0.1495	0.5472		
Average	23.98	29.91	23.50	20.92				

Source: Statistical Yearbook of China, Beijing, 1984, 1988, 1991.
Notes: M0 = currency in circulation. M2 = M0 + urban savings deposits + farmer households deposits. M3 = M2 + agricultural collective units deposits + township enterprises deposits + enterprise deposits + capital construction deposits + rural deposits + other deposits. M* = M3 + treasury deposits + deposits of government agencies and organizations.

domestic economy [IFS lines 12a, 12d, and 12e] and *IR* is international reserve [gold and foreign exchange held by the state]). Domestic credit expansion (DCE) causes an increase in money supply but will not create external reserve.[24] The Polak coefficient *(p)* is used to express the external drain of reserves and money in one year associated with one unit of domestic credit expansion, ceteris paribus. The Polak coefficient is defined as

$$p = mv/(1 + mv)$$

where *m* is the import/GNP ratio. The Polak coefficient provides a useful link between DCE and change in money supply. For example, if $p = 0.33$, it implies that out of one unit of gross money creation, 0.33 will have been drained out of the money stock within a year and the remaining 0.67 will be the observed increase in the money stock. The domestic credit expansion money multiplier, $(1+p)e$, measures the extent of domestic credit expansion associated with one unit increase in the credit base.

Table 2.11 shows the various monetary parameters. The Polak coefficient, shown in column 4, is generally low, though it peaked in 1985. Increase in money stock has been high and expanded since 1985. On the contrary, the domestic credit expansion multiplier, shown in column 5, has been low even though the money multiplier has increased

Table 2.11
Monetary Parameters

Year	v = GNP/M2	e = M2/(Q+IR)	m = IM/GNP	p = mv/(1+mv)	(1+p)e
1978	8.48		0.0522	0.3096	
1979	7.29		0.0608	0.3071	
1980	6.00		0.0668	0.2861	
1981	5.19		0.0770	0.2855	
1982	4.66		0.0688	0.2428	
1983	4.08		0.0726	0.2285	
1984	3.47		0.0891	0.2362	
1985	3.28	0.87	0.1468	0.3250	1.1528
1986	2.81	0.96	0.1540	0.3020	1.2499
1987	2.50	1.11	0.1422	0.2623	1.4023
1988	2.36	1.21	0.1467	0.2572	1.5212
1989	2.11	1.23	0.1403	0.2284	1.5109
1990	2.04		0.1456	0.2414	

Sources: Statistical Yearbook of China, Beijing, 1984, 1988, 1991; *International Financial Statistics,* Washington, D.C.: International Monetary Fund, 1990.

Notes: v = velocity of circulation, e = money multiplier, m = import/income ratio, p = Polak coefficient, (1+p)e = domestic credit expansion money multiplier.

by over 40 percent from 0.87 to 1.23 between 1985 and 1989. These parameters suggest that monetary policy has not been able to constrain the growth of money supply in line with real economic growth and that price stability was difficult to maintain.

The role of the interest rate has not been accepted as a major economic instrument since 1949. There were over twenty different interest rates in 1949, but they had been reduced to seven by 1979.[25] Four major unfavorable features account for the malfunctioning of the role of interest rate in China.[26] One is a consistently low interest rate. Enterprises do not need to consider the frugal use of loans, and the interest rate charged on rural-sector loans is even lower. The second feature is the overcentralization of control, while the third feature is uniformity. The last feature is isolation. The interest rate has not been used in association with other prices, tax, and the amount of loans, which are highly connected to each other.

As early as 1981, various suggestions have been made to improve the role and functioning of the interest rate.[27] First, the scope should be broadened to cater for different kinds of deposits by depositing institutions. Lending rates should be raised and made greater than deposit rates, for this will discourage and reduce unnecessary lending. Rates on long-term loans should be greater than short-term loans, though rates to agriculture and technology-related purposes should be kept low.[28] The principles governing the new role of the interest rate include (1) the use of market rate, (2) the decentralization of interest rate management, (3) maintaining a higher average rate, and (4) the introduction of differentiated rates and limiting the use of the best lending rate.[29]

A formula has been set to calculate the deposit rate. The basis of the formula depends on the average profit that banks derive from their assets. A bank's profit is derived from the difference between lending and deposit rates.[30] Letting P = average profit rate, R = lending rate, r = deposit rate, K_0 = bank's asset, K_1 = sum of all kinds of deposits, and c = cost to the bank except payment of r, it follows that $P > R > r$. The determination of R and r can be worked out from the bank's income equation:

$$\text{Bank's income} = K_0P = [R(K_0 + K_1) - K_1r - c]$$

Hence,

$$R = (K_0P + K_1r + c) / (K_0 + K_1) \text{ and}$$

$$r = [R(K_0 + K_1) - K_0P - c] / K_1$$

One suggestion is that there should be a two-stage reform of the interest rate. The first stage involves a partial reform, while the second involves a complete and across-the-board effort to implement reform. Major interest rate changes on deposits and loans were made in 1982, 1985, and 1988. Tables 2.12 and 2.13 show the various interest rates on deposits and loans. One observation is that these rates are low in general, particularly the short-term rates. In the case of loans, enterprises simply keep borrowing at short-term rates. In the case of deposits, long-term deposits become unattractive at a time of high inflation. Reform in China has not been able to make the rate of interest an effective economic instrument in regulating the supply and demand of funds. A consistently low-interest-rate policy eases credit creation and increases money supply without taking into consideration the real side of the economy. A policy of easy credit gives rise to a situation where banks "give as many loans as are needed whenever they are needed" (Li 1981). Chen Yun, the deputy governor of the PBC, remarked first that, due to the government's preferences, Chinese banks were often required to extend loans to projects which were not viable from a commercial point of view. Second, due to the lack of a money market, the relationship between the Central Bank and commercial banks was out of balance.[31]

STATE BUDGET AND FISCAL REFORM

The reinstatement of economic and budgetary balance in 1978 was not novel to the reformists. Back in 1957 when the first Five-Year Plan was drafted, Chen Yun believed that financial balance could bring a balance between aggregate demand and aggregate supply and could avoid inflation and market disruption.[32] Budgetary balance was seen as crucial in promoting financial reform. The reformists believed that budgetary deficits distort resource allocation, weaken macro control, and disturb various relationships. Chinese scholars distinguished a "push effect" and a "burden effect" of deficit budgeting. The "push effect" occurs when a budget deficit accelerates economic development and rapid economic results are achieved in the short run. The "burden effect" becomes effective when the enlarged purchasing power soon leads to inflation, which requires a larger deficit in the following year.[33] National debt and public borrowing can be a good solution, but the latter can be a double-edged sword. If used effectively, public borrowing can facilitate economic growth, but the ability to repay depends on how fast economic growth takes place. If the growth rate cannot exceed the rate of repayment, a "deficit breeds deficit" vicious cycle will be developed.[34]

Table 2.12
Readjustment of Interest Rates on Bank Deposits (Monthly Interest Percentage)

Item	1/10/1971	1/4/1979	1/4/1980 Fix. dep. 1/7/1980 Curr. dep.	1/1/1982 1/4/1982 Saving deposit	1/4/1985	1/8/1988	1/9/1988	1/2/1989
(1) Institution unit deposits (Enterprises and Groups)								
(a) Current	0.15	0.15	0.15	0.15	0.15	0.15	0.24	
(b) Fixed								
One-year				0.30	0.36			
Two-year				0.36	0.42			
Three-year				0.42	0.48			
(2) Deposits by urban and rural residents								
(a) Current	0.18	0.18	0.24	0.24	0.24	0.24	0.24	0.24
(b) Fixed								
Six-month	0.27	0.30	0.36	0.45	0.51	0.54	0.75	
One-year	0.27	0.33	0.45	0.48	0.57	0.60	0.72	0.95
Three-year	0.27	0.38	0.51	0.57	0.66	0.69	0.81	1.10
Five-year	0.42	0.57	0.66	0.69	0.78	0.90	1.25	
Eight-year				0.75	0.75	0.87	1.04	1.47

Source: *China Report: Social and Economic Development 1949–1989*, 1990. Hong Kong: Zie Yonder Company Ltd., p. 432.

Table 2.13
Changes in Interest Rates on Bank Loans (Monthly Interest Percentage)

Item	Before 4/1982	1/4/1982	1/8/1985	1/9/1988
Banks' industrial-commercial loans				
(a) Circulation-fund	0.42	0.60	0.66	0.75
(b) Short-term:				
1 year	0.42	0.42	0.66	0.75
1-3 years	0.42	0.48	0.72	0.83
3-5 years	0.42	0.54	0.78	0.90
5-10 years		0.60	0.84	1.35
10 years +		0.66	0.90	
Banks' agricultural loans				
(a) State farm for:				
1. Production	0.36	0.48		
2. Buying equipment	0.36	0.42		
(b) Communes and subunits for:				
1. Production	0.36	0.48		
2. Buying equipment	0.18	0.36		
3. Develop crop growing and animal breeding	0.36	0.48		
4. Buying equipment for developing crop growing and animal breeding	0.18	0.36		
5. Buying farm machinery	0.18	0.36		
6. Used as deposit	0.36	0.48		
7. Individual commune members	0.42	0.48-0.60		

Sources: Scherer, John, ed. 1982. *China Facts and Figures Annual,* vol. 5. Gulf Breeze, Fla.: Academic International Press, p. 92; *People's Republic of China Year Book,* 1986. Beijing: Xinhua Publishing House, p. 324; *People's Republic of China Year Book,* 1989. Beijing: Xinhua Publishing House, p. 152; *China Official Annual Report 1982/3,* 1983. Hong Kong: Kingsway International Publications Ltd., pp. 454–455.

At the macrolevel, the concept of economic balance is applied to the areas of loans, material and foreign reserve. A basic principle of budgetary balance is that "expenditure relies on the amount of income," which implies that a proper proportion between accumulation and consumption, between accumulation funds and liquidity funds, as well as between government revenues and expenditures should be kept.[35] Donnithorne (1986) summarizes the Chinese fiscal reform into four headings: (1) a switch from paying the profits of state enterprises to the Ministry of Finance and from the local finance bureau to a system in which enterprises pay taxes while themselves retaining most of the remainder, (2) taxes on collective and private enterprises, (3) taxes on foreign enterprises operating in China and on Sino-foreign joint ventures, and (4) a revamping of the fiscal relations between different levels of administration.

The substitution of profit tax for profit remittance began in 1980 with the payment of three taxes—industrial and commercial tax, enterprise income tax, and fixed assets tax. From October 1984, the change extended to all state enterprises. This feature of profit tax substitution led to a continuous decline of total fiscal revenue as a ratio of GNP, from about 31 percent in 1978 to 17.8 percent in 1989, as shown in column 1 of Table 2.17. Four methods of division between state and enterprise tried out in 1983 were (1) proportionate sharing, (2) a quota responsibility system, (3) a proportionately increased responsibility system, and (4) an adjustment tax. Donnithorne (1986) notes that these measures were all cumbersome and liable to abuse. Furthermore, tax changes were ad hoc. For example, a construction tax of 10 percent was introduced in 1983; a resource tax was introduced in October 1984; and a value-added tax was applied in 1984 on machinery, agricultural implements, automobiles, motor boats, and a host of other household products. In 1982, the Ministry of Finance instituted a new tax of 10 percent on banks' income, and an export tax was introduced in the same year. In March 1985, custom duties were raised, followed by an additional "regulatory tax" a few months later. A personal income tax law was introduced in 1980, with progressive rates ranging from 5 percent to 45 percent.[36] Wu (1989) discusses the reform on profit substitution in a two-phase development. The first phase began in 1983 when tax payments were substituted for profit delivery. The second phase began two years later when profit delivery was replaced by tax payment to mitigate the contradictions caused by distorted prices.[37]

Fiscal relations between the central government and the provinces have undergone radical changes. In February 1980, the State Council decided to embark on a process of delineating central finances and local finances. Local finances grew, but the reform led to a decline in central government revenues. Nambu (1991, p. 2) points out that in

March 1985, when the State Council decided to separate completely the fiscal affairs of the various levels of government based on a differentiation of taxes so as to clarify the authority and responsibility of each level, the purpose of fiscal management reform was to raise local enthusiasm and that the central government continued to maintain a tight control over regions. In actuality the old method of overall revenue division continued to be used, and four major problems developed: (1) interference of local government in enterprises; (2) overinflated investment and superfluous construction due to the "local ownership" attitude; (3) the creation of fiscal deficits in central finances due to the decentralization of revenue collection, coupled with the continuation of vast state expenditures; and (4) the tacking on of surcharges by the local governments. The State Council attempted to improve the situation in 1988, making the distribution of fiscal revenue between the central and local government more transparent.[38] The major problems are that macroeconomic controls by the central government over local governments became weaker; that local government began to concentrate on short-term projects; and that locally monopolized markets emerged, causing bottlenecks in industrial supply on a national level and detracting from the optimum use of resources.

Table 2.14 summarizes the proportional shares between central and local governments. As far as revenues are concerned, though their proportions are small, the share of the central government increased from 20.6 percent in 1981 to 39.8 percent in 1988 in the case of budgetary revenue and from 33.7 percent in 1982 to 40.8 percent in 1987 for extrabudgetary revenue. In the case of budget expenditure, the proportion spent by the central government has reduced from more than 50 percent in 1981 to less than 40 percent in 1988. Local governments have a bigger say in their expenditures. The situation in the case of extrabudgetary expenditure is different. Extrabudgetary expenditure made by the central government expanded from about 30 percent to 40 percent between 1982 and 1987, though the proportion spent by local governments is still larger with a nearly 60:40 division.

Blejer and Szapary (1990b), however, argue that there are "unintended consequences" of fiscal reform in China. First, the contract responsibility system has introduced a degree of regressiveness into the enterprise income tax. The contract usually stipulated a minimum amount of profit to be taxed each year. Profits above the contracted amount are fully retained by the enterprise, and enterprises that fail to reach their profit target must pay their minimum tax obligation. Since below-quota profits are subject to a flat tax and above-quota profits are taxed at a lower rate, enterprises end up retaining an increasingly larger portion of their total profits as output. This results in a continuously decreasing average tax rate and an elasticity of less than unity for the enterprise

Table 2.14
Proportional Shares of Budget Revenue and Expenditure

Year	Revenue			
	Budgetary		Extrabudgetary	
	Central	Local	Central	Local
1981	20.6	79.4		
1982	23.0	77.0	33.7	66.3
1983	29.8	70.2	37.2	62.8
1984	34.9	65.2	39.6	60.4
1985	37.9	62.1	41.6	58.4
1986	40.6	59.4	41.2	58.8
1987	38.2	61.8	40.8	59.2
1988	39.8	60.2		
	Expenditure			
1981	54.0	46.0		
1982	49.9	50.1	30.9	69.1
1983	49.7	50.3	34.3	65.7
1984	47.8	52.2	37.3	62.3
1985	45.3	54.7	40.9	59.1
1986	41.3	58.7	40.6	59.4
1987	42.1	57.9	40.3	59.7
1988	39.2	60.8		

Source: China Statistical Yearbook, Beijing, 1990, pp. 222–223.

profit tax. Furthermore, the contract system works toward reducing the tax/GNP ratios, as well as reducing the ability of the central government to introduce measures in order to meet changing economic circumstances. To permit enterprises to deduct from pretax profits on the payment of interest on loans and the repayment of loans principal not only caused profit to decline but also led to higher enterprise losses.

Profit-making enterprises are faced with a falling average tax rate, while loss-making enterprises have their loss covered by the budget. The budget, therefore, seems to experience the worse of both worlds. Technically, the way in which fiscal reforms have been implemented have led to the emergence of a long-term income elasticity of tax revenue below unity and have weakened the tax base, resulting in a reduction of revenue transferred to the central government as shown in Table 2.15.[39] The income elasticity of tax revenue fell from 3.12 in 1979 to 0.90 in 1984. The same trend applied after there was a change in tax submission in 1985. The elasticity ratio fell from 5.98 in 1986 to 0.96 in 1989.

Table 2.15
Tax/Income Ratios and Income Elasticity of Tax Revenue

Year	Tax/GNP	Elasticity
1978	14.5	
1979	13.5	3.12
1980	12.8	1.92
1981	13.2	0.67
1982	13.5	0.79
1983	13.4	1.10
1984	13.6	0.90
1985	23.8	(0.20)
1986	21.6	5.98
1987	18.9	6.98
1988	17.1	2.06
1989	17.1	0.96
1990	16.0	3.21

Source: China Statistical Yearbook, Beijing, 1984, 1988, 1991.
Note: Income elasticity of tax revenue is defined as $(\Delta GNP/\Delta T)/(T/GNP)$, where T is total tax revenue and Δ represents the change. Figures from 1985 are not comparable to other years due to the practice of profit substitution by taxes and to other factors.

On the whole, the experience of fiscal reform and experience in the period of 1978–1989 exhibited a typical case of "soft budget," as advocated by Kornai (1986, pp. 41–44). Table 2.16 shows three calculations of fiscal balance in columns 1, 4, and 7. Column 1 shows the difference between total revenue and expenditure. With the exception of 1978 and 1985, the Chinese authority has experienced budget deficits. The "real budget deficit," shown in column 4 as defined by Nambu (1991), takes into account both domestic and foreign borrowings; and the amount of deficit becomes much larger. Column 7 shows the soft budget which included extrabudgetary revenue and expenditure figures. In all years, extrabudgetary revenues are higher than extrabudgetary expenditures, the soft budget deficits in most years from 1982 to 1987 were smaller than the real budget deficits in column 4.

There are three aspects in China's soft budget. One is that both the extrabudgetary revenue and expenditure figures are rising rapidly, as shown in columns 5 and 6 of Table 2.16, despite huge fiscal deficits before and after 1985. The second aspect is that the extrabudgetary revenue's percentage share in state-budgeted revenue has risen sharply from 31 percent in 1978 to 94 percent in 1989. The extrabudgetary expenditure's percentage share in total budget expenditure, on the other hand, has expanded from 63.7 percent in 1982 to 75.9 percent in 1987, as shown in columns 2 and 4 of Table 2.17. The fiscal budget over the years has become a weaker financial mechanism in steering the econ-

Table 2.16
Budgetary Performance I (Rmb Billions)

Year	Fiscal Balance (1)	Bond Debt (2)	Foreign Debt (3)	Real Fiscal Deficit (4)	Extrabudgetary		The Soft Budget (7)
					Revenue (5)	Expenditure (6)	
1978	+ 1.02			+ 1.02	34.71		
1979	-17.07		3.53	-20.60	45.29		
1980	-12.75		4.30	-17.05	55.74		
1981	- 2.55	4.38	7.31	- 9.86	60.11		
1982	- 2.93	4.16	4.00	-11.31	80.27	73.45	-4.49
1983	- 4.53	4.25	3.78	-12.29	96.77	87.58	-3.10
1984	- 4.45	6.06	3.48	-12.18	118.85	111.47	-4.80
1985	+ 2.16	6.25	2.92	- 6.82	153.00	137.50	+8.68
1986	- 7.06	6.31	7.57	-20.88	173.73	157.84	-4.99
1987	- 7.96	9.21	10.65	-24.92	202.89	184.08	-6.11
1988	- 7.86	13.89	13.86	-30.94	227.00		
1989	- 9.23	19.59	14.41	-37.53			
1990	-15.04	19.00	16.21	-50.90			
1991	-13.35		16.24	-48.59			

Sources: China Statistical Yearbook, Beijing, 1984, 1988, 1991; Nambu, Minoru. 1991. Problems in China's Financial Reforms. *China Newsletter*, JETRO, 92 (May/June):2–10.

Notes: (1) Fiscal Balance = fiscal revenue − fiscal expenditure. (4) Real Fiscal Deficit = (1) − (2) − (3). (7) Soft Budget = (4) + (5) − (6).

Table 2.17
Budgetary Performance II (Rmb Billions)

Year	State-budgeted revenue/GNP	Extra-budgetary revenue as percentage of state-budgeted revenue	Expenditure/ GNP	Extra-budgetary expenditure as percentage of state-budgeted expenditure	Price subsidies	Price subsidies growth rate
1978	31.25	31.0	30.96		1.11	
1979	26.71	42.4	31.84		7.92	613.5
1980	22.32	53.5	27.13		11.77	48.6
1981	21.29	59.1	23.36		15.94	35.4
1982	20.87	74.1	22.20	63.69	17.22	8.0
1983	20.85	79.9	22.24	67.76	19.74	14.6
1984	21.07	81.0	22.21	72.09	21.83	10.6
1985	21.44	83.3	21.52	74.54	26.18	19.9
1986	22.46	79.5	23.96	67.72	25.75	-1.6
1987	19.93	89.7	21.38	75.85	29.46	14.4
1988	17.76	91.2	19.31		31.68	7.5
1989	17.76	94.8	19.23		37.03	16.9
1990					38.08	2.8

Source: China Statistical Yearbook, Beijing, 1984, 1988, 1991.
Note: State-budgeted revenue does not include foreign borrowing.

omy. Its performance certainly did not exhibit a balancing trend as envisaged in 1978. The third aspect is the amount spent on price subsidies shown in column 5 of Table 2.17. Huang Hsiao (1987, p. 52) points out that the professed principle of "balanced budget with a slight surplus" had been abandoned in the first decade of reform in China and that deficit financing was integrated with budget planning.

State subsidies are divided into three broad categories: (1) social welfare payments, which are cash payments to workers in state enterprises, amounting to Rmb 54 billion in 1988; (2) budgeted price subsidies – which cover payments to specified commodities, essential imports, agricultural imports, and enterprises' losses – amounting to Rmb 97 billion in 1989 and equivalent to 32 percent of budget expenditure; and (3) other price subsidies, including the provision of services, subsidized interest rates on bank loans, group consumption, and price differentials and totaling Rmb 22 billion in 1987.[40] Although state subsidies are intended to serve some basic purposes, such as welfare payments to assist the needy, the negative economic impact includes the increasing burden to the state and increasing difficulty for macroeconomic control.

The level of state subsidies has jumped both in absolute and relative terms since 1978. In the state budget, the ratio of price subsidies to expenditure increased from 20 percent in 1978 to 32 percent in 1989, indicating that these subsidies have grown faster than the budget itself. In value terms, state price subsidies to urban consumers have increased from Rmb 5.56 billion in 1978 to Rmb 35 billion in 1989, and the corresponding share of state budget expenditure has increased from 5 percent to 11.6 percent in the same period. The scope of subsidized products has also expanded from one item (cotton wool) in 1953 to a small group of basic items, such as grain and vegetables, in 1978 but has expanded to cover more than 120 items in 1989. Rapidly growing subsidies contributed to excess growth in incomes, consumption, and the budget deficit during the 1980s. China has attempted to reduce subsidies, but attempts so far have been insufficient and sometimes inappropriate.[41] Growing subsidies have also cut into the budgetary allocation for investment and have reduced the state's ability to promote development and restructure the economy. Consequently, while the share of subsidies in budget expenditure has increased, the share of investment has dropped from more than 50 percent in the late 1970s to approximately 25 percent in 1991. Because subsidies cannot be cut easily, the government has less flexibility in reducing the budget deficit.

SAVINGS AND INVESTMENT

Savings are considered as a means to influence production and direct consumption. Paul Reynolds (1982) argues that savings in China have to provide a major portion of the capital required for modernization, and capital formation through savings has been one of the success stories in Chinese economic history since 1949. Furthermore, a domestic saving policy has important implications for foreign financing. For example, the reason China was forced to reschedule several major contracts in 1980 was because of the domestic deficit.[42] However, Reynolds also points out that a high savings rate must be partially attributed to a scarcity of certain staples and consumer products. Lorenzen (1989) concludes that enforced savings in Chinese private households are widespread, especially in the countryside, and the amount of cash hoardings accumulated between 1978 and 1985 constituted a threat to economic stability.

Although government saving and state-enterprise saving can be substituted for each other within limits, the latter has certain advantages because it gives enterprise managers a stronger incentive to cut cost and increase profits and because it enables enterprises to function as autonomous economic units. The problem of state-enterprise saving is that profits intended for enterprise saving are diverted into bonuses and worker benefits if other aspects of system reform lag behind and that inappropriate motivation and distorted prices have led enterprise managers to make wrong investment decisions. Nonstate enterprises can contribute to savings and improve efficiency through competition and microeconomic structural change. If nonstate enterprises are allowed to make substantial profits and to invest more freely, they will have a strong incentive to increase their profits through cost reduction and greater attention to customer needs and to save and reinvest their profits.

In the case of household savings, the introduction of the rural production responsibility system has given farm households strong incentives to make their income grow faster through greater saving and reinvestment. The World Bank (1985, p. 147) finds that saving for housing is important in both the rural and urban areas, and saving for retirement has been increased substantially. Savings propensity, shown in Table 2.18, seems to vary inversely with GNP growth rate. This can be seen in 1981–1982 when GNP growth rate was low and in 1984–1985 and 1988 when GNP growth rates were high. The average savings propensity for the period 1978 to 1989 was 66.6 percent. The highest propensities were 78 percent in 1982 and 1987, and the lowest was 51.7 percent in 1988.

Qian (1988) points out that China's savings rate is higher than the average rate for developed and developing countries and explains that the higher marginal propensity to save in the post–1979 years is due to the increase in the amount of repressed inflation in the consumer goods markets and the shift in household economic behavior. Both

Table 2.18
Households Savings Propensity

Year	(1) Change in Savings Deposits (urban & rural)	(2) Change in Currency	(3) = (1)+(2) Household Money Accumulation	(4) = (1)/(3) Savings Propensity	(5) GNP Growth Rate
1978	29.0	16.6	45.6	63.6	
1979	70.4	55.7	126.1	55.8	11.4
1980	118.5	78.5	197.0	60.2	11.8
1981	124.2	50.1	174.3	71.3	6.8
1982	151.7	42.8	194.5	78.0	8.9
1983	217.1	90.7	307.8	70.5	11.9
1984	322.2	262.3	584.5	55.1	19.8
1985	407.9	195.7	603.6	67.6	22.9
1986	615.0	230.6	845.6	72.7	13.3
1987	835.7	236.1	1071.8	78.0	16.5
1988	728.2	679.5	1407.7	51.7	23.7
1989	649.6	210.0	859.6	75.6	12.9

Sources: China Statistical Yearbook, Beijing, 1984, 1988, 1991; Peebles, Gavin. 1986. Chinese Monetary Management 1950–1982, in *China's System Reform Conference*, Paper No. 34. Hong Kong: Centre of Asian Studies, University of Hong Kong.
Note: Figures in columns 1, 2, and 3 are expressed in Rmb 100 millions.

Qian (1988) and Feltenstein, Lebow, and van Wijnbergen (1990) use the absolute income hypothesis, the permanent income hypothesis, and the asset adjustment hypothesis to examine China's marginal savings rate. Qian looks at the urban sector only and found that there is a distinct increase in China's marginal savings rate in all the three hypotheses employed. In the case of absolute income hypothesis, the rate increased from 0.04 in 1955–1978 to 0.26 in 1979–1985. The corresponding figures for the permanent income hypothesis were from 0.01 to 0.27, while the rate for the asset adjustment hypothesis was from 0.09 to 0.28.

Investment in the prereform period had concentrated on heavy industry. The decision at the Fifth National People's Congress in June 1979 aimed to restore balance among industries. Agriculture is considered as the base, and investment in both agriculture and light industry had increased in 1979. Much of the increased investment expenditures went into small, light industrial factories. This had drained resources from more efficient large plants, and the power of local governments to allocate extra funds for construction increased. Investment in fixed assets is an important means of expanding production. Through the construction and purchase of fixed assets, it is thought that advanced technology and equipment can be absorbed and that new industries can be established. Investment in fixed assets contains the amount of work done in construction and purchase of fixed assets and includes investment in state-owned units, in urban and rural collective units, and in individual households. Investment in fixed assets of state-owned units consists of investment in capital construction, in technical-updating and transformation, and in other fixed assets. Investment in urban and rural collective units includes investment in collective units in cities, towns, and rural areas. Investment in urban and rural individual households includes housing investment by individuals in cities, towns, and industrial or mining areas; investment in housing; and in the purchase of productive fixed assets by rural individuals.[43]

There are four sources of funding for investment in fixed assets: appropriation from the state budget, domestic loans, foreign investment, and self-raised funds and others. Investment from the state budget is included in the state investment plan. State budget investment in capital construction includes appropriations from the state budget, both from central and local government budgets according to the state unified plan, and bank loans in substitution of budget appropriations, as well as appropriations for special construction projects from the budget of the central government. State budget investment in technical updating and transformation also includes appropriations for technical updating and transformation from both the central and local governments.

Domestic loans refer to investment funded by loans from construction banks, industrial, and commercial banks; loans from the local budget; and other domestic loans. Foreign investment refers to investment in domestic projects by utilization of foreign capital (including equipment, materials, and technology). The domestic investment funded by foreign capital raised by the Bank of China (BOC) and the China International Trust and Investment Corporations (CITIC) is included but excludes the purchase of foreign equipment and materials which used China's foreign exchange reserve and equipment from Eastern European countries through credit trade arrangements. Self-raised funds and other investment refer to funds raised by various ministries of the State Council, by provinces, autonomous regions and municipalities, prefectures, counties, and enterprises and other investment. Table 2.19 shows China's total investment in fixed assets by ownership and by source of funds. Between 1980 and 1990, the nominal value of total investment in fixed assets increased by 388.5 percent, and with the exception of 1989, annual increase peaked in 1985 with 38.8 percent. State-owned enterprises are the largest group of institutions carrying out fixed asset investments. However, the proportions have declined from 81.9 percent in 1980 to 65 percent in 1990. Fixed asset invest-

Table 2.19
Total Investment in Fixed Assets (Rmb 100 Millions)

Year	By Ownership							
	Total		State-owned		Collective		Individual	
	Value	Per-centage	Value	Share	Value	Share	Value	Share
1978			668.7					
1979			699.4					
1980	910.9		745.9	81.9	46.0	5.0	119.0	13.1
1981	961.0	5.5	667.5	69.5	115.2	12.0	178.3	18.5
1982	1230.4	28.0	845.3	68.7	174.3	14.2	210.8	17.1
1983	1430.1	16.2	952.0	66.6	156.3	10.9	321.8	22.5
1984	1832.9	28.2	1185.2	64.7	238.7	13.0	409.0	22.3
1985	2543.2	38.8	1680.5	66.1	327.5	12.9	535.2	21.0
1986	3019.6	18.7	1978.5	65.5	391.7	13.0	649.4	21.5
1987	3640.9	20.6	2298.0	63.1	547.0	15.0	795.9	21.9
1988	4446.6	22.1	2762.8	62.1	711.7	16.0	1022.1	22.9
1989	4137.7	-6.9	2535.5	61.3	570.0	13.8	1032.3	24.9
1990	4449.3	7.5	2918.6	65.6	529.5	11.9	1001.2	22.5

Year	By Source							
	State budget		Domestic loan		Foreign invest.		Self-raised funds & others	
	Value	Share	Value	Share	Value	Share	Value	Share
1981	269.8	28.1	122.0	12.7	36.4	3.8	532.9	55.5
1982	279.3	22.7	176.1	14.3	60.5	4.9	714.5	58.1
1983	339.7	23.8	175.5	12.3	66.6	4.7	848.3	59.3
1984	421.0	23.0	253.5	13.9	70.7	3.9	1082.7	59.2
1985	407.8	16.0	510.3	20.1	91.5	3.6	1533.6	60.3
1986	440.6	14.6	638.3	21.1	132.2	4.4	1808.5	59.9
1987	475.5	13.1	835.9	23.0	175.4	4.8	2154.0	59.2
1988	402.7	9.1	914.6	20.6	254.5	5.7	2874.8	64.7
1989	341.6	8.3	716.4	17.3	274.2	6.6	2805.6	67.8
1990	387.7	8.7	870.9	19.6	278.3	6.3	2912.5	65.5

Source: China Statistical Yearbook, Beijing, 1984, 1988, 1991.

ments by both collective-owned and individuals have expanded. State-owned enterprises, however, is still the largest investment sector. In the source of funding, investment from state budget has declined drastically from 28.1 percent in 1980 to 8.7 percent in 1990, while the other sources of funding have all increased. Although foreign investment still occupies the smallest proportion, it has almost doubled—from 3.8 percent in 1980 to 6.3 percent in 1990.

The productivity of investment can be seen from output figures. Furthermore, one of the primary objectives of reform is the balance of agriculture, light, and heavy industries. Table 2.20 shows the level of nominal value of agriculture and industrial outputs. As a proportion of gross output, agriculture's share has increased in the mid-1980s but falls back to its prereform level. However, this is only a relative measurement; agricultural output value went up by 298.4 percent between 1980 and 1990. The proportional share between light and heavy industrial output improved slightly between 1977 and 1990; light industrial output share expanded merely from 32.9 percent in 1977 to 37.4 percent in 1990. The decline in the proportional share of heavy industrial output was small; it fell considerably in the early 1980s from 41.9 percent in 1977 to 34.5 percent in 1981 but rose to 38.3 percent in 1990. On the whole, the share of heavy industrial output did not decline, while the increased proportion of light industries expanded at the expense of agriculture. In growth terms, between 1980 and 1990, total industrial and agricultural output expanded by 346.3 percent. However, the growth rate in light industry was slightly bigger than heavy industry between 1980 and 1990. The rigidity of the industrial structure obvi-

Table 2.20
Output Value (At Current Price, Rmb 100 Millions)

Year	Total	Agri-culture	Industrial			Proportions		
			Total	Light	Heavy	Agric.	Light	Heavy
1977	4978	1253	3275	1638	2087	25.2	32.9	41.9
1978	5634	1397	4237	1826	2411	24.8	31.2	42.8
1979	6379	1698	4681	2045	2636	26.6	32.1	41.3
1980	7077	1923	5154	2430	2724	27.2	34.3	38.5
1981	7581	2181	5400	2781	2619	28.8	36.7	34.5
1982	8294	2483	5811	2919	2892	29.9	35.2	34.9
1983	9211	2750	6461	3135	3326	29.9	34.0	36.1
1984	10831	3214	7617	3608	4009	29.7	33.3	37.0
1985	13335	3619	9716	5106	5107	27.1	34.6	38.3
1986	15207	4013	11194	5330	5864	26.4	35.0	38.6
1987	18489	4676	13813	6656	7157	25.3	36.0	38.7
1988	24089	5865	18224	8979	9245	24.3	37.3	38.4
1989	28552	6535	22017	10761	11256	22.9	37.7	39.4
1990	31586	7662	23924	11813	12111	24.3	37.4	38.3
Growth rate 1980-1990	346%	298%	364%	386%	345%			

Source: China Statistical Yearbook, Beijing, 1984, 1988, 1991.

ously has not permitted the balance to till in good favor of light industries in the first decade of reform.

Between 1980 and 1989, total investment in fixed assets increased by 354.3 percent. Comparing with the total output growth rate of 303.4 percent, one cannot conclude that investment in fixed assets has been too productive. The comparison is even weaker when looking at the growth rates of light and heavy industries. This, however, is not surprising, for much of investment in fixed assets was geared to basic construction and infrastructural development. The total output/investment in fixed assets ratio fell gradually from 7.77 in 1980 to its lowest at 5.04 in 1986 and stayed at 6.90 in 1989. Efficiency in fixed assets investment did not improve in the 1980s.

Reform at the industrial and enterprise levels needs to be deepened. Poor enterprise management and output performance have been reported. For example, a report in 1987 illustrated that the incentive system was inappropriately applied. A chemical factory offered a bonus system of five yuan to each worker for every additional ton above the production target. Workers responded by heating chemicals faster than before, resulting in more coal being used and raised production cost and lowered profits. The management did a quick reversal, making the bonus payable only for every ton of coal saved. Workers responded by slowing down the heating process to such a level that production fell to an all-time low and the factory verged on bankruptcy, though the workers saved much coal.[44] Enterprise management must become independent from political influence. Managers should have the overall responsibility on output and production; cadres should not be given the authority to interfere with production work. It was reported that inexperienced cadres had added an unnecessary burden to production.[45] Despite the bold step taken on the separation of party and government by the previous Prime Minister Zhao Ziyang in the Thirteenth Party Congress in 1987, the involvement of party politics in output and production is detrimental to the efficiency of investment. Despite the adequate supply of investment funds both locally and from abroad, the industrial structure in China is basically outdated with too many inefficient state-owned enterprises. The problem does not seem to rest with the supply of funds, but the focus should be their efficient use.

Table 2.21 shows total investment in fixed assets by state-owned enterprises. Investment in capital construction remained at nearly 75 percent before 1980, but it declined gradually to 57.7 percent in 1988. The percentage of newly added fixed assets in capital construction has been high and constantly remained at above 70 percent. Before 1984, over 60 percent of fixed investment in state enterprises came from the central budget, but the percentage has fallen to only 38 percent. Profit retention by state enterprises expanded drastically from 2.1 billion

Table 2.21
Total Investment in Fixed Assets by State Enterprises

Year	Total (Rmb 100 million)	Capital Construction		Share of total in renovation, upgrading and other investment
		Share of total	Share of newly added	
1978	668.72	74.9	74.3	25.1
1979	699.36	74.9	83.7	25.1
1980	745.90	74.9	79.1	25.1
1981	667.51	66.4	86.6	33.6
1982	845.31	65.7	74.4	34.3
1983	951.96	62.4	76.3	37.6
1984	1185.18	62.7	71.8	37.3
1985	1680.51	63.9	68.2	36.1
1986	1978.50	59.4	79.1	40.6
1987	2297.99	58.4	71.4	41.6
1988	2726.76	57.7	71.1	42.3
1989	2509.98	61.3	70.5	38.7

Source: China Report: Social and Economic Development 1949–1989. 1990. Hong Kong: Zie Yonder Company, pp. 229 and 238.

yuan in 1978 to 11.8 billion yuan in 1981 and further escalated to 31.3 billion yuan in 1984.[46] It was reported that in 1982 and 1983, state enterprises made a loss of US$ 2 billion and US$ 1.3 billion, respectively, and that the percentage of state enterprises losing money was 26.1 and 15.8, respectively.[47]

The pursuance of rapid growth has given rise to the serious problem of shortages of raw materials and electricity. Chinese media reports suggest that key reform goals are being undermined by the rapid growth, and high output in some cases is caused not by efficiency gains but by the use of large amount of inputs. Rapid growth is wearing out equipment at excessive rates, increasing occupational hazards in factories. High output levels have been possible due to the import of large amounts of raw materials. For example, imports of rolled steel in 1985 were equivalent to one half of domestic production, yet China experienced shortages of rolled steel and other raw materials. The shortages have actually eased pressure on firms to maintain quality standards, since low product quality remains a serious problem throughout China.[48]

FOREIGN TRADE AND INVESTMENT

The establishment of the Shenzhen Special Economic Zone (SEZ) in 1979 marks the opening up of China to the outside world for trade and foreign-direct investment. Its primary aim is to utilize foreign funds, and to promote China's foreign economic and technological cooperation and expanding foreign trade. Subsequently, three more SEZs were established in 1984. The Chinese authority maintained four principles governing the use of foreign resources, namely (1) equity, mutual benefit, and lawful right; (2) good faith and appropriate terms; (3) ability to repay; and (4) funds raised in proportion to China's available foreign exchange reserve. Beijing's formal takeover of China's membership in the International Monetary Fund (IMF) from Taiwan on April 17, 1980, further confirmed and consolidated China's intention of opening her economy to the outside world. China also became a member of the Asian Development Bank on March 10, 1986, while Taiwan was designated Taipei, China. Beijing was seeking a seat on the board of directors of the bank, and subscribed 114,000 shares of the bank's capital stock valued at $1.3 billion, the largest subscription after the United States and Japan.[49]

China can obtain foreign savings from three sources: exports, trading agreements, and foreign capital inflows. About one third of exports is primary products, and its volume is unlikely to change much, mainly because of supply constraints and competing domestic demand. Export prospects for manufactured goods are more favorable.[50] Trading agreements include joint ventures, joint production or management, joint exploration, compensatory trade, processing raw materials and assembling parts for companies abroad, leasing, and securities sold to foreign institutions.

There are two categories of foreign capital inflows. One is loan and foreign borrowing from foreign governments; the other is financial aid from the World Bank and the IMF. Loans from foreign banks are divided into short-term credit loans, intermediate-term credit loans, and long-term credit loans. In general, short-term credit loans have a term of one year or less. Foreign borrowing has become a major earner of foreign savings. There was a considerable degree of goodwill in the late 1970s, and two reasons explained the warm relationship between China and the World Bank. One was China's 4-percent annual growth rate, its healthy balance of payments, and its prudent external debt in the early 1980s. The other was its good repayment record.[51]

Imai (1991) points out that China has rapidly increased its foreign loan intake in 1985, and loans had vastly exceeded the amount of external foreign-direct investment. By 1986, foreign loans accounted for 69.1 percent of all foreign capital inflows. Fears began to arise in 1986 over the size of the foreign debt, but by 1988, the loan value reached US$ 6.4 billion. Economic sanctions imposed by Western nations in response to the Tiananmen crackdown of June 1989 had made acquisition of new foreign loans difficult for about a year. In 1990, China had contracted for a smaller increase in loans than in 1989, and credit lines remained low. Extension of loans by the World Bank and foreign investment loans such as yen credits resumed in the latter half of 1990. Imai observes that the use of foreign loans is divided between local governments (about 40 percent) and central government organizations (about 60 percent). Japan alone accounted for over 40 percent of all foreign loans, followed by the World Bank at 16 to 17 percent.

The principle of debt management in China is centralized control but decentralized responsibility. The State Council exercises overall control while the responsibility for managing plans and approving cases is divided among the individual government ministries. The State Planning Commission formulates plans for the use of foreign capital, the PBC manages the foreign loans, and the Ministry of Finance manages the foreign borrowings of the central ministries and commissions and the local governments. The Ministry of Foreign Economic Relations and Trade (MOFERT) manages direct investment from other countries, while the Committee for Guidance of the Special Economic Zones of the State Council manages foreign loans of the SEZs and directly administered cities.[52]

By the end of 1988, China had entered into nearly 16,000 direct foreign contracts, with an operation rate near 40 percent.[53] Shen (1990) emphasizes that initial direct foreign investment performance has made a significant contribution to China's economy, but by 1988–1989, direct foreign investment had reached a critical stage in which fundamental socioeconomic problems were destined to hinder its further development. Shen (1990, pp. 61–62) summarizes China's experience with direct foreign investment as a cyclic pattern of development, accompanied by frequent policy adjustments and changes. There were four periods of major changes in the first decade of economic reform. In 1979–1982, China's overall policy remained restrained, and the value of direct foreign investment was limited. In the second period of 1983–1985, China promoted her direct foreign investment policy, and foreign investment surged into China. In 1986–1987, however, rising economic problems forced a policy of retrenchment that reversed direct foreign investment's growth. In the spring of 1988, a call for "gold coast development" set off another boom, which lasted until spring 1989.

Shen (1990) argues that the problems of direct foreign investment reflect both economic constraints and systemic constraints. The major economic constraint is foreign exchange shortage. In approving direct foreign investment projects, foreign enterprises have to demonstrate an ability to balance their foreign exchange accounts by exporting part of the output. Most foreign investments, therefore, are not able to sell domestically. The situation is worse for those foreign enterprises

62

Financial Repression and Economic Reform in China

which needed foreign exchange to import technology and raw materials. Furthermore, foreign exchange is difficult for domestic customers to obtain and is reluctant to spend on local assembled goods rather than on imports. In some cases, local production is even more expensive than imports. Thus, the industrial output is not competitive both at home and in the international market.

The major systemic constraint is the centralized system that has been modified by recent reforms. A typical example is the supply of industrial inputs. Demands are decided by government planners at various levels, and although a materials market emerged, it ends up with more speculations than proper allocation of material inputs. The traditional policy of work allocation by the state also comes into conflict with foreign enterprises in China. Foreign employers insisted on the right to hire and fire workers, but in practice, workers are provided by local government agencies. The problem of bureaucracy has been particularly onerous; foreign investment participants have to fight hard against red tape.

Table 2.22 shows the three major sources of foreign resources inflows: foreign loans, direct foreign investment (FDI), and exports. Between 1983 and 1989, exports were the major source of foreign resource inflow, because the share was constantly maintained at over 80 percent.

Table 2.22
Inflow of Foreign Resources (US$ 100 Millions)

Year	Total	Foreign Loans (percentage share)	FDI (pecentage share)	Exports (percentage share)
1979-1982	895.47	10.85	1.79	87.36
1983	242.11	4.40	3.78	91.82
1984	288.45	4.46	4.92	90.62
1985	319.97	8.40	6.12	85.48
1986	381.98	13.13	5.87	81.00
1987	478.92	12.12	5.53	82.35
1988	577.46	11.23	6.47	82.29
1989	625.99	10.04	6.03	83.93
Percentage change 1983-1989	159	490	312	136

Sources: China Report: Social and Economic Development 1949–1989. 1990. Hong Kong: Zie Yonder Company, p. 351; *China Statistical Yearbook,* Beijing, 1984, 1988, 1991.

The share of foreign loans was steady at about 10 percent, while the FDI's share did not exceed 7 percent. In growth terms, foreign loans grew nominally by 490 percent between 1983 and 1989, and FDI grew by 312 percent, while exports grew by only 136 percent. Foreign loans have occupied a growing important position as a form of foreign resource inflow.

Table 2.23 gives the breakdown of foreign loan items used. There is no general pattern of development for each of the five items of government loans, loans from international financial organizations, export financing, commercial loans, and bond issues. The largest share of government loans was in 1984 at 56 percent. Loans from international financial institutions increased drastically in the mid-1980s, with a largest share of 27 percent in 1986, then leveled off to a share of less than 20 percent. Export financing enjoyed a steady increase in value terms, although the share in total foreign resource inflow remained small at less than 14 percent in 1988. Commercial loans have taken up the largest share among all the five categories at close to 40 percent since 1987. Bond issues have been irregular. They became quite important in the mid-1980s but dropped to less than 3 percent of the total in 1989.

The breakdown in FDI is shown in Table 2.24. Equity joint venture has become more important, increasing from a share of 5.55 percent between 1979 and 1982 to 54 percent in 1989, and growth in nominal

Table 2.23
Foreign Loans Used (Percentage Share)

Year	Total (US$ 100 millions)	Govern-ment Loan	Interna-tional Financial Organiza-tion	Export Financing	Commercial Loans	Bond issues
1982	17.83	31.02	0.17	10.60	48.23	9.98
1983	10.65	67.23	6.85	9.95		15.96
1984	12.86	56.22	14.23	10.34		19.13
1985	25.06*	19.39	24.10	5.03	20.99	30.41
1986	50.16	16.77	26.75	3.55	29.80	23.11
1987	58.05	13.75	12.32	8.15	44.44	21.34
1988	64.87	18.17	17.31	13.69	37.54	13.29
1989	62.86	34.19	17.24	10.21	36.10	2.24

Source: Imai, Satoshi. 1991. China's Foreign Debt—Where It Stands Today. *China Newsletter,* JETRO, 93 (July/August):17.
*There is a discrepancy in this value between the source quoted here and the sources of Table 2.22.

64   *Financial Repression and Economic Reform in China*

Table 2.24
Foreign-Direct Investment (Percentage Share)

Year	Total (US$100 millions)	Equity Joint Venture	Contractual Joint Venture	Cooperative Development	Solely Funded Operation
1979-1982	17.67	5.55	30.11	28.07	2.27
1983	9.16	8.08	24.78	31.88	4.69
1984	14.19	17.97	32.77	36.86	1.06
1985	19.59	29.71	29.86	24.55	0.66
1986	22.44	35.83	35.38	11.59	0.71
1987	26.47	56.14	23.42	6.91	0.94
1988	37.39	52.82	20.86	5.70	6.04
1989	37.73	53.99	19.93	6.15	9.83
Percentage 1983-1989	312	265	231	-21	763

Source: China Report: Social and Economic Development 1949–1989. 1990. Hong Kong: Zie Yonder Company, p. 351.

terms between 1983 and 1989 was 2,653 percent. Cooperative development which experienced not only a declining share from 28 percent between 1979 and 1982 to 6 percent in 1989 but also a growth rate of 20.5 percent between 1983 and 1989. The share of contractual joint venture has declined considerably since 1988. Solely funded operation has remained small but has expanded considerably since 1988. Overall FDI has increased by 312 percent between 1983 and 1989. Table 2.25 shows that a large portion of FDI has been geared to tourism and the hotel industry.

Table 2.25
Foreign-Direct Investment in China, July 1979 to December 1985

Kinds of Investment	Joint Ventures (percentage)	Cooperative Business (percentage)	Wholly Foreign Owned (percentage)
Hotels & Apartments	48.5	50.0	10.0
Machinery & Electronics	15.1	2.0	35.0
Textile & Light Industries	21.0	5.0	30.0
Energy	10.0	15.0	0.0
Materials	0.0	10.0	20.0
Agriculture	0.0	8.0	0.0
Services	5.0	10.0	5.0

Source: Oborne, Michael. 1986. China's Special Economic Zones. Paris: OECD Development Centre, p. 17.

One should not be carried away with the amount of foreign resource inflows because there are matching outflows. Taking into account of imports and all foreign debts, Table 2.26 shows that China has experienced an outflow of resources since 1983, especially in 1985 and 1986. Although the foreign debt needs not to be repaid until years later, China's import bill is excessively large. As Table 2.27 shows, although the export/GNP ratios are rising, they are very low. Furthermore, both the export/total foreign resources ratios and the export/FDI ratios have fallen since the mid-1980s. The ability of foreign resources in raising exports has remained weak, implying that the ability for China to repay foreign debt and borrowing will become difficult. One solution certainly is the reduction of imports or to improve productivity and allow output and export to expand.

PRICES AND INFLATION

China's prices do not reflect relative market scarcities or the cost of production. State-set prices have been changed infrequently since the 1950s. Some goods have accumulated large inventories, while others are in severe shortage. Between 1979 and 1986, there have been six principal changes to the price structure. For example, in 1979 the purchase prices of farm and sideline products were raised by a big margin and additional price rises were set for above-quota purchases of the major farm products, the sale prices of eight nonstaple foods were raised

Table 2.26
Total Available Foreign Resource (US$ 100 Millions)

Year	(1) Total Foreign Loans	(2) FDI	(3) Balance of Trade	(4) Foreign Debt	(5) = (1)+(2)+ (3)-(4)
1982	17.83		30.3	21.6	
1983	10.65	9.16	8.4	19.2	9.01
1984	12.86	14.19	-12.7	15.7	-1.35
1985	26.88	19.59	-149.0	9.9	-112.43
1986	50.14	22.44	-119.7	21.6	-68.72
1987	58.05	26.47	-37.7	28.6	18.22
1988	64.87	37.39	-77.5	37.3	-12.54
1989	62.86	37.73	-66.0	38.7	-4.11

Sources: China Report: Social and Economic Development 1949-1989. 1990. Hong Kong: Zie Yonder Company, p. 351; *China Statistical Yearbook,* Beijing, 1984, 1988, 1991; Imai, Satoshi. 1991. China's Foreign Debt – Where It Stands Today, *China Newsletter,* JETRO, 93 (July/August):17.

Table 2.27
Export/GNP, Export/Total Foreign Resource, and Export/FDI Ratios

Year	Export/GNP	Export/Total Foreign Resource	Export/FDI
1978	0.0467		
1979	0.0530		
1980	0.0607		
1981	0.0770		
1982	0.0797	12.54	
1983	0.0755	20.87	24.27
1984	0.0834	20.33	18.42
1985	0.0944	10.17	13.96
1986	0.1113	6.17	13.79
1987	0.1295	6.79	14.90
1988	0.1261	7.33	12.71
1989	0.1248	8.36	13.93

Sources: China Report: Social and Economic Development 1949–1989. 1990. Hong Kong: Zie Yonder Company, p. 351; *China Statistical Yearbook,* Beijing, 1984, 1988, 1991; Imai, Satoshi. 1991. China's Foreign Debt – Where It Stands Today, *China Newsletter,* JETRO, 93 (July/August):17.

by 30 percent in the cities, and city dwellers were subsidized accordingly.[54] The 12th Central Committee at the Third Plenery Session held in October 1984 acknowledged the irrational price system in the forms of (1) inadequate price differentials for a given product with diverse quality; (2) irrational price ratios between different commodities, particularly the relative low prices for some mineral products and raw and semifinished materials; and (3) the retail price of major farm and sideline products set lower than their state purchasing price. It was pointed out that the irrational price system is closely related to the irrational system of price control. The overcentralized system of price control must be reformed by reducing the scope of uniform prices set by the state and appropriately enlarging the scope of floating prices within certain limits and of free prices.

Prices should respond rather quickly to changes in labor productivity and the relation between market supply and demand. The guiding principles of price reform were as follows: (1) the irrational price ratios should be adjusted on the basis of exchange of equal values and changes in the relation between supply and demand; (2) when the prices of some mineral products and raw and semifinished materials are raised, the processing enterprises must substantially cut down consumption so that the increased production cost can be basically offset within the enterprise, with only a small part of the increase being borne by the state through tax reductions and exemptions; and (3) in solving the problem of the state purchasing farm and sideline products at prices higher than their selling prices and in readjusting the prices of consumer goods, effective measures must be adopted to ensure that the real income of urban and rural inhabitants do not go down as a result of price readjustments.[55]

The subsequent price reform in 1985 contained four objectives: (1) rationally readjust the purchasing and marketing prices of grain and the purchasing price of cotton in the rural areas and introduce the practice of state purchase according to contract; (2) appropriately raise charges for short-distance railway transport to facilitate the restructuring of the transportation system; (3) properly widen price differences for products of different quality and increase regional price differences; reduce or eliminate expensive and unmarketable products of inferior quality; and encourage a rapid increase in the manufacture of brand-name, high-quality products in order to facilitate rational commodity circulation; and (4) leave basically unchanged the prices of those raw and semifinished materials, fuels, and other major means of production which are distributed according to state plan, while the prices of those marketed by enterprises through their own channels according to specific regulations are determined by market forces.[56]

It is widely believed that price reform has led to inflation. As soon as reform on prices was announced in 1984, policies restricting inflation growth was on its way. China's 1985 budget called for narrowing the budget deficit by slowing the growth of government spending. The 1985 antiinflation package included a 10-percent cut in administrative expenditures and a tight money policy. In April 1985, interest rates on time deposits and on loans for working funds were raised. In order to reduce excess currency, the authority set aside $2 billion in foreign exchange reserves to be used to import scarce consumer durables. Many of the administrative controls were employed through China's banking system. Chinese leaders were very concerned with inflation, excessive investment spending, and its large trade deficit.[57] It was reported that inflation was as high as 15 percent in 1985.[58]

Chen and Hou (1986) summarize the four sets of prices under the current Chinese reform system: planned, floating, negotiated, and free market. The most important one is the planned price, which covers all of those commodities and services essential to production and consumption and is set by the state and changed infrequently. These commodities account for 65 to 70 percent of total retail sales, and these prices are uniform throughout the country. Floating price was introduced in 1980 as a result of the authority's attempt to introduce some degree of flexibility to the price structure. A floating price is usually set in accordance with market conditions by industrial and commercial enterprises, and the limit of floating is determined by the state at a range of 5 to 30 percent of the planned price.

The negotiated price refers to those prices agreed on between the buyer and seller within predetermined limits. It is applied to most of the agricultural products within the state procurement scheme once the purchase quotas for these products are fulfilled. Usually these negotiated prices are lower than those prevailing in free markets. Last, the free market prices cover a wide variety of agricultural and sideline products in the countryside and in cities throughout China. The free market prices are determined by demand and supply, though they are subject to government regulations. In terms of total retail sales in 1981, the planned and floating prices accounted for 92.5 percent; negotiated prices, 3.7 percent; and free market prices, 3.8 percent. The price indexes thus compiled by the State Statistical Bureau principally reflect the movement in the government-fixed prices.

There are various explanations to the causes of inflation in the first decade of reform in China. Naughton (1991) argues that increases in consumer prices are caused basically by changes in relative prices; for example, the permission to let food price rise has accounted for most of the increase in the overall price level. The price structure in China is distorted; low prices in agriculture have ensured that the bulk of national saving is occurred to the state-owned modern industrial sector. Heavy reliance on revenues coming from the modern industrial sector has been the special feature of the Chinese budget. But relative price changes have rapidly reduced the profitability of modern industry, leading to a huge decline in the share of budget revenues in GNP, and require large public borrowing. Naughton (1991) concludes that this has created a source of inflationary pressure which is independent from that created by the direct effect of relative price changes. The monetary policy has been very accommodating since the end of 1984 and provided sufficient liquidity for price increases which led to an explosion of inflation in 1988. Beginning from 1987, prices of all important consumer goods began to increase, and price increases became quantitatively more important than changes in relative prices. Price realignment is not complemented by reforms in the tax and fiscal system. Flaws in the sequencing of reforms is the primary cause of inflation in China.

Yunqi Li (1989) categorizes the causes of inflation into reform inflation—price reform and changes in the economic structure associated with economic reform—and excess demand inflation—mistakes made in the process of formulating and implementing economic policy, resulting in the expansion of excess aggregate demand. Yang (1989) associates inflation in China with the monetary crisis in the second half of the 1980s. Expansion of fiscal deficits since the mid-1980s, coupled with falls in enterprise deposits, an easy credit policy, and a huge quantity of money circulated outside the formal monetary system, are the major causes of inflation. For example, enterprises did not deposit their cash receipts into banks but rather made direct wage payments without going through the banks. In 1985, the interest rate did not rise in response to an inflation rate of 8.8 percent and resulted in a negative interest rate. By 1988 when inflation reached 10 percent or more, instead of depositing money in banks, commodity hoarding replaced cash deposits. The unwanted cash circulated outside the banking system, and informal markets emerged, thereby further eroding the role of banks as a financial intermediary.

Free market prices are also available from Chinese data sources. Table 2.28 shows the discrepancy of free market and retail prices. By examining the annual change indexes, one can see that the free market prices did not deviate too much from retail prices, and it is only toward the second half of the 1980s that the free market price index exceeded the official retail price index by a large margin. On the contrary, in the late 1970s, the free market price was below that of the government set retail price. In constant terms, both the free market price and the retail price have more than doubled between 1977 and 1989. Wage increases were rapid in the first decade of reform as shown in columns 6 and 7 of Table 2.28. In most years, workers in collective-owned units enjoyed a higher wage increase than their counterparts in state-owned units. Severe wage increases were notable in years of high inflation.

Chen and Hou (1986) point out that economic reform in China has led to new demands for money. Economic decentralization has increased monetization of the economy, resulting in a situation whereby enterprises holding cash in excess of that prescribed by government regulations. The implementation of the production responsibility system, the increased autonomy of state, and collective enterprises are causes of growth in currency demand. Two causes of inflation in China are suggested: one is the adjustment of official or planned prices; the other is the increase in the volume of currency in circulation, due specifically to huge state budget deficits. Chen and Hou's analysis focuses on the relationship between currency supply and the retail sector. In China, most of the producer goods and wholesale transactions are handled by state enterprises according to planned prices. The use of cash is limited to wage payments. As a result, the effect of changes in the quantity of currency in circulation on prices or on the supply of producer goods in the state sector is limited. However, in the retail sector, currency is the regular means of payment. The currency sector is, therefore, closely linked to the retail sector.[59]

By using the Fisher's equation of exchange

$$MV = PT$$

Table 2.28
Prices and Wages Indexes

Year	Free Market Price Index		Retail Price Index		Price difference (1) - (3)	Real Wage Index	
	Previous year=100 (1)	1977=100 (2)	Previous year=100 (3)	1977=100 (4)	(5)	State-owned units (6)	Collective-owned units (7)
1977	97.6	100.0	102.2	100.0	-4.4	2.8	5.2
1978	93.4	93.4	100.7	101.5	-7.3	9.4	11.8
1979	95.5	89.2	102.0	103.6	-6.5	11.0	15.0
1980	101.9	90.9	106.0	111.0	-4.1	12.6	17.3
1981	105.8	96.2	102.4	113.9	3.4	2.8	8.0
1982	103.3	99.3	101.9	116.0	1.4	5.4	6.6
1983	104.2	103.5	101.5	117.4	2.7	4.0	6.2
1984	99.6	103.1	102.8	119.4	-3.5	14.3	33.4
1985	117.2	120.8	108.8	130.9	-3.6	12.8	14.2
1986	108.1	130.5	106.0	139.1	2.1	15.0	10.2
1987	116.3	151.8	107.3	149.4	9.0	5.0	5.5
1988	130.3	197.8	118.3	177.8	12.0	5.5	0.9
1989	110.8	219.2	117.8	209.0	-7.0	-4.3	-8.2

Source: China Statistical Yearbook, Beijing, 1984, 1988, 1991.
Notes: (6) = nominal annual wage index of state-owned units less annual retail price changes. (7) = nominal annual wage index of collective-owned units less annual retail price changes.

where M is the quantity of currency, V is the velocity of currency circulation, P is the retail price, and T is the commodity supply, Chen and Hou (1986) argue that V is quite stable in China because of the role of state banking in handling the receipts and expenditures of industrial and commercial enterprises. Thus, a change in M may not cause PT (retail sales) to change to the same degree. In an inflationary period, growth in M tends to be greater than growth in PT, the difference reflects suppressed inflation. Chen and Hou (1986, p. 822) define suppressed inflation as "a catchall for all sorts of inflationary pressures not captured in the retail price index largely because of price controls." Open inflation, measured by the retail price index, reflects only the extent of price increases for retail commodities controlled by the government and those sold on free markets. By using Chen and Hou's formula of suppressed inflation, Table 2.29 indicates the figures of open inflation, total inflation, and suppressed inflation for the first decade of reform in China. One can see from column 7 of Table 2.29 that China has experienced two periods of inflationary pressures. The first period began in 1979 and lasted until 1982, while the second period began in 1982 and lasted until 1987. The year 1988 also experienced rapid inflation but was quickly overcome by events in 1989. When comparing columns 1 and 7 in Table 2.29, those years which experienced severe suppressed inflation (1980, 1981, 1984, and 1988) corresponded to years of rapid currency growth.

A major criticism in Chen and Hou's (1986) measurement is that the velocity of circulation varies. An improvement is Feltenstein and Ha's (1991) construction of the "true" price inflation, which is based on the following formula:

$$\log P_T = \log P + \alpha \log(M2/PR)$$

where P_T is the true price, P is the official retail price, R is the real volume of consumer retail sales, and $M2$ is the stock of currency plus household bank deposits. Another parameter on the expectation adjustment (β) is also constructed from an output equation. Constant velocity is equivalent to the hypothesis that α equals to unity. The true rate of price inflation represents the opportunity cost of holding money. A simultaneous search process to find the optimal value of α and β is done by locating their log-likelihood values. The searching range for α is [0, 3] and β is [0, 1] with an interval width of 0.01. The values of α and β are 0.89 and 0.92, respectively. Using $\alpha = 0.89$, the yearly "true" price inflation rates are shown in column 8 of Table 2.29. As compared to the total inflation rate, "true" price inflation has a narrower gap of fluctuation, and the trend seems to be smoother than total inflation.

Table 2.29
Indicators of China's Inflation, 1976–1989 (Percentage Change)

Year	Currency in Circulation (1)	Retail Sales at Current Price (2)	Retail Sales at Constant Price (3)	General Retail Price Index (4)	Inflation Total (5)	Inflation Open (6)	Inflation Suppressed (7)	True Price Inflation (8)
1976	11.6	5.4	5.1	0.3	6.2	0.3	5.9	
1977	-4.1	7.0	4.9	2.0	-8.6	2.0	-10.6	
1978	8.7	8.8	8.0	0.7	0.6	0.7	-0.1	3.49
1979	26.1	15.5	13.2	2.0	11.4	2.0	9.4	13.14
1980	29.3	18.9	12.2	6.0	15.3	6.0	9.3	19.40
1981	14.5	9.8	7.2	2.4	6.8	2.4	4.4	13.59
1982	10.8	9.4	7.3	1.9	3.2	1.9	1.3	11.61
1983	20.6	10.9	9.2	1.5	10.4	1.5	8.9	15.03
1984	49.5	18.5	15.3	2.8	29.7	2.8	26.9	20.08
1985	24.7	27.5	17.2	8.8	6.4	8.8	-2.4	10.75
1986	23.3	15.0	8.5	6.0	13.7	6.0	7.7	20.17
1987	19.4	17.6	9.6	7.3	8.9	7.3	1.6	18.15
1988	46.7	27.8	7.9	18.5	36.0	18.5	17.5	21.18
1989	9.8	8.9	-7.6	17.8	18.8	17.8	1.0	34.33

Sources: China Statistical Yearbook, Beijing, 1984, 1988, 1991; Chen, Nai-Ruenn, and Chi-ming Hou. 1986. China's Inflation, 1979–1983: Measurement and Analysis, *Economic Development and Cultural Change*, 34(4):823; Feltenstein, Andrew, and Jiming Ha. 1991. Measurement of Repressed Inflation in China, *Journal of Development Economics* 36:279–294.
Notes: Column 4 = column 6. Column 5 is computed by dividing column 1 by column 3 after figures in both columns were converted to link indexes. Column 7 = column 5 − column 6.

In conclusion, different evidence tend to suggest that poor monetary management in the reform period has led to unprecedented rates of inflation. Huge budget deficits, easy credit policy, decentralization of authority to industrial enterprises, the expanded rural income resulting from the family responsibility system, the drive to consumption and the severe shortages in industrial inputs and consumption goods, and an extremely low interest rate ceiling for loans and deposits are the driving forces behind the inflation crisis, which is further deepened by abnormal or speculative behavior of commodity and industrial material hoarding in the late 1980s.

THE CHINESE VERSION OF FINANCIAL REPRESSION

The data discussed in this chapter suggest that the Chinese reform experience can be analyzed within the general framework of financial repression. Several major features of financial repression can be identified. In the area of money and banking, China experienced a very unsteady growth in currency circulation, an easy bank credits and loans policy, and a negative real interest rate in most years due to a low interest rate ceiling. In budgetary performance, China experienced continued fiscal deficits, and very large extrabudgetary revenues and expenditures. Together with large price subsidies, China has a very "soft budget" policy. Furthermore, state borrowing was forced upon enterprises and individuals in most cases. Savings were regarded as forced, mainly due to the inadequate supply of consumables, especially in the rural areas. The rise in wages was not in line with production of consumption goods, resulting in shortages in industrial inputs and speculative activities. China did not experience any major difficulties in securing foreign resources inflows in the forms of foreign loans, direct foreign investment, and foreign borrowing. At the same time, the amount of foreign resources inflow was limited by the size of imports, particularly in the mid-1980s.

A large supply of financial resources coexisted with a rather rigid and restrictive economic structure. Inflation has led to speculative activities as well as hoarding of industrial inputs and consumption goods. Currency circulated outside the formal banking systems, and the store of value function of money was overshadowed and dominated by the medium of exchange function. It might not be possible to measure the degree of financial repression, but the various injections of financial resources illustrate the extent of "shallow" finance in China. Table 2.30 shows the aggregate figures of financial resources injected into the Chinese economy. Column 1 is the net budgetary injection (i.e., fiscal balance + extrabudgetary balance + price subsidies); column 2 shows the net state borrowing (i.e., inflow of national debts less out-

Table 2.30
Injection of Financial Resources (Rmb Billions)

Year	(1) Net budgetary and extra-budgetary injection	(2) Net state borrowing	(3) Self-raised funds in fixed assets investment	(4) Change in national bank loans	(5) Net foreign resources	(6) Total of (1) to (5)	(7) Resource injection/ output ratio	(8) Resource injection/ GNP ratio	(9) True price inflation
1980		1.44		374.67					
1981		1.02	53.29	350.37					
1982		2.83	71.45	287.60					
1983	13.33	3.69	84.83	378.78	5.56	487.74	0.19	0.30	15.03
1984	14.88	4.84	108.27	988.52	3.19	1123.72	0.22	0.34	20.08
1985	18.90	5.03	153.36	1485.94	-30.32	1472.53	0.11	0.17	10.75
1986	8.52	8.81	180.85	1684.89	-16.48	1874.99	0.27	0.42	20.17
1987	16.92	8.77	215.40	1441.95	17.45	1702.18	0.27	0.45	18.15
1988	18.61	18.44	287.48	1518.98	9.21				
1989				1858.04	12.88				

Sources: China Statistical Yearbook, Beijing, 1984, 1988, 1991; Feltenstein, Andrew, and Jiming Ha. 1991. Measurement of Repressed Inflation in China, *Journal of Development Economics* 36:279–294.

flow or debt repayments); column 3 is the self-raised funds for investment in fixed assets; column 4 is the change in national banks' total loans; column 5 is net foreign resource inflows (i.e., trade balance + FDI + total foreign loans). Due to the limited availability of extrabudgetary expenditure figures, the aggregate shown in column 6 does not reflect the performance of the entire decade. However, the size of financial resources injected into the Chinese economy has been large and has increased rapidly. With the exception of 1985 when the injection was shortened by an extraordinary huge trade deficit, financial resources had increased by 249 percent between 1983 and 1987, while total output (agricultural and industrial) and GNP had increased by only 100.7 percent and 95.4 percent, respectively, for the same period.

Columns 7, 8, and 9 in Table 2.30 show the resource/output ratio, the resource/GNP ratio, and "true" price inflation. Increase in these ratios did not keep pace with the size of resources injection. In the case of the resource/output ratio, the figures between 1986 and 1987 remained constant. Among the five types of financial sources, net budgetary injection is fairly low, though the lowest was net state borrowing. Resources injection arising from self-raised funds was large, implying a relatively good ability on the part of enterprises in raising funds themselves. Foreign resources did not have a steady inflow, largely due to import fluctuations. However, changes in bank loans were the largest share of resource injection. The real negative interest rate, resulting from a low interest rate ceiling, and the easy credit policy have accounted for the large injection. The most crucial aspect of financial repression in China, therefore, is a weak control of the banking sector and a loose financial credit policy exercised by national banks.

One can conclude that the major feature of financial repression in China is internal. The easy credit policy and the low interest rate ceiling have encouraged unproductive investment at the expense of productive investment. The solution would be to relax interest rate ceilings and let the market rate work more extensively in order to eliminate inefficient investment and regulate productive investment activities. It is only through a high return on investment that output can be increased and shortages eliminated over time. Rising outputs, in turn, increase supply and check inflation from deteriorating further. Once money functions as the store of value, then the McKinnon (1973) argument of complementarity between money and capital can be materialized. Rising outputs also generate consumption and income, which would lead to higher tax revenue and ease the pressure on the state budget. The chain relationship starts with the correction of financial policy by removing the interest rate ceiling. A proper reallocation of investment funds through an increased role of interest rate would gradually remove major economic problems facing the authority currently.

NOTES

1. World Bank, *China: Socialist Economic Development,* vol. 1 (Washington, D.C.: World Bank, 1983), 80.

2. Zhaoxiang Dong and Heihu Li. 1981. "A Fundamental Principle for Achieving Rural Prosperity and Raising Economic Effectiveness," *Jingji Yanjiu [Economic Research]* (May 1981):30–34.

3. Peter Nolan and Fureng Dong, eds., *The Chinese Economy and Its Future* (Cambridge, Mass.: Polity Press, 1990), 18.

4. C. T. Wu, "Impacts of Rural Reforms," in *China's Economic Reforms,* ed. Joseph Chai and Chi K. Leung (Hong Kong: University of Hong Kong, 1987), 265–292.

5. Nolan and Dong, *Chinese Economy,* 9.

6. *China Report: Social and Economic Development 1949–1989* (Hong Kong: Zie Yonder Company, 1990), 21.

7. Ryutaro Komiya, "Macroeconomic Development of China: Overheating in 1984–87 and Problems of Reform," *Journal of the Japanese and International Economies* 3(1989):64–121.

8. *Sing Dao Daily,* April 29, 1988, Hong Kong.

9. See, for example, *Sing Dao Daily,* May 27, 1988, Hong Kong.

10. *Hong Kong Standard,* China Special, December 9, 1987, Hong Kong.

11. Xu Meizheng, "Structural Reform and Financial Reform in China," in *Financial Reform in Socialist Economies,* ed. Christine Kessides et al., Economic Development Institute Seminar Series (Washington, D.C.: World Bank, 1989).

12. Charles E. Greer, ed., *China Facts and Figures Annual,* vol. 12 (Gulf Breeze, Fla.: Academic International Press, 1989), 378. For a detailed breakdown of foreign financial institutions, see *People's Republic of China Year Book 1987* (Beijing: Xinhua Publishing House, October 1987), 292–293.

13. Joh Scherer, ed., *China Facts and Figures Annual,* vol. 9 (Gulf Breeze, Fla.: Academic International Press, 1986), 98.

14. Xu Meizheng, "Structural Reforms."

15. *South China Morning Post,* May 15, 1993.

16. Ibid., July 11, 1993.

17. Ibid., July 9, 1993.

18. See Y. C. Jao, "Financial Reform in China 1978–89: Retrospect and Reappraisal," *Journal of Economics and International Relations* 3(4[1990]): 279–309.

19. John Scherer, ed., *China Facts and Figures Annual,* vol. 10 (Gulf Breeze, Fla.: Academic International Press, 1987), 92.

20. Charles Greer, ed., *China Facts and Figures 1988 Annual,* vol. 11 (Gulf Breeze, Fla.: Academic International Press, 1989), 243.

21. Zhiqiang Liu, "China's National Debt," *Beijing Review* 31 (August 1988):28–29, 40.

22. Enhua Zhang, "Yen Snag in Bond Issues Abroad," *China Daily* (Business Weekly), September 7, 1987, p. 2.

23. For a detailed comparison, see Kui-Wai Li and Michael T. Skully, "Fi-

nancial Deepening and Institutional Development: Some Asian Experiences," *Savings and Development* 15(2[1991]):147–165; and idem, "Accumulation of Financial Resources in Asian Economies," *Savings and Development* 16(3[1992]): 225–241.

24. Walter T. Newlyn, ed., *The Financing of Economic Development* (Oxford: Claredon Press, 1977). Newlyn assumed that in an open economy, the relationship between the external reserve and credit expansion could be the ultimate constraint on credit expansion.

25. *Renmin daxue fu yin—Jinrong he Caimao* (Beijing: People's University, People's University Reprint Series–Money and Finance), vol. 3, 1979, p. 65.

26. Ibid., vol. 6, 1985, p. 103.

27. See, for example, *Zhongguo jinrong [China Finance]*, 1981, no. 11.

28. For a discussion on the political acceptability of the interest rate reform, see Kui-Wai Li, *The Reform and Management of Economic Reform in the PRC,* Working Paper No. 28, Department of Business and Management, City Polytechnic of Hong Kong, May 1988.

29. *Renmin daxue fu yin,* vol. 5, 1985, p. 104.

30. Ibid., vol. 12, 1981, p. 83; and idem, vol. 6, 1985, p. 106.

31. *South China Morning Post,* May 8, 1992.

32. *Renmin daxue fu yin,* vol. 5, 1981, pp. 5–13.

33. Ibid., vol. 8, 1985, pp. 8–50.

34. Ibid., pp. 8–52.

35. *Zhongguo jinrong,* 1984, no. 6, pp. 13–16.

36. For a detailed discussion of tax reforms, see Audrey Donnithorne, "Banking and Fiscal Changes in China since Mao," in *China's System Reforms Conference,* Paper No. 31 (Hong Kong, Centre of Asian Studies, University of Hong Kong, March 1986).

37. For a detailed discussion on profit substitution, see Cuilan Wu, "China's Reform of the Financial and Tax Systems," in *Financial Reform in Socialist Economies,* ed. C. Kessides et al., Economic Development Institute Seminar Series (Washington, D.C.: World Bank, 1989); and Henry C. Y. Ho, "Distribution of Profits and the Change from Profit Remission to Tax Payments for State Enterprises in China," in *China's System Reform Conference,* Paper No. 35 (Hong Kong, Centre of Asian Studies, University of Hong Kong, March 1986).

38. For details, see M. Nambu, "Problems in China's Financial Reforms," *China Newsletter,* Japan External Trade Organization (JETRO), 92 (May/June 1991):2–10.

39. Figures from 1985 were not comparable to other years due to the practice of profit substitution by taxes and to other factors. Nonetheless, the tax/GNP ratios declined between 1978 and 1984 as well as between 1985 and 1988.

40. "The Heavy Burden of State Subsidies," *China Briefing,* Hong Kong Bank, China Services Ltd., No. 38, March 1991.

41. For example, in attempting to control the growth of the total wage bill, the state has introduced various control measures such as a ceiling on basic wages and a progressive tax on bonuses. By so doing, too much attention is given to control the growth of basic wages and not in wage subsidies. See ibid.

42. Paul Reynolds, *China's International Banking and Financial System* (New York: Praeger, 1982), 10.

43. For the various definitions, see Explanatory Notes, *China Statistical Yearbook* (Beijing: State Statistical Bureau of the People's Republic of China, 1988), 919–946.

44. *Hong Kong Standard* (China Special), December 9, 1987, p. 3.

45. Ibid. This reproduces a Xian radio commentary. It said that relations with the party and the administration within enterprises is not well coordinated. Some factory party committee secretaries feel that they do not have power in their hands and that their words do not carry weight; therefore, they are dispirited and in an antagonistic mood. Some factory directors worry about the possibility of separating themselves from the party leadership and dare not boldly exercise their functions and powers. Some factory directors only like to see their party committees act as guarantors and are not keen on having their party committees act as their supervisors. Neither understand nor support the work carried out by their party committees. Factory directors are overburdened with work and spend a considerable part of their time on attending meetings, receiving visitors, and attending all kinds of examinations. A factory worker said he attended eight types of examinations within half a year, including an examination concerning knowledge of family planning.

46. Greer, *Facts and Figures*, vol. 12, pp. 148–149.

47. *Asian Wall Street Journal Weekly*, May 21, 1984, p. 12.

48. Scherer, *Facts and Figures*, vol. 9, p. 97.

49. *Beijing Review*, May 12, 1987, pp. 7–8; and *New York Times*, March 11, 1986, p. 50.

50. The World Bank Country Report of 1983 reported that in the aggregate, foreign exchange earnings from exports would grow only moderately in constant prices and that the growth was unlikely to reach 6 percent a year in the first half of the 1980s, though it could accelerate to 11 percent in the second half. World Bank, *China: Socialist Economic Development*, vol. 1 (Washington, D.C.: World Bank, 1983), 204.

51. *China Business Report*, January 1983, p. 4; and *Business PRC*, September/October 1983, vol. 6, no. 4.

52. For a detailed account, see S. Imai, 1991. "China's Foreign Debt–Where It Stands Today," *China Newsletter*, JETRO, 93 (July/August 1991):16–23.

53. "The Utilization of Foreign Capital: 1979–1988," *Beijing Review*, March 6–12, 1989, pp. 26–29.

54. *Beijing Review*, August 15, 1986, p. 15.

55. John Scherer, ed., *China Facts and Figures Annual*, vol. 8 (Gulf Breeze, Fla.: Academic International Press, 1985), 141.

56. Ibid., vol. 9, p. 66.

57. Joint Economic Committee, U.S. Congress, "China: Economic Performance in 1985," (mimeo, 1986) pp. 7–8.

58. *Beijing Review*, August 12, 1985, p. 12.

59. Nai-Ruenn Chen and Chi-ming Hou, "China's Inflation, 1979–1983: Measurement and Analysis," *Economic Development and Cultural Change* 34(4): 811–835. These authors found that about 80 percent of the quantity of currency

in circulation is in the hands of individual consumers. Generally, more than 40 percent of the quantity comes from wage and bonus payments and more than 30 percent from state procurement of agricultural and sideline products and state agricultural loans. Currency generated through these channels eventually expanded the purchasing power in the retail sector.

3

The Equity Market: Trend and Prospects

GENERAL DEVELOPMENTAL PROBLEMS

Patrick (1966) identifies two probable phenomena of causality relationship between financial development and economic growth. One is a "demand-following" phenomenon, in which "the creation of modern financial institutions, their financial assets and liabilities, and related financial services is in response to the demand for these services by investors and savers in the real economy." The other is "supply-leading," in which "the creation of financial institutions and the supply of their financial assets, liabilities, and related financial services is in advance of demand for them." The direction of causality changes over the course of development. Typically, as the process of real growth occurs, the financial "demand-following" response becomes dominant. Financial development through the establishment and well functioning of the equity market makes financial resources more productive since they are managed by private business organizations which put more emphasis on economic efficiency and productivity. Hemming and Mansoor (1988) argue that financial liberalization and equity market development can quicken privatization of enterprises, since market forces in the financial sector can influence enterprise behavior. Yoon (1986) also raises the presence of inefficiencies in financial liberalization without the efficient functioning of the equity markets.

To develop an equity market from a politics-driven, monobanking system in China is difficult. The first major problem is political acceptability. It was reported that when China conducted experiments with the shareholding system among enterprises and publicly issued stocks for the first time in 1986, people's attitude was indifferent. Staff members had to go from door to door selling stocks, and only one half of stocks issued was sold. The change took place in 1989 when the stock system was seen as "the product of socialization and commercialization of production, and not the sole property of capitalism."[1]

Dickie (1981) notes that the difficulties encountered in establishing equity markets in developing countries are obstacles affecting the supply of and demand for shares. As far as supply is concerned, three types of enterprises may go public: state-owned, locally-owned, and foreign-owned enterprises. Various problems in the primary market can be identified. First, due to a poor administration of tax laws and differences in bookkeeping practices, enterprises are reluctant to comply with disclosure requirements for public offerings. Second, the price of shares is kept low when offered in the primary market, investors can gain a favorable return when stock prices soared in the secondary market. Usually foreign enterprises face the difficulty on the method of determining the "fair" price for the shares. The loss of control makes enterprises reluctant to go public. The availability of alternative channels, such as bank borrowing, to raise capital will also be considered. If enterprises can secure loans from banks easily, the need to raise capital from the primary market is reduced. The lack of institutions willing to underwrite public offerings is another obstacle, since underwriting is indispensable to a healthy primary market.

On the demand side, the first problem is the existence of an inverted yield curve; that is, interest rates on short-term debt exceeding those on long-term debt adversely affect the demand for shares. Such a bias toward short-term debt makes it difficult for enterprises to secure long-term capital. The experience of other developing countries shows that investors are yield conscious and tend to compare the dividend rate with the yield on other forms of investment. Small investors mistrust paper investments or investments dominated in local currency. Tangible assets can be a more attractive form of portfolio diversification. The inability to understand the available financial statements and to evaluate independently the investment risk is another cause of reluctance of small investors to enter the security market.

In addition to the will to develop an equity market, institutional changes are needed. One is improvement in taxation policy so that both the share issuers and investors know exactly the extent of financial involvement. The other is the establishment of sound regulations stating the various registration requirements and exemptions so that investors are protected against malpractices such as insider abuse and market manipulation.[2]

THE DEVELOPMENT TREND

The development of the equity market in the first decade of economic reform in China is considered as slow. According to Tam (1991), capital market development in China's economic reform has gone through three qualitatively distinct phases. The first stage began in 1978 with the rapid development of the informal credit sector. The second stage began late in 1984 when enterprises and specialized banks tried to raise capital directly from their own employees and the public. The third stage began late in 1987 when the central government banned state enterprises from issuing equities without special approval. The intention then was to control rising inflationary pressures, but its side effect was to build up formal institutional arrangements, including the establishment of stock exchanges to promote secondary markets. The total estimated value of aggregate enterprise shares/bonds only amounted to Rmb 10 billion in 1985, Rmb 12 billion in 1986, Rmb 21 billion in 1988, and to Rmb 31 billion in 1989, while the number of stock-broking companies increased from 33 in 1988 to 44 in 1989. The amount of shares issued by joint stock companies was Rmb 2.4 billion in 1986, increasing to Rmb 5 billion in 1989.[3]

Despite both private and public bonds and shares being issued as early as in 1985,[4] value of shares traded in stock exchanges increased from Rmb 0.2 billion in 1988 to Rmb 2.3 billion in 1989. Total securities issued (including treasury bonds and other government bonds) were Rmb 67 billion, Rmb 100 billion, and Rmb 145 billion in 1987, 1988, and 1989, respectively.[5] Although many cities and provinces had been clamoring to open stock exchanges, the central government was only prepared to back the two stock exchanges in Shenzhen and Shanghai so as to maintain quality and a unified market.[6]

If one defines Tobin's q as the ratio between the value of shares traded and total securities issued, the values of q for 1988 and 1989 were 0.002 and 0.0159, respectively. It does need a rather matured capital market in order to have a higher q value. Goldsmith's (1969, p. 44) financial interrelations ratio (FIR), defined as the ratio of the aggregate market value of all financial instruments to the value of the country's national wealth, reflects the basic feature in financial development. The numerator of the FIR shows the kind and amount of aggregate financial capital in the economy, while the denominator of the ratio shows the economy's aggregate monetary wealth, which can be indicated by the level of national income. The FIR is a wider concept than the money/income ratio as it incorporates all financial capital in the economy. Less-developed countries tend to have a much lower FIR, but this improves as economic growth proceeds. It is no different for China, as Table 3.1 shows. Indeed, China's FIR was below 0.3 in the

Table 3.1
Financial Interrelations Ratios (FIR), 1981–1990

Year	Fixed Capital Investment* (Rmb billions)	GNP (Rmb billions)	FIR
1981	96.11	477.3	0.2013
1982	123.03	519.3	0.2369
1983	143.01	580.9	0.2462
1984	183.29	696.2	0.2633
1985	254.31	855.8	0.2972
1986	301.96	969.6	0.3114
1987	364.08	1130.1	0.3222
1988	444.66	1401.8	0.3201
1989	413.78	1591.6	0.2600
1990	444.93	1768.6	0.2516

Sources: Statistical Yearbook of China, Beijing, 1984, 1988, 1991; *China Statistical Yearbook,* Beijing, 1984, 1988, 1991.
*Sources of fixed capital investment include state budget, domestic loans, foreign funds, and self-raised funds.

first half of the 1980s, and slightly improved to over 0.3 in 1986–1988.

National attention on the stock market was raised in 1989 when interest and dividends were drawn from the stocks of the Development Bank, the first institution that sold stocks in Shenzhen. The interest rate reached 30 percent. The sluggish stock market suddenly became brisk as the news spread, and the price of the Development Bank stock rose from Rmb 20 to Rmb 180 per share.[7] On December 9, 1990, the Shanghai Stock Exchange was set up; the Shenzhen Stock Exchange was set up on July 3, 1991. By the end of 1991, the total value of stocks approved by the state and publicly issued in Shanghai and Shenzhen had reached Rmb 3.3 billion, of which 84.8 percent were public stocks and 15.2 percent were individual stocks. There were 89 enterprises which had publicly issued stocks, of which 34 had put their stocks on sale in the stock market. There were more than 3,200 pilot enterprises by the end of 1991 experimenting with various types of stock systems. Stocks trading volume had reached Rmb 120 billion in November 1991. Trading in government securities had declined from 90 percent in November 1990 to 70 percent in November 1991, while shares issued by enterprises had expanded from 5 percent to 25 percent in the same period and the number of stockbroking companies had increased from 46 to 60.

The China Stock Exchange Association was established on August 26, 1991, with a total membership of 158, of which 35 are individual members.[8] In Shanghai, most of the stocks are small to medium state enterprises, while in Shenzhen, they are mostly joint-venture manufacturing concerns with an emphasis on exports. Some of the companies listed earlier have expanded rapidly from being insignificant trading and manufacturing firms to sizeable property development companies. Shares are classified as A shares, which are geared for the domestic market, and B shares, which are reserved for foreign investors only. Between February and June 1992, B shares in Shenzhen had risen more than 93 percent.[9] Recent experience suggests that China's stock markets do not face any supply problem, but the sluggish demand makes the authority reluctant to let the two stock markets develop too rapidly and become out of pace with institutional and legal development.

INSTITUTIONS AND MARKETS

Tam (1991) reports that there were 6,000 enterprises adopting the share system in 1988, and the number of nonbank financial institutions permitted to trade in primary and secondary markets was 800 for the same year. Wang (1988) shows a more detailed breakdown of different forms of financial institutions between 1985 and 1987. Larger ones include postal depository services (2,974), trust and investment companies (538), share-issuing banks (2), mutual deposit unions (14,000), and rural service companies (87). Some banking institutions, shown in Table 2.5, are engaged in the issue and trading of shares.

Financial institutions that have emerged since 1978 include insurance companies, trust and investment companies, share-issuing banks, credit cooperatives, and fund-adjustment centers. Trust and investment companies, first established in 1979, include state-owned trust companies, the Chinese International Trust and Investment Corporation (CITIC), and collective-owned companies. Trust and investment companies can underwrite stock and bonds for enterprises. Rural cooperatives resumed their cooperative functions, while other nonbank financial institutions – such as financial companies – act as "cross regional go-betweens for borrowers and lenders" (Wang 1988, p. 32). Fund-adjustment centers were set up in industries in large cities and provided interfirm, short-term credit and services for member enterprises. In general, the unofficial financial institutions are emerging to become more and more significant in resource allocation, breaking the monopolistic element of the state banks.

There are four types of financial markets in China: the informal credit market, the commercial paper market, the interbank loan market, and the long-term capital market. Both Wang (1988) and Tam (1991) have given a descriptive account on the development of these markets. The discounting of commercial papers started in 1982, but its utilization and bank acceptances remain very limited, mainly due to the informal practice of oral agreements and handwritten notes among small enterprises. On the contrary, the market for interbank loans was more active. By the end of 1986, there were nearly 100 interbank loan networks which facilitated cross-regional "horizontal" capital floats. The path of development was rapid between 1986 and 1987. Loans expanded from Rmb 30 billion to Rmb 200 billion, though most of these networks, as Wang (1988) observes, are primary loan markets characterized by negotiation rather than securitization and outdated operational techniques.

In the case of the long-term capital market, some collectively-owned enterprises were allowed to issue shares and bonds in 1983, while the Tianqiao Department Store in Beijing was the first state-owned enterprise permitted to sell shares in 1984. Usually financial institutions and local authorities made use of the primary equity market to raise funds directly from the public. However, there is no general law on securities. In 1987, the state council released an interim regulation on management of enterprise bonds. Quite a number of enterprises do not follow the standardized stock system, and some pilot enterprises have violated the principle of equity equality and equal interest for equal shares. Some enterprises ensure both interest earnings and dividends, while others lack a shareholder congress, a board of directors, and a supervisory committee.[10]

The concept of risk probably has not been understood in China. As soon as new stocks have been put on sale, residents rushed to buy without fear of risk or financial crisis. Demand has been very high, and long queues of investors outside securities outlets are common. For example, when the two listed corporations sold their stocks in Shanghai in 1986, queues were formed. Chaos and riots broke out in Shenzhen in August 1992 when investors formed queues to pick up share application forms from distribution centers.[11] Table 3.2 summarizes the major features of the four types of enterprise issued shares (equity shares, employment shares, worker shares, and public shares). Enterprises can issue more than one type of equity and market them informally. Long-term government bonds and bank bonds are not transferable in secondary markets, thereby limiting the liquidity of assets and the effectiveness of secondary markets.

The informal credit sector is considered to be active in China. Informal credit activities have a high positive real rate of interest, ranging from 2 to 15 percent monthly (Wang 1988). The major characteristics are that money supplied by private lenders are used for income-producing activities and for the financing of rural housing and other major consumption items. Tam (1991) concludes that the informal credit market played a dominant role as a source of loans to rural households. It provided the needed competition and circumvented the existing

Table 3.2
Enterprise Stock Issues

Equity Shares - Issued to reorganize the properties of communes and enterprises.

Employment Shares - Issued by collective and state enterprises, common among rural townships and villages. Holders are entitled to nominate a position within the enterprise. Interest payments are normally higher than bank deposit rates and can enjoy dividend payments. Shares are redeemable upon request. This is a way to get family member employed.

Worker Shares - Common in both rural and state enterprises. Resources raised are used to expand production facilities, and to raise wage and bonus payments. Interest rates are higher than bank deposit rates, in addition to fixed dividend payments. Quantity of each issue is small as compared to total enterprise capital, and it is not intended to improve workers' participation in management. Not all purchases are voluntary.

Public Shares - Public subscription through brokerage agency, raise initial capital to form new enterprises and/or diversify activities. Funds are used as a substitute for bank loans during tight credit conditions.

Source: Tam, O. K. 1991. Capital Market Development in China. *World Development* 19(5):511–532.

government regulations on interest rates and the scope of lending. Successful private money lenders later became financial intermediaries as private money shops. Wang (1988) agrees that the informal money market can induce competition and reduce the financial resource distortions created by the fragmented and inefficient nature of the formal capital market.

Recently, there has been an increasing number of researchers working on the stock market in China. For example, Hu (1993) has discussed both the historical and theoretical background of China's capital market and a follow-up on the two stock markets in Shanghai and Shenzhen. Shen (1993) traveled to China himself and examined the various structural aspects of the security market, giving emphasis on national regulations governing the trading of securities.

PROSPECTS OF THE EQUITY MARKET

Equity markets in China are far from perfect, and their development lagged behind the need of the economy. Problems of the equity markets in China include (1) the inadequate legal framework; (2) the poor timing of new stock release; (3) the method of new issues being cumbersome, inconvenient, and liable to abuse; (4) lack of price standardization (i.e., same share has different prices in different stock trading centers); (5)

lack of standardization in share specifications (e.g., differences in interest earnings and dividend payments); and (6) lack of a proper regulatory framework.[12] Wang (1988) singles out three major problems which need attention and improvement. One is the lack of legislation and regulations. The lack of security laws is largely responsible for the poorly defined stocks in China. Second, owing to poor communications and primitive operational techniques, China's financial market is fragmented. Lack of uniformity and regional monopolies exist. Diversifications in both financial institutions and instruments can improve market efficiency. The nontransferability of government bonds restricts the use of other policy instruments such as open-market operation in the management of the economy.

The development, or rather the lack of development, in the equity market shows that the Chinese authority is really facing a "crossroad" situation. On the one hand, traditional socialist ideology prefers a monobanking financial system. This is reflected in the unwillingness to consolidate the capital market and in the delay in establishing security laws and regulations to govern the various practices. On the other hand, the deepening of economic reform cannot succeed without further development of private capital market. The permission to issue bonds and shares granted to both collectively-owned and state-owned enterprises shows the authority's determination to deepen economic reform. The fact is that development of the capital market and the establishment of a shareholding system has to be complemented with enterprise reform. The introduction of the contract responsibility system in the rural areas in 1978 is considered an improvement in public ownership and productivity increase, while the call in 1987 for the separation between ownership and management in public enterprises is the solution proposed by the reformists.

Taking a more positive viewpoint, however, development of the Chinese equity market in the 1980s was a significant stepping stone. The mayor of Guangzhou, Mr. Li Ziliu, remarked on the riots in Shenzhen in August 1992: "It is not chaos, it's just like a baby learning to walk."[13] The various problems in the equity market are temporary; once regulations and practices relating to the operational function of the capital market are established, problems will subside. Given the huge demand and the enthusiasm shown in the form of long queues at share-release centers in Shenzhen and the resulting riots in the summer of 1992, supply of shares by different enterprises will increase. Increased supply in the primary market will then call for standardization of practices in the secondary market.

In conclusion, despite the low q and FIR ratios in China, the equity market will have to develop and become a major arm in the overall financial development. The 1980s saw a process of slow development, but statistics suggest that there is no shortage in both demand and supply of equities. Such a "demand-following" phenomenon in the equity market will create trading problems which will hopefully lead to the establishment of standardized practices. The equity market offers additional channels and instruments in which financial resources can be utilized more efficiently if economic reform is to be deepened.

NOTES

1. "Stocks: New Excitement in China's Economic Life," *Beijing Review,* August 10–16, 1992, pp. 14–17.

2. For a more recent study on capital market development, see Sung Soo Koh, The Korea Stock Market: Structure, Behavior and Test of Market Efficiency, Ph.D. Thesis, Department of Banking and Finance, City University Business School, London, November 1989.

3. On Kit Tam, "Capital Market Development in China," *World Development* 19(5[1991]):511–532.

4. Shares and bonds issued by enterprises in the 1980s were acquired by their own workers. The Shanghai Stock Exchange was opened in December 1990, while the Shenzhen Stock Exchange was opened in July 1991. Shares have been traded in the Shanghai as early as 1983, but trading was very insignificant. (See "The Shanghai Stock Exchange Market – From Infancy to Maturity," *Zhongguo jinrong [China Finance],* October 1990, pp. 9–12; and "The Development of China's Capital Market in 1991," *Zhongguo jinrong [China Finance],* January 1992, pp. 26–27.)

5. Tam, "Capital Market Development."

6. "Too Few Options," *China Trade Report,* June 1992, p. 1.

7. "New Excitement," pp. 14–17.

8. "Development of China's Capital Market," pp. 26–27.

9. "Too Few Options," p. 1.

10. "New Excitement," pp. 14–17.

11. "Irrational Rationing," *Far Eastern Economic Review,* August 20, 1992, p. 65; "Shenzhen Shares Frenzy," *South China Morning Post,* August 9, 1992; "Anger over Shares Chaos in Shenzhen," *South China Morning Post,* August 10, 1992; and "Bank May Shoulder Blame in Shenzhen," *South China Morning Post,* August 14, 1992.

12. "Development of and Suggestions on China's Stock Market," *Zhongguo jinrong [China Finance],* April 1992, pp. 28–29.

13. "Irrational Rationing," p. 65.

4

Financial Relationships and Productivity

AN ANALYTICAL FRAMEWORK

The core issue is the relationship between financial resources and output. The available financial resources, if invested efficiently, lead to a rise in output, namely

$$\text{Financial Resources} \rightarrow \text{Output}$$

The availability of financial resources takes different forms: foreign-direct investment and foreign loans, government fiscal expenditures, private capital raised through the equity market and the issue of bonds by enterprises, and bank loans. In a financially matured economy, the financial sector and the agents in the sector, such as banks and the stock market, will ensure that financial resources will be used most efficiently. A process of financial deepening suggests that the financial sector is able to channel the resources to productive investment and increase in output. Financial repression, however, suggests the contrary.

McKinnon's (1973) financial repression model is relevant in providing a framework to examine why, given the available financial resources, output does not rise proportionately. The complementarity of money and capital is a relevant financial mechanism to look at the productivity of investment. In developing countries where money is the most popular form of financial asset, the willingness to hold (demand) money tells the extent of investment productivity. If investment is productive, the return to investment activities will be high. And since the return to investment is measured in money terms, the demand for money rises.

To ensure a high return to investment, financial repression advocates recommend the use of a positive and considerably large interest rate. The argument is that the interest rate is the opportunity cost of financial resources. If it is set at a low or negative level, financial resources become cheap. Both productive and unproductive investment can have equal access to low-cost resources. If public enterprises are the major investment agents, their loss need not be accounted for, unproductive investment will likely be promoted. Investment returns are low and financial resources cannot promote output. On the contrary, if financial resources are properly priced and their scarcity is reflected in the high opportunity cost, unproductive investment cannot secure the fundings; and only productive investment can succeed in securing the funds. By raising the interest rate, the allocation of financial resources will be redirected from unproductive to productive investment activities. In this process of removing the price distortion of financial resources and promoting productive investment, output gradually rises.

There are two components in the real interest rate. One is the nominal value fixed by the central authority, the other is the inflation rate. The analysis on inflation becomes another major aspect in the financial repression framework. A high level of inflation gives a low real interest rate, the opportunity cost of financial resources becomes low, and it becomes easy for unproductive investment to secure fundings. Accordingly, investment return is low. Furthermore, a high level of inflation leads to a fall in the value of money, and the store of value function of money is diminished. Money becomes only the medium for transactions, holding money is unattractive, and demand for money falls. Households are prepared to get rid of cash in exchange for something more tangible. In turn, the demand for physical assets and commodities – such as industrial raw materials – increases, leading to a situation of excess demand and a further rise in price.

A vicious cycle develops as inflation accelerates. From the supply side, rapid inflation leads to speculation on the price of industrial inputs. Suppliers become unwilling to sell the raw materials in anticipation of a further rise in price. The hoarding of industrial raw materials actually leads to a fall in output. Thus, excess demand is coupled with a fall in supply, accelerating the pace of inflation further. On the external front, export falls as domestic price rises, and import rises to supplement the falling domestic supply. The economic crisis is the direct result of a low interest rate, unproductive investment, high inflation, and simple speculative activities. The monobanking system and the lack of development in banking intermediaries can hardly help to remove financial repression.

COMPONENTS OF FINANCIAL REPRESSION IN CHINA

From economic data discussed in Chapter 2, this section attempts to identify the various aspects of financial repression in China. One can classify five different but related components of financial repression during China's first decade of economic reform: low marginal productivity of loans, large money supply, a soft fiscal policy, large trade deficit and falling efficiency of external resources, and a prolonged negative real interest rate.

Component 1: Marginal Productivity of Loans

Bank loans are a major source of investment. If the price of loans is not distorted, bank loans will be directed to productive investments. Eventually, the rate of growth in output exceeds the rate of growth in loans. The improvement in output expands at a rate faster than loan requirements. The change in loans (ΔL) declines relatively to change in total output (ΔY). Over time, one expects a rising marginal productivity of loans ($\Delta Y/\Delta L$) ratio. On the contrary, a declining $\Delta Y/\Delta L$ ratio can imply inefficiency in investment and loan deployment. If loans are not used for productive investment activities (e.g., loans being used to repay interests of previous loans), output will not expand. Since the interest rate for loans is set at a low level, low-cost bank loans encourage low-return investment activities.

Table 4.1 shows that the $\Delta Y/\Delta L$ ratio first increased in the early 1980s but declined rapidly in the mid-1980s, reaching only 1.11 in 1986. The rise in output in 1988, however, brought the ratio up to 3.69 before it fell again. The changes in total output in excess of loans in the early and late 1980s were both short lived. Financial resources in the form of bank loans did not maintain a high level of output. When compared with the interest rate on bank loans (shown in Table 2.13) and the inflation rates (shown in Table 2.29), one can see that the loan rate is constantly lower than the "true" price inflation rate. It shows that a low loan rate ceiling has encouraged inefficient investment at the expense of more efficient ones. Inefficient investment usually requires additional loans to cover losses. A vicious cycle then appears: loose bank credits geared to inefficient investment result in losses which require further loans to finance the losses, the amount of bank loans made available to efficient investment is then further diminished, and output declines as more and more inefficient investments are held.

Table 4.1
Marginal Productivity of Loans, 1980–1990

Year	(ΔTotal Output/ ΔLoan) x 100
1980	1.8622
1981	1.4388
1982	2.4814
1983	2.4213
1984	1.6393
1985	1.6863
1986	1.1111
1987	2.2779
1988	3.6900
1989	2.4038
1990	1.1004

Sources: Statistical Yearbook of China, Beijing, 1984, 1988, 1991; *China Statistical Yearbook,* Beijing, 1984, 1988, 1991.

There are, however, limitations to this interpretation of a low marginal productivity of loans. If a large portion of investments were geared to infrastructural activities, the marginal productivity of loans may not rise. This is particularly true in the case of state investments. As nonstate-financed investments rise, however, the marginal loan rate is still expected to rise. There may also be an identification problem involved. As shown in Figure 4.1, if the $(\Delta Y/\Delta L)_{t+1}$ line has shifted outward as compared to the $(\Delta Y/\Delta L)_t$ line, then the marginal productivity of loans would have increased. If bank loans (L) are expanding faster than the productivity is increasing, one would expect a decline in $\Delta Y/\Delta L$, as shown by point B when compared with point A in Figure 4.1.[1]

Component 2: Money Supply

The rate of growth of money in the mid-1980s was larger than the growth rates of GNP, output, and consumption. The money multiplier of M2 shown in Table 2.11 has expanded by 50 percent, from 0.87 in 1985 to 1.23 in 1989. The money/income ratios in the same period did not increase as rapidly, implying that the growth of money was inflationary.

Figure 4.1
Marginal Productivity of Loans

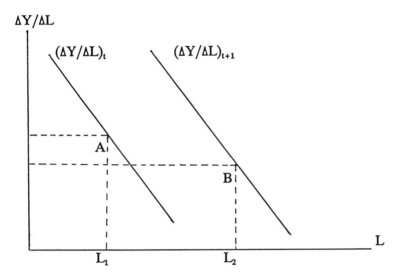

Kapur (1976b) raises the possibility of money losing its store of value function in a situation of financial repression; money is used purely for transactionary purposes. Money circulation increases when it comes to a point where households get rid of cash held in anticipation of deteriorating inflation, and workers demand wages to be paid in kind instead of in cash terms. Hoarding of commodities and industrial raw materials as a hedge against rapid inflation has made the holding of money unpopular, as happened in 1988. The velocity of circulation shown in Table 2.11 declined rapidly from 8.48 in 1978 to 4.08 in 1983 and further down to 2.11 in 1989. The "falling" velocity of circulation reflects that the growth rate of money (M2) was constantly higher than the growth rate of GNP, as confirmed in Tables 2.1 and 2.10.

There was ineffective control over inflation, and the state responded by increasing money supply through bank credits and subsidies in order to keep up with a constant purchasing power. Households are unwilling to hold money in the face of rapid inflation. The loose monetary policy seems to be the direct consequence of a large money supply and a falling value of money.

Component 3: A Soft Fiscal Policy

State investment through fiscal expenditures is another source of investment capital. The annual budget in China over the years has experienced huge deficits and extrabudgetary figures. The large proportional share of extrabudgetary expenditures and revenues effectively has reduced the ability of the state in directing its investment activities. The disproportionate share of extrabudgetary figures shown in Tables 2.14 and 2.17 and the net budgetary and extrabudgetary injection of financial resources shown in column 1 of Table 2.30 show that China has managed state financial resources poorly.

Typically, the official budget was constantly in severe deficit, though the extrabudgetary revenue figures in some years were generally larger than extrabudgetary expenditure figures. The tax/GNP ratios and tax elasticity changed from year to year, while price subsidies grew by more than 10 percent except 1982, 1986, and 1988, as shown in Tables 2.15 and 2.17, respectively. Constant fiscal deficits increase money supply and fuel inflation, lowering real interest rate and the opportunity cost of investment.

Component 4: External Resources

Despite a steady flow of foreign loans over the years, the trade imbalance has been extremely large since 1985. Table 2.26 shows that in net terms, China has experienced a negative inflow of foreign resources. The large trade deficits over the years primarily reflected the shortages of both capital and consumer goods at home. As shown in Table 2.27, a falling export/FDI ratio does not seem to support China's export-led strategy, which is basically a duplication from the experience of the Asian Newly Industrializing Economies. By the late 1980s, rapid inflation in China made exports less attractive, since the domestic price had caught up with the export price. The role of import in an export-led strategy is to expand the economy's capital ability so that both output and export expand to cover the import bill. In China's experience, with the exception of 1982 and 1983, trade has been in deficit. The weak performance in China trade and export may be due to two things: (1) imports were mainly expensive consumer goods and (2) outputs originally geared to exports were supplemented for domestic shortage at a time of high domestic inflation.

A successful export-led strategy will produce a rising marginal export rate and a falling marginal import rate. If imports of capital goods are export promoting, the marginal export rate should rise, while the marginal import rate should decline. Table 4.2 works out the marginal export and import ratios. With the exception of 1981, 1986, and 1987, the marginal export rate has remained basically unchanged and indeed has declined after reaching a peak in 1987. The marginal export rate was larger than the marginal import rate from 1980–1982, but the

Table 4.2
China's Marginal Export and Import Ratios

Year	ΔGNP (Rmb 100 millions)	ΔExport (Rmb 100 millions)	ΔImport (Rmb 100 millions)	ΔExport/ ΔGNP	ΔImport/ ΔGNP
1979	410	44.1	55.5	0.1076	0.1354
1980	472	59.5	55.9	0.1261	0.1184
1981	303	96.4	68.9	0.3182	0.2274
1982	420	46.2	-10.2	0.1100	-0.0243
1983	616	24.5	64.3	0.0398	0.1044
1984	1153	142.2	198.7	0.1233	0.1723
1985	1596	228.4	637.3	0.1431	0.3993
1986	1138	273.2	240.5	0.2401	0.2113
1987	1605	387.9	115.9	0.2417	0.0722
1988	2717	296.7	441.1	0.1092	0.1623
1989	1898	189.3	144.6	0.0997	0.0762
1990	1770	1029.8	374.4	0.5818	0.2115

Source: Statistical Yearbook of China, Beijing, 1984, 1988, 1991.

trend was reversed in 1983–1985. In the case of marginal import rate, the trend was unsteady, with a negative in 1982 but a large positive in 1985.

Component 5: Inflation

The last aspect of financial repression is the large and fluctuating inflation, shown in Table 2.29. Inflation can be regarded as the outcome of the other components. Recent studies on the measurement of inflation have come to different findings (Chow 1987, Feltenstein and Farhadian 1987, Szapary 1989). In addition to the official retail price, there is also the free market price for consumer goods; Chen and Hou's (1986) "total inflation," which comprises also the suppressed inflation; and Feltenstein and Ha's (1991) "true" price inflation. When compared with the annual interest rates on resident deposits and bank loans, real interest rates in China are mostly negative.

These five components of financial repression in China are closely related to each other. For example, the huge increase in money supply has led to price inflation. Huge budget deficits lead to rising income and consumption; but if there is a supply shortage and a negative real deposit rate, price inflation emerges. In turn, inflation penalizes savings and encourages speculative and hoarding activities, which further exacerbates the shortages.

China's first decade of economic reform has shown that an improper and poor financial development have restricted the full potentials of economic reform. The five components of financial repression reflect that the economic ills in the latter half of the 1980s were financial in nature. The Chinese authority's attempt to solve economic problems on an ad hoc basis can at best provide a partial solution: the root of all problems seems to be the misuse, not the shortage, of financial resources. A major financial policy in China has been a deliberately low rate of interest ceiling so that the provision of low-cost borrowing encourages state enterprises to invest. A low rate of interest charged by state banks on loans makes credit creation, and hence, the supply of money easily becomes uncontrollable. This financial policy has definitely contributed to inefficient investments by state enterprises.

LINEAR EQUATIONS

This section constructs various financial relationships in order to examine the impact of different macroeconomic and financial variables on economic reform. In China, where there is a problem of data availability, the construction of financial relationships in the form of simple linear equations is most suitable.[2]

Three groups of linear equations (eight equations in all) are constructed. The first group is composed of three equations involving demand for money and investment, and their structure closely follows those of McKinnon (1973) and Fry (1979, 1980b). The purpose is to demonstrate that the McKinnon-Shaw hypothesis is applicable to the Chinese economy. Analysis of the demand for money gives an indication of investment returns, if we assume that money and capital complement each other. The second group of equations contains two equations on inflation, the independent variables of which are money supply and expectation, amended from the studies by Feltenstein and Farhadian (1987), Szapary (1989), and Feltenstein and Ha (1991), and real consumption, the latter an improved version of Chow's (1987) construction. These two equations point out that inflation in China is caused by price expectations, expectation adjustment, and money supply, and inflation has reduced real consumption considerably. The third set of three equations examines the productivity of different financial resources by looking at their regression coefficients.

Each set of equations reflects the different aspects of financial repression in China. The first set shows that the Chinese economy has experienced repression along the lines of the McKinnon-Shaw framework. The second set aims to explain the cause of inflation in a financially repressed economy. The third set shows the empirical relationship between financial capital and output. The availability of financial capital is the necessary condition; efficient performance is the sufficient condition for output growth.

The Demand for Money and Investment

1. The Demand-for-Money Equation. Table 4.3 summarizes the six recent studies on China's demand for money (Chow 1987, Portes and Santorum 1987, Feltenstein and Farhadian 1987, Feltenstein and Ha 1991, Szapary 1989, Burton and Ha 1990, Peebles 1991). Chow (1987) uses the quantity theory of money as a theoretical starting point and confirms that the quantity theory of money provides a reasonable first approximation in explaining the demand for money in China. Portes and Santorum (1987) incorporate the nominal interest rate in their equation formulation and carried out the Granger causality test and the Huang test; their results were used to construct a consumption model.

Other studies employ a similar approach of using lagged values of income, price and money stock, and inflation. Feltenstein and Farhadian (1987) construct their money demand function by using a money supply identity and a behavioral equation describing the demand for real cash balances. Szapary (1989) finds that the relatively high degree of responsiveness of money demand to changes in real incomes is explained by increased monetarization and the role of time deposits as a major form for holding household savings. Peebles (1991) reworks Chow's (1987) results but extends the analysis to include purchasing power and concludes that changes in narrow money supply are not a separate independent cause of price increases.

McKinnon (1973) and Fry (1978a, 1978b) have incorporated the importance of the real interest rate in their demand-for-money function. They believe that a demand-for-money function that does not incorporate the effect of the interest rate is inadequate for determining the extent to which financial variables affect income and investment performance. The McKinnon-Fry construction of the demand-for-money function can be described as follows:

$$(M/P)_t = f_1[(GNP/P)_t, (I/GNP)_t, (d - i)_t] \qquad (4.1)$$

where M is the nominal money stock, M/P is the demand for money, P is the retail price index, I is the total investment in fixed assets, d is the annual deposit rate, and i is the inflation rate. The investment/income ratio is included as one of the determinants of the real stock of money. McKinnon (1973) argues that such a construction incorporates the demand for money that arises directly from the process of capital

Table 4.3
Summary of Recent Studies on China's Demand for Money

Author(s)	Special Features	Results
Chow (1987)	Quantity Theory of Money.	Provides a reasonable first approximation in explaining demand for money in China.
Portes and Santorum (1987)	Lagged values of money stock, price and disposable income, nominal interest rate.	M0 is a more suitable monetary variable than M2.
Feltenstein and Farhadian (1987)	Real income, rate of inflation based on adaptive expectation formulation, real balance lag.	Inflationary expectation effect is low.
Feltenstein and Ha (1991)		Strong support for the existence of repressed inflation, forced savings reduced money velocity.
Szapary (1989)	Formulation of expected inflation based on market price.	Money balances adjust slowly to long run levels. One percentage point increase in expected inflation is estimated to reduce the demand for real broad money by 1.8 to 3 percent.
Burton and Ha (1990)	Calculation of real household balance for long run equilibrium, average inflation rate.	One percentage point increase in the annual inflation rate would reduce real household money balance by about one half percentage point.
Peebles (1991)	Use purchasing power as the indicator.	Money stock and its growth rate are a consequence of monetary demand imbalance.

Sources: Chow, Gregory C. 1987. Money and Price Level Determination in China, *Journal of Comparative Economics* 11 (September):319–333; Portes, Richard R., and Anita Santorum. 1987. Money and the Consumption Goods Market in China, *Journal of Comparative Economics* 11:354–371; Feltenstein, Andrew, and Ziba Farhadian. 1987. Fiscal Policy, Monetary Targets and the Price Level in a Centrally Planned Economy: An Application to the Case of China, *Journal of Money, Credit and Banking* 19(2): 137–156; Feltenstein, Andrew, and Jiming Ha. 1991. Measurement of Repressed Inflation in China, *Journal of Development Economics* 36:279–294; Szapary, G. 1989. Monetary Policy and System Reforms in China, *Ninth Latin American Meeting of the Econometric Society*, Santiago, Chile; Burton, David, and Jiming Ha. 1990. *Economic Reform and the Demand for Money in China*, Asian Department, WP/90/42, Washington, D.C.: International Monetary Fund; Peebles, Gavin. 1991. *Money in the People's Republic of China*, Sydney: Allen & Unwin.

accumulation itself. The first independent variable still captures the conventional transaction motive for holding money, while the last variable measures the real return on holding money. If the deposit rate is kept constant for a long time while inflation fluctuates, the last variables *(d − i)* effectively show the impact of inflation on money demand.

The necessary condition for money to complement capital is that the partial derivative of the second explanatory variable is positive, namely

$$\delta(M/P) \,/\, \delta(I/GNP) > 0 \qquad (4.2)$$

McKinnon (1973) emphasizes the *indirect* link of *(d − i)* → *M/P* → *I/GNP*. If money is viewed as a "conduit" through which accumulation takes place, the demand for money rises with the productivity of capital. The desire to hold money depends on the real return; a positive real return raises investment/savings propensities because of the importance of money as a store of value. If the attractiveness of holding money is high, the partial derivative of the real return variable *(d − i)* is large and positive, namely

$$\delta(M/P) \,/\, \delta(d − i) > 0 \qquad (4.3)$$

The corollary is that a small partial derivative signals the presence of financial repression.

2. *Investment Equation.* Investment often involves the issue of savings. Two studies, by Qian (1988) and Feltenstein, Lebow, and van Wijnbergen (1990), estimated the marginal propensity to save in China. Qian (1988) starts by pointing out that China's savings rate, at about 30 percent, is higher than the average rate in developed and developing countries. Like Chow (1985), Qian (1988) believes that the quantity theory of money is an appropriate postulate as a generalized form-of-money equation for China. Urban and rural savings data in China are tested against three hypotheses of the Keynesian absolute income model, Friedman's permanent income model, and the asset adjustment model. The permanent income hypothesis yields the lowest while the asset adjustment model yields the highest marginal propensity to save in the urban sector. Qian (1988) also notes that there was a regime change in 1979 and that the marginal propensity to save in the post–1979 years has been greater than in the pre–1979 decades but concludes that the rapid increase in the household savings rate in recent years is explained by the increase in the magnitude of repressed inflation in the consumer goods market and the shifts in the economic structure of household behavior.

A special feature in the empirical study by Feltenstein, Lebow, and van Wijnbergen (1990, p. 240) is their use of "virtual price," which is defined as "the real discount factor at which consumers would be willing to consume the volume of goods available to them today, with the same level of utility that holds if today's effective demand could be satisfied at official prices." Feltenstein, Lebow, and van Wijnbergen

(1990) employ four savings specifications from the permanent income model. Savings were deflated by the virtual price. For the period 1953–1983, the marginal propensity to save estimates are similar to Qian's (1988), but they argue that the use of virtual price produces a superior result and does not reflect the regime change.

Fry (1978a, 1978b) estimates a demand-for-money function but avoids the investment function by arguing that domestic saving is equal by definition to domestically financed investment, a saving function based on Fry's (1978b) real GNP, and that an additional independent variable of the real rate of interest, $(d - i)$, can be constructed as follows:

$$(S/GNP)_t = f_2[(GNP/P)_t, (d - i)_t] \tag{4.4}$$

where (S/GNP) is the gross national savings and (GNP/P) is real income. Fry (1978b) postulates that the coefficient estimates can be used as an indication of complementarity. By using Nepal's experience, Thornton and Poudyal (1990) estimated a two-equation model – a demand-for-money equation and a savings equation. The explanatory variables in the saving function are M/P, the per-capita income, and the growth rate. Multicolinearity may occur in the last two explanatory variables. One problem with Thornton and Poudyal's (1990) inclusion of M/P in the savings equation is that if a broader definition of money is used, then savings (S/P, the dependent variable) are correlated with the monetary aggregate (M/P, the explanatory variable). As such, it is more appropriate to include M/P in the investment equation and $(d - i)$ in the savings equation.

As compared with the two theoreticals set up by Qian (1988) and Feltenstein, Lebow, and van Wijnbergen (1990), the advantage of McKinnon's (1973) approach is that the substitution of real rate of return for the price variable avoids the debate as to which is the most appropriate price. In McKinnon's (1973) construction, complementarity can equally be seen in an investment function of the following form:

$$(I/GNP)_t = f_3[(R)_t, (L - i)_t] \tag{4.5}$$

where R is the average return on physical capital and L the loan rate. If we start from a situation of financial repression with low real cash balances, the complementarity effect as indicated by the partial derivative is

$$\delta(I/GNP) / \delta(L - i) > 0 \tag{4.6}$$

If cash balances are already attractive to hold and the economy is already liquid with cash, further increases in the real deposit rate reduce the propensity to save so that the direction of equation 4.6 is reversed and money and capital revert to the neoclassical case of a "competing asset" effect.

McKinnon's (1973) indirect link can be reformulated by substituting M/P for $(L - i)$ as the explanatory variable in equation 4.5. The monetary variable will then have a direct impact on the investment/income ratio. Such a direct formulation becomes

$$(I/GNP)_t = f_4[(R)_t, (M/P)_t] \qquad (4.7)$$

By including M/P in the investment function, the two equations, 4.1 and 4.7, become the two-equation system employed in Thornton and Poudyal's (1990) study on the Nepal economy.

Inflation and Real Consumption

3. The Inflation Equation. Recent studies of China's savings behavior (Qian 1988; Feltenstein, Lebow, and van Wijnbergen 1990) have come across a common problem in identifying a set of "prices" for empirical study. Different technical manipulations have been tried, including virtual price (Ellis and Naughton 1990; Feltenstein, Lebow, and van Wijnbergen 1990), the adaptive expectation formulation (Feltenstein and Farhadian 1987; Feltenstein and Ha 1991), market price (Szapary 1989), and the long-run average inflation rate (Burton and Ha 1990).

As shown in Table 2.29, "total" and "true" price inflation are generally large and the real interest rates are negative in most years. Chow (1987) finds that the price level can be reasonably explained by the money/income ratio. Feltenstein and Farhadian (1987) work out the expected rate of inflation by using an adaptive expectation scheme. Feltenstein and Ha (1991) use an opportunity cost variable, measured by the adaptive expected rate of inflation in the "true" price index. Szapary (1989) finds that a formulation for the expected inflation based on the past rate of change in market prices performed best in his demand-for-money equation. Burton and Ha (1990) use a "testing down" process to determine the structure of a dynamic model. Chen and Hou (1986) point out that there are four sets of prices in China and that any estimation of price inflation cannot ignore their effects; their construction of "total" inflation has the advantage of being simple and provides a "catch-all" web to include all kinds of inflationary pressures which existed in the Chinese economy, while Feltenstein and Ha's (1991) construction of true price inflation assumes a constant velocity.

Inflation $(\Delta P/P)_t$ in China, as most recent studies have shown, is caused by two explanatory variables, namely, the previous period's money supply $(M/P)_{t-1}$ and expected inflation $(\Delta P/P)^e_{t-1}$. The following equation can be constructed:

$$(\Delta P/P)_t = g(M/P)_{t-1} + h(\Delta P/P)^e_{t-1} \tag{4.8}$$

By using an adaptive expectation scheme, the following expectation equation can be formulated:

$$(\Delta P/P)^e_t - (\Delta P/P)^e_{t-1} = k[(\Delta P/P)_t - (\Delta P/P)^e_{t-1}] \tag{4.9}$$

and after rearranging, the equation can be expressed as follows:

$$
\begin{aligned}
(\Delta P/P)^e_{t-1} &= k[(\Delta P/P)_{t-1} - (\Delta P/P)^e_{t-2}] + (\Delta P/P)^e_{t-2} \\
&= k(\Delta P/P)_{t-1} - k(\Delta P/P)^e_{t-2} + (\Delta P/P)^e_{t-2} \\
&= k(\Delta P/P)_{t-1} + (1 - k)(\Delta P/P)^e_{t-2}
\end{aligned}
$$

Using a process of Koyck transformation, equation 4.8 becomes:

$$
\begin{aligned}
(\Delta P/P)_t &= g(M/P)_{t-1} + kh(\Delta P/P)_{t-1} + (1 - k)h(\Delta P/P)^e_{t-2} \\
&= g(M/P)_{t-1} + kh[g(M/P)_{t-2} + h(\Delta P/P)^e_{t-2}] + (1 - k)h(\Delta P/P)^e_{t-2} \\
&= g(M/P)_{t-1} + (khg)(M/P)_{t-2} + h^2k(\Delta P/P)^e_{t-2} + (1 - k)h(\Delta P/P)^e_{t-2} \\
&= g(M/P)_{t-1} + (khg)(M/P)_{t-2} + kh^2(\Delta P/P)^e_{t-2} + h(\Delta P/P)^e_{t-2} \\
&\quad - kh(\Delta P/P)^e_{t-2}
\end{aligned}
$$

Since $(\Delta P/P)_{t-1} = g(M/P)_{t-2} + h(\Delta P/P)^e_{t-2}$, then

$$(\Delta P/P)^e_{t-2} = (1/h)(\Delta P/P)_{t-1} - (g/h)(M/P)_{t-2}$$

The final reduced equation becomes

$$
\begin{aligned}
(\Delta P/P)_t &= g(M/P)_{t-1} + (khg)(M/P)_{t-2} + (h^2k + h - kh)[(1/h)(\Delta P/P)_{t-1} \\
&\quad - (g/h)M/P_{t-2}] \\
&= g(M/P)_{t-1} + (khg)(M/P)_{t-2} + (hk + 1 - k)(\Delta P/P)_{t-1} \\
&\quad - (khg + g - kg)M/P_{t-2} \\
&= g(M/P)_{t-1} + (kg - g)(M/P)_{t-2} + (hk + 1 - k)(\Delta P/P)_{t-1} \tag{4.10}
\end{aligned}
$$

Inflation depends on the impact of money supply in the last two periods and inflation in the last period. The three unknowns of g, h, and k can be solved easily from the three estimates in equation 4.10. The values of g, h, and k show, respectively, the impact of money supply, the impact of expectation, and the impact of expectation adjustment on inflation. In general, equation 4.10 becomes

$$(\Delta P/P)_t = f_5[(M/P)_{t-1}, (M/P)_{t-2}, (\Delta P/P)_{t-1}] \qquad (4.11)$$

The advantage of the Koyck transformation process is that the adaptive expectation is absorbed into the last two explanatory variables and a separate process to identify the expected inflation rate is not needed. This should be an improvement on the studies by Feltenstein and Farhadian (1987), Feltenstein and Ha (1991), and Szapary (1989).

4. The Real Consumption Equation. The increase in income since 1979 has improved household consumption. When the economy is financially repressed and money holding is penalized by inflation, however, one expects households to consume as soon as they receive their pay. The marginal propensity to consume is bound to be very high. Portes and Santorum (1987) look at the Chinese consumption-goods markets by using models applied to Eastern European countries. Their consumption equation includes previous savings, disposable income, and an exponential time trend in consumption for the period 1954–1983. Their result shows excess demand existed in the early 1980s. Lorenzen (1989) regresses real income on real consumption but looks at the difference between urban and rural households. Three results are produced: the current year figures, the first difference figures, and the natural logarithm figures. The marginal propensity to consume for urban households is similar and large, while the result for rural households declined in the first two formulations, implying that rural households have more restricted consumption possibilities.

Real income $(GNP/P)_t$ certainly affects real consumption $(C/P)_t$, but inflation from the previous period $(\Delta P/P)_{t-1}$ can also influence current period consumption. A general expression can be constructed in the following form:

$$(C/P)_t = f_6[(GNP/P)_t, (\Delta P/P)_{t-1}] \qquad (4.12)$$

Equation 4.12 aims to see the impact of real income and inflation on real consumption. Real income is expected to have a positive relationship with real consumption, while inflation would have a negative relationship. The estimated coefficient of GNP/P is the marginal propensity to consume.

Financial Productivity

A direct and simple way to look at the productivity of various financial resources is to regress output on all financial resources. In the case of China, data on agricultural and industrial output are available. A slightly disaggregated formulation is to regress separately the two output series on the different forms of financial capital. Assumptions are made regarding the source of capital. In the case of agriculture, state budget expenditures and agricultural loans are the major sources of financing. In the case of industrial output, five sources of capital are available: state budget expenditures, foreign-direct investment, self-raised funds, bank loans for circulating funds, and bank loans for fixed assets.

5. *Agricultural Output.* Given the injection of various forms of financial resources, one can regress them on total output, and the resulting estimation can be used as an efficiency measure. There are four types of financial resources: real state budget expenditures *(SB/P)*, self-raised funds measured in real terms *(SRF/P)*, real foreign-direct investment *(FDI/P)*, and different types of bank loans. How efficient and productive each of these four financial resources is in regard to total (industrial and agricultural) output can be seen from the coefficient estimates. Consider a Harrod-Domar output equation employed by Mathieson (1979):

$$Y = \alpha K \qquad (4.13)$$

where Y is domestic output, K is total real working capital, and α is the output/capital ratio. A simple extension of Mathieson's (1979) construction is to look at total output in terms of agricultural and industrial output and working capital in terms of different financial resources.

In the case of real agricultural output *(YA/P)*, there are basically two sources of funding: previous real state-budget expenditure $(SB/P)_{t-1}$ and the last period's loans for agriculture measured in real terms $(MLA/P)_{t-1}$. The following linear relationship can be formulated:

$$(YA/P)_t = f_7[(SB/P)_{t-1}, (MLA/P)_{t-1}] \qquad (4.14)$$

The estimate of both independent variables should be positive. Since bank loans need to be repaid, they should be more efficient than state budget estimates. If banks hold an easy credit policy, however, the estimate can be equally small.

6. *Industrial Output.* Industrial investment can be financed through state-budget expenditures *(SB/P)*, foreign-direct investment *(FDI/P)*, bank loans for circulating funds *(MCFL/P)*, bank loans for fixed assets *(MLFA/P)*, and self-raised funds *(SRF/P)*, all measured in real terms. While state-budget expenditures and bank loans for circulating funds are short term in nature (lag one quarter), all other explanatory vari-

ables should take a year (lag four quarters) before any impact can be realized. The linear regression equation becomes

$$(YI/P)_t = f_8[(SB/P)_{t-1}, (SRF/P)_{t-4}, (MCFL/P)_{t-1},$$
$$(FDI/P)_{t-4}, (MLFA/P)_{t-4}] \qquad (4.15)$$

The estimated coefficients provide information as to which type of financial resource is more productive, or efficient, in promoting industrial output $(YI/P)_t$. State budget financed investment (SB/P) mainly is concerned with state enterprises, which are notorious for their inefficiency. The estimated coefficient is expected to be low or even negative. Self-raised funds (SRF/P) are carried out by collective enterprises which have greater freedom in their management and investment activities. One would expect that the estimated coefficient would be positive and could even be larger than the coefficient (SB/P). One point worth noting, however, is the way the money is raised. Enterprises can raise funds by selling enterprise bonds. These bonds, however, are not freely tradable and very often are purchased by the enterprise's own employees. As such, these funds are nothing more than "wage pools" and nowhere near the investment funds that are used in developed market economies. If the workers do not have a say in the use of these wage pools, funds so raised are not efficient. They only provide another channel for the enterprise to obtain extra funds.

Foreign-direct investment (FDI/P) should be more efficient in productive terms, since management and technology are brought from overseas; these manufacturing plants are geared to the export market, so the estimated coefficient should be positive and large. Since the interest rate on bank loans is low and state banks are obliged to support domestic enterprises, credit policy in China is regarded as loose; its estimated coefficient should be low.

Equations 4.14 and 4.15 measure financial productivity in terms of agricultural and industrial outputs. The resulting estimates can be used as guidelines in redirecting investment and financial activities. A poor estimate shows a low-quality investment and makes a small contribution to real economic activities. A good and significant estimate reflects high investment efficiency. The coefficient estimates can be interpreted as the marginal efficiency of investment ratios. Galbis (1977, 1982) and Fry (1982, 1984) considered the ex-ante conditions on investment efficiency. Typically, a low or negative real rate on bank loans discourages productive investment. These two equations show the ex-post realization of investment efficiency.

7. Total Output. If banks are holding an easy credit policy and bank resources are given to inefficient investments, the real loan rate $(L - i)$

will have a weak impact on total output *(Y/P)*, as the following simple linear relationship shows:

$$(Y/P)_t = f_9[(L - i)_{t-1}] \tag{4.16}$$

If the loan rate *(L)* is held constant and stable for a long time, the coefficient estimate really reflects the impact of inflation *(i)* on real output. If the real loan rate has been high and positive, the coefficient estimate should be large. When banks are holding a negative real loan rate and loans are given out easily, the coefficient estimate remains low, reflecting a weak impact on total output.

THE DATA PROBLEM

A major problem in any empirical work on China's economic reform is the availability of data. Yearly data used in Chapter 2 cannot be used for statistical testing, because there are only a few observations. The use of quarterly data is more appropriate, but quarterly data in China are either unavailable or, in the case of quarterly GNP and consumption data, confidential. Where quarterly data are not available, proxy quarterly data have to be constructed from yearly data. With the quarterly or proxy quarterly data, the number of observations for any variable increases to around forty, which becomes adequate for any statistical testing. Table 4.4 shows and summarizes the availability of Chinese data, while Table 4.5 shows the alternative data set that is employed to work out the quarterly proxies. A major assumption used in constructing the proxies is that seasonal fluctuations are held constant.

Yearly data appear in two different forms. Typically, consumption, GNP, agricultural output, and investments in fixed assets are whole-period yearly data, while M2 are end-of-year figures. End-of-year figures are equivalent to the figure for the fourth quarter. The construction of quarterly proxies has to take into account such differences. In constructing proxy quarterly data based on end-of-year data, the formula is simple. First, the natural logarithmic M2 figures of 1980Q1 to 1989Q4 are regressed on constant (C1), first-quarter dummy (Q1), second-quarter dummy (Q2), and third-quarter dummy (Q3) in the following form:

$$\log (M2, 80Q1 - 89Q4) = C1 + \beta_{11}Q1 + \beta_{12}Q2 + \beta_{13}Q3 \tag{4.17}$$

The constant always takes the value of unity, while respective quarters will have the value of unity for some and zero for others. The four estimates of C1, β_{11}, β_{12}, and β_{13} can then be worked out from equation 4.17.

Table 4.4
China's Quarterly Data, 1977-1990

	1977	78	79	80	81	82	83	84	85	86	87	88	89	90
C	Y	Y	Y	Y	Y	Y	Y	Y	Y	Y	Y	Y	Y	-
GNP	-	Y	Y	Y	Y	Y	Y	Y	Y	Y	Y	Y	Y	-
Ind.Out.	Y	Y	Q	Q	Q	Q	Q	Q	Q	Q	Q	Q	Q	Q
Agr.Out.	Y	Y	Y	Y	Y	Y	Y	Y	Y	Y	Y	Y	Y	-
FixInv	-	-	-	Y	Y	Y	Y	Y	Y	Y	Y	Y	Y	-
MCFL	-	-	-	Q	Q	Q	Q	Q	Q	Q	Q	Q	Q	Q
MLA	-	-	Y	Y	Q	Q	Q	Q	Q	Q	Q	Q	Q	Q
SB	-	-	-	-	Y	Y	Y	Y	Y	Y	Y	Y	Y	-
MLFA	-	-	Y	Q	Q	Q	Q	Q	Q	Q	Q	Q	Q	Q
FDI	-	-	-	-	Y	Y	Y	Y	Y	Y	Y	Y	Y	-
SRF	-	-	-	-	Y	Y	Y	Y	Y	Y	Y	Y	Y	-
M2	Y	Y	Y	Q	Q	Q	Q	Q	Q	Q	Q	Q	Q	Q
Int.Rate	Q	Q	Q	Q	Q	Q	Q	Q	Q	Q	Q	Q	Q	Q
Loan Rate	Q	Q	Q	Q	Q	Q	Q	Q	Q	Q	Q	Q	Q	Q

Sources: China Finance, Beijing, 1978-1991; *Monthly Bulletin of Statistics,* 1978-1991. Beijing: State Statistical Bureau, Department of Data Base and Programme Bank Management, 1981-1991. Beijing: State Information Center.
Notes: Y = yearly data available; Q = quarterly data available; - = no data available.
Description: C = consumption; GNP = Gross National Product; Ind.Out. = industry output; Agr.Out. = agricultural output; FixInv = investment in fixed assets (included SB, MLFA, FDI, and SRF); SB = state budget; MLFA = bank loans for fixed assets; FDI = foreign direct investment; SRF = self-raised funds; MCFL = loans for circulating funds; MLA = loans for agriculture; M2 = currency in circulation plus domestic deposits; Int.Rate = one year deposit rate; Loan Rate = banks' industrial and commercial loans for circulation funds.

Second, these four estimates will then be added onto the logged end of year M2 figures to derive the quarterly proxies.

The construction of proxy quarterly data based on whole-period figures is more complicated. The first step is to find the quarterly fluctuations by regressing the proxy base figures; in the case of consumption, these are peasants' cash income and workers' cost-of-living expenditures on constant (C2), first-quarter dummy (Q1), second-quarter dummy (Q2), and third-quarter dummy (Q3) as follows:

$$\log (Z, 84Q1 - 87Q4) = C2 + \beta_{21}Q1 + \beta_{22}Q2 + \beta_{23}Q3 \quad (4.18)$$

where Z = (peasants' cash income per capita $\times$ rural population) + (workers' cost-of-living expenditures per capita $\times$ urban population). In equation 4.19, let X be the end-of-year consumption figures, and a1, a2,

Table 4.5
Construction of Proxy Quarterly Data

Variable	Quarterly Data	Basis of Proxies
1. Consumption	1984 Q1 - 1987 Q4	(Peasants' cash expenditure per capita x rural pop.) + (workers' cost-of-living expenditure per capita x urban pop.)
2. GNP*	1984 Q1 - 1987 Q4	(Peasants' cash income per capita x rural pop.) + total retail sales + industrial output.
3. Agriculture	1984 Q1 - 1987 Q4	(Peasants' cash income per capita x rural pop.)
4. Investment in fixed assets	1984 Q1 - 1986 Q4	Investment in fixed assets by state-owned enterprises (total, state budget, foreign direct investment, self-raised funds)
5. M2	1980 Q1 - 1989 Q4	M2 (M0 + rural savings + urban savings)

Sources: Burton, David, and Jiming Ha. 1990. *Economic Reform and the Demand for Money in China,* Asian Department, WP/90/42. Washington, D.C.: International Monetary Fund; *China Finance,* 1978–1991; *Monthly Bulletin of Statistics.* 1978–1991. Beijing: State Statistical Bureau.

*Burton and Ha (1990, Appendix 1) assume that annual income data were broken down into three components: agriculture, commerce, and industry. The variables used to work out the proxies are, respectively, rural household income, industrial production, and total retail sales.

$a3$, and $a4$ are quarterly components of consumption in a particular year. Hence

$$X = a1 + a2 + a3 + a4 \qquad (4.19)$$

and the natural logarithmic form is

$$\log X = \log (a1 + a2 + a3 + a4) \qquad (4.20)$$

The relationships of different quarterly data are

$$\log a1 = \log a4 + \log b_{21} \qquad (4.21)$$
$$\log a2 = \log a4 + \log b_{22} \qquad (4.22)$$
$$\log a3 = \log a4 + \log b_{23} \qquad (4.23)$$

where $\beta_{21} = \log b_{21}$, and so on.

Anti-logging these equations, yields

$$a1 = a4 \cdot b_{21} \qquad (4.24)$$
$$a2 = a4 \cdot b_{22} \qquad (4.25)$$
$$a3 = a4 \cdot b_{23} \qquad (4.26)$$

Substituting equations 4.24, 4.25, and 4.26 into equation 4.20 yields

$$\log X = \log (a4 \cdot b_{21} + a4 \cdot b_{22} + a4 \cdot b_{23} + a4)$$
$$\log X = \log a4(b_{21} + b_{22} + b_{23} + 1)$$
$$\log X = \log a4 + \log (b_{21} + b_{22} + b_{23} + 1) \qquad (4.27)$$

Rearranging:

$$\log a4 = \log X - \log (b_{21} + b_{22} + b_{23} + 1) \qquad (4.28)$$

Once a4 and the estimate of βs are known, the values of a1, a2, and a3 can be determined from equations 4.21, 4.22, and 4.23.

In the absence of quarterly data, these constructed proxies are second-best solutions. In their econometric analysis on China, Burton and Ha (1990) also constructed quarterly proxies for GNP. The formula for the construction of the proxies is comparable to Burton and Ha's (1990). The proxies are used only where the true quarterly data are not available. Table 4.6 shows the database from which the proxies are constructed, while Table 4.7 shows the constants (Cs) and the estimated β_{ij} ($i = 1, 2, j = 1, 2, 3$) in equations 4.17 and 4.18.

REGRESSION ANALYSIS

The eight equations for macroeconomic and financial relationships are divided into three sets:

1. Financial repression (equations 4.1, 4.5, and 4.7)
2. Inflation and consumption (equations 4.11 and 4.12)
3. Financial productivity (equations 4.14, 4.15, and 4.16)

Table 4.8 shows the classification of endogenous and exogenous variables in each set of equations. The variables, which are endogenous in one equation but are exogenous in another, include the monetary aggregate (M2), the investment/income rate (I/GNP), and the inflation rate. The lagged dependent variable is considered as an exogenous explanatory variable in some equations. It is assumed that the most recent past will receive the greatest weight, and the influence of past

Table 4.6
Base of Proxy Data

Year/Quarter	Workers' Consumption (Rmb/Mth)	Peasants' Income (Rmb/qr)	Peasants' Expenditure (Rmb/qr)	Rural Population (Million)	Urban Population (Million)	Total Retail Sale (Rmb 100 Million)	Industrial Output* (Rmb 100 Million)	Investment in Fixed Assets (Rmb 100 Million)		
								SB	FDI	SRF
1984 1	47.67	80.22	85.98	766.46	263.97	744.2	1642.81	2.56	0.32	15.61
1984 2	42.43	64.19	65.84	746.77	286.43	749.6	1876.39	8.72	0.56	37.52
1984 3	44.80	77.16	71.10	727.09	308.90	767.4	1896.31	10.73	0.54	45.73
1984 4	46.62	130.94	105.53	707.40	331.36	944.4	2082.47	23.47	1.36	70.12
1985 1	63.17	108.05	106.02	697.05	344.64	1072.5	2098.05	2.75	0.48	14.08
1985 2	56.62	97.41	89.46	686.69	357.91	1025.1	2447.97	7.55	0.54	37.65
1985 3	61.11	94.59	86.42	676.34	371.19	1016.2	2370.50	7.81	0.61	41.78
1985 4	61.02	129.44	107.29	665.98	384.46	1186.0	2501.28	5.02	3.54	125.72
1986 1	73.90	109.45	115.24	655.55	398.60	1176.5	2401.73	2.45	0.93	20.16
1986 2	64.70	93.00	92.23	645.12	412.75	1174.5	2802.58	2.80	1.46	60.03
1986 3	68.84	104.69	98.67	634.69	426.89	1198.1	2749.04	5.31	2.23	68.15
1986 4	72.12	164.90	137.87	624.26	441.03	1400.9	3071.95	9.63	3.03	179.63
1987 1	75.31	122.25	131.24	612.47	456.68	1383.4	2881.54			
1987 2	65.99	106.72	108.35	600.69	472.33	1381.4	3437.14			
1987 3	68.83	124.57	116.66	588.90	487.97	1413.4	3432.35			
1987 4	73.72	189.95	159.22	577.11	503.62	1641.8	3761.39			

*The data are generated from constant price (1980Q4 = 100) figures.

Table 4.7
Estimates of Quarterly Variations

		End-of-Year Figures				
	M0	Rural Savings	Urban Savings	Loans for Circulating Funds	Fixed-Asset Loans	Agriculture Loans
C1	6.8591	6.2618	6.8830	8.4549	6.1146	5.9357
β_{11}	-0.2497	-0.1920	-0.2133	-0.1947	-0.4789	-0.0159
β_{12}	-0.2764	-0.1630	-0.1392	-0.1772	-0.3344	0.0276
β_{13}	-0.1741	-0.1176	-0.0715	-0.1270	-0.2184	0.0580

Whole Year Figures

	Consumption	GNP	Industrial Output*	Agricultural Output	State-Owned Fixed-Asset Investment †	State Budget	Foreign Direct Investment	Self-Raised Funds	Retail Sales	Retail Price†
C2	11.9743	8.2188	7.6328	6.8817	6.5066	2.3447	0.6789	4.6556	6.9538	4.8708
β_{21}	-0.0943	-0.1781	-0.1277	-0.3217	-1.7881	-1.3839	-1.3285	-1.8470	-0.0993	-0.0506
β_{22}	-0.2513	-0.1023	-0.0291	-0.4971	-0.8804	-0.6057	-0.9524	-0.8729	-0.1157	-0.0342
β_{23}	-0.1856	-0.1140	-0.0655	-0.4098	-0.7478	-0.3120	-0.8006	-0.7705	-0.1223	-0.0189

*Quarterly variation is based on constant price (1980 = 100) of period 1981Q1–1990Q4.
†Quarterly variation is based on 1981Q1–1990Q4.

113

Table 4.8
Endogenous and Exogenous Variables

Equation	Endogenous Variables	Exogenous Variables
(4.1) Demand for Money	M2PP	GNPPP, IPGNP, DDI1YR
(4.5) Investment	IPGNP	DDI1YR
(4.7) Investment	IPGNP	M2PP
(4.11) Inflation	IYR	M2PP
(4.12) Real Consumption	CPP	GNPPP, IYR
(4.14) Agricultural Output	YAPP	SBPP, MLAPP
(4.15) Industrial Output	YIPP	SBPP, MCFLPP, FDIPP, MLFAPP, SRFPP
(4.16) Total Output	YPP	LDI1YR

Notes: P replaces the slash; for example, GNP/P becomes GNPPP. IYR = yearly inflation ($\Delta P/P$). DDI1YR = real annual deposit rate (d − i). LDI1YR = real loan rate (L − i).

observations will fade uniformly with the passage of time. In general, using distributed lag models considers a one-time change in the explanatory variable on the equilibrium of the dependent variable to be its marginal effect. In particular, autoregressive distributed lag models allow the adjustment pattern to vary for each explanatory variable. Goldfeld and Sichel (1990) conclude that general distributed models have been increasingly used as an improvement on partial adjustment models.

In the first set of equations on financial repression, the demand-for-money equation follows the construction of McKinnon (1973). Goldfeld and Sichel (1990) raise various econometric issues in regard to the demand for money. They specify that the partial adjustment model that has been used for estimation requires a short-run dynamic specification. Typically, partial adjustment is motivated by cost-minimizing behavior wherein the costs of disequilibrium are balanced against adjustment costs. Criticisms of the partial adjustment model are also raised. For example, first difference specifications may only reflect the inability of parameter constancy tests to detect shifts in the first difference specification. Goldfeld and Sichel (1990) conclude that general distributed lag models have been used increasingly to estimate money demand. Furthermore, the autoregressive distributed lag model allows the adjustment pattern to vary for each independent variable. The demand for money specified in equation 4.1 can be improved by making the lag of the dependent variable another explanatory variable. The justification is that demand for money in this quarter is influenced by the situation in previous quarters.

The same can be applied to the two investment equations – that the lag of the dependent variable can be included as an explanatory variable. The two versions of the investment equations are McKinnon's (1973) original version, which uses the real rate of borrowing as the explanatory variable, and replacement of the real rate of borrowing, using the money aggregate as the explanatory variable. The justification is that such a measurement produces a more direct estimate of the demand for money on investment.

China's price inflation index is either manipulated or inaccurately recorded, and a number of price indicators exist. Of the two officially recorded retail price and free market price indexes, the free market price for consumer goods is the one that reflects the market demand-and-supply conditions, while the official price index is passively influenced by the free market price. The relationship between the two price indexes is described as one in which the free market price is the leading indicator, since the demand for consumer goods has remained huge and at the same time reflects the general consumption situations, while the official price index has to take into account various considerations. In general, the official price inflation index is milder than the free market price index.

The theoretically more suitable inflation figures are based on Feltenstein and Ha's (1991) construction of the true price, given in equation 2.1. With $a = 0.89$, the quarterly true prices are then constructed. The real value of different variables is the nominal value, deflated by the true price; the yearly rate of change of the true price is the inflation rate used in the regression estimation.

The division into agricultural and industrial output is possible because of the availability of the quarterly data on bank loans for the two sectors. Other explanatory variables which would affect both sectors, such as state-budget expenditures and self-raised funds, do not have such division in the data. Foreign-direct investment and bank loans for fixed assets are included in the industrial output equation, because their usage is geared mainly to the industrial sector and has very little impact on agriculture. A considerable amount of foreign-direct investment is directed to the service sector in such areas as hotels and tourism; such division is not possible because the data are not broken down.

With the exception of the inflation rate and deposit and loan rates, all other variables are regressed in natural logarithmic form. In the process of finding the best estimates to subject to various diagnostic tests, the lag dependent variable, quarterly dummies, and/or the time trend will be added. The Microfit computer software (see Pesaran and Pesaran 1987) and the ordinary least square (OLS) method will be used; and the maximum likelihood estimation and the Guass-Newton iterative method (option 5 in the Microfit estimation manual) are applied to equations in which serial correlation is detected; the autoregressive order is determined by the Lagrange multiplier test.[3]

CONCLUSION

Based on the statistical analysis in Chapter 2, five components of financial repression in China's first decade of economic reform are identified. The eight linear equations, divided into three groups, describe the macroeconomic and financial relationships and aim to explain the cause and extent of financial repression. The first set contains the three equations on the demand for money and investment, with the real rate of return as an explanatory variable. The monetary variable is substituted for the rate of return variable in order to examine a direct effect of money on investment. While inflation is caused by both money supply and expectation in the second set of equations, the real consumption equation tries to see the impact of income and inflation on consumption. The first two output equations in the third set of equations measure the influence of state-budget expenditures, activities of financial intermediaries, and foreign resources deployment on output expansion, while the total output equation measures the impact of inflation on real output.

Quarterly data are used in the empirical analysis. In the case of consumption, income, agricultural output, fixed-asset investment, state-budget expenditures, foreign-direct investment, and self-raised funds, proxy quarterly data are constructed, assuming a constant seasonal fluctuation. The remaining variables contain mostly true quarterly data and a few proxies. This is a second-best solution, since some quarterly data such as consumption and GNP are held confidential by the state. Ways to improve the second-best situation include ensuring that all diagnostic tests are passed before the results are derived and constructing simple linear relationships and using the true quarterly data wherever possible.

This chapter summarizes the various financial equations in an econometrically testable form. The ordinary least squares method is used, and the Microfit computer software package is suitable for the regression exercise.

NOTES

1. The author would like to thank Dr. Ann Horowitz for raising this point.
2. Financial linear regression relationships were applied in the simulation work by Newlyn and Avramides in W. T. Newlyn, ed., *The Financing of Economic Development* (Oxford: Claredon Press, 1977).

3. The estimation method can be found in the Appendix of the Microfit manual (M. H. Pesaran and B. Pesaran, *Microfit: An Interactive Econometric Software Package User Manual* [London: Oxford University Press, 1987]) and also in Andrew Harvey, *The Economic Analysis of Time Series,* 2nd ed. (London: Philip Allan, 1990), 268–269.

5

Pricing of Financial Resources

EMPIRICAL RESULTS

The ordinary least squares (OLS) method is applied to the eight individual linear equations. The likelihood ratio test is applied to the demand-for-money and real consumption equations. A nested test is applied to the two investment equations. Two equations (industrial output and true price inflation) require the Guass-Newton iteration method to determine the order of autoregression. The number of observations ranges from thirty-two to forty-seven. Variables' natural logarithm values, except the growth rates, are used in the regression. The quarterly dummy variables and the time trend have to be applied to some cases. In deciding whether to add the quarterly dummies or the time trend, various combinations are tested in the regression exercise until the best result is found—best in the sense that the estimates satisfied all or most diagnostic tests and the T-ratio significance test. For example, neither quarterly dummies nor the time trend are used in the industrial output equation, but both are included in the total output equation. On the whole, although a few T-ratios are not significant, the overall results and most estimates have the correct signs and expected values. The empirical results of variables which depend entirely on proxy quarterly data, such as GNP, turn out to be good and acceptable. The results of each set of equations are examined in turn.

Demand for Money and Investment

Table 5.1 reproduces the findings of the other five studies on demand for money in China. First, there are differences in the use of data and in the formulation of equations. Chow (1987) uses income as the only explanatory variable. Portes and Santorum (1987) also use retail sales price index, while Szapary (1989) and Burton and Ha (1990) use in addition the expected inflation and average inflation, respectively, as the second explanatory variables. With the exception of Feltenstein and Ha (1991), the income coefficient estimates of the four studies

Table 5.1
Empirical Works on the Demand for Money

Chow (1987, p. 325) 1952–1983 Dependent Variable: ln M/P	
ln Y	
0.3504	

Portes and Santorum (1987, p. 362) 1955–1983 Dependent Variable: M2	
$Y_t = C_t + S_t$	Retail Sales Price Index
1.46	-0.07

Szapary (1989, p. 17) 1983Q1–1987Q4 Dependent Variable: M2/P	
Real National Income	Expected Inflation
0.15	-0.28

Burton and Ha (1990) 1983Q1–1988Q3 Dependent Variable: Household Money Balances	
ΔY	Average Inflation
0.910	-1.583

Feltenstein and Ha (1991) 1979Q1–1988Q4 Dependent Variable: Quasi Money	
Adjusted Real Income	"True" Price Inflation
0.392	-0.548

Sources: Chow, Gregory C. 1986. *The Chinese Economy.* Hong Kong: Chinese University of Hong Kong Press, p. 325; Portes, Richard R., and Anita Santorum. 1987. Money and the Consumption Goods Market in China, *Journal of Comparative Economics* 11, p. 362; Szapary, Gyorgy. 1989. Monetary Policy and System Reforms in China, *Ninth Latin American Meeting of the Econometric Society.* Santiago, Chile, p. 17; Blejer, Mario, David Burton, Steven Dunaway, and Gyorgy Szapary. 1991. *China: Economic Reform and Macroeconomic Management.* International Monetary Fund, Occasional Paper 76, p. 33; Feltenstein, Andrew, and Jiming Ha. 1991. Measurement of Repressed Inflation in China, *Journal of Development Economics* 36, p. 287.

have a wider range (from 0.15 in Szapary's result to 1.46 in Portes and Santorum's result).

In the case of the second coefficient estimates of the inflation variable by the various authors (Portes and Santorum, Szapary, and Burton and Ha), their negative coefficient estimates suggest that inflation has a negative impact on demand for money. Such a simple relationship, however, lacks explanatory power in the case of China. The narrowness in both the choice of consumption items and of income-earning assets simply implies that households in general demand more money to maintain their consumption pattern when prices rise. Feltenstein and Ha (1991) have similar results when their true price inflation is used.

McKinnon's (1973) demand-for-money function is an extension of Chow's (1987) equation. Whether the former's inclusion of investment/income in the demand-for-money function gives a better explanation depends crucially on the log-likelihood ratio test (Greene 1991, p. 356). Table 5.2 shows the empirical result of Chow's (1987) equation using the "true" price.

As compared to Chow's (1987) result of 0.3504, the coefficient of 0.2816 shown in Table 5.2 is smaller. Chow's (1987) equation, however, does not have a strong explanation, it does not relate money and income to capital, and it cannot explain anything about the financial sector. By including the variables of the investment/income ratio (IPGNP) and the yearly real interest rate (DDI1YR), McKinnon's (1973) demand-for-money equation is an improvement, since both the size and the sign of the coefficients have different interpretations. To show the significance of each of the two variables (DDI1YR and IPGNP), an interme-

Table 5.2
Chow's Formulation of Money Demand (M2PP), 1981Q1–1989Q4
(36 Observations)

Explanatory Variable	Coefficients	T-Ratios	Diagnostic Test
Const	-1.4462	-2.7931*	R-Squared = 0.9898
GNPPPT	0.2816	3.5784*	F-Statistics = 583.1126*
M2PPT(-1)	0.9447	49.9912*	D-h Statistics = 1.2978
Q1	-0.0781	-4.6531*	Heteroscedasticity = 1.8396
Q2	-0.1327	-7.9629*	LM Test (4) = 0.6127
Q3	-0.0895	-4.8110*	Max. of Log-likekihood = 72.6129

Source: Based on Chow, Gregory C. 1987. Money and Price Level Determination in China, *Journal of Comparative Economics* 11 (September):319–333.
*1 percent level of significance. LM Test (4) is the Lagrange Multiplier test of residual serial correlation of order 4 (F distribution). Heteroscedasticity (F distribution) is based on the regression of squared residuals on squared fitted values.

diate result can be obtained by adding the real interest rate (DDI1YR) to the regression in the first instance. Table 5.3 shows the empirical result when the real interest rate is first added to Chow's (1987) work. The coefficient of DDI1YR (0.2586) is positive, and both the T-ratio of the variable and the F-Statistics for the equation are significant. The result of the joint test of zero restrictions on the coefficients of the newly added variable (DDI1YR) is shown by the significant F-Statistic, which is $F(1, 41) = 12.7061$. The real interest rate, therefore, has a positive and significant impact on the demand for money.

To complete McKinnon's (1973) demand-for-money equation, the investment/income ratio (IPGNP) is finally added to the the regression. Table 5.4 shows that all coefficient estimates have the correct signs. The positive estimate of IPGNP(-4) (0.3926) is in line with McKinnon's (1973) argument of complementarity for money and capital. The estimate on the real return of holding money (DDI1YR) has a positive of 0.1657, implying that an improvement in the negative real interest (either a higher deposit rate or lower true price inflation) will have a positive impact on the demand for money. Again, the result of the joint test of zero restriction on the coefficient of the added variable (IPGNP) is shown by the significant F-Statistic, which is $F(1, 28) = 8.2961$. The addition of the investment/income variable can contribute positively to the explanatory power of the regression.

Finally, adding the two variables simultaneously also gives a significant F-Statistic of $F(2, 28) = 6.0706$. The simultaneous inclusion of the two variables (IPGNP and DDI1YR) is also supported by the likelihood ratio test. If $\ln L^*$ is the log-likelihood evaluated at the restricted estimates, the likelihood ratio statistics for testing the restrictions are (Greene 1991, p. 356)

$$\lambda = -2(\ln L^* - \ln L) \tag{5.1}$$

Table 5.3
Impact of Real Interest Rate (DDI1YR) on the Demand for Money (M2PP), 1978Q1–1989Q4 (48 Observations)

Explanatory Variable	Coefficients	T-Ratios	Diagnostic Tests
Const	0.3660	0.7901	R-Squared = 0.9937
GNPPP	-0.3027	-0.4893	F-Statistics = 1078.9*
M2PP(-1)	0.9963	74.4955*	D-h Statistics = 0.5802
DDI1YR	0.2586	3.5646*	LM Test (4) = 0.4867
Q1	-0.0744	-5.3341*	Heteroscedasticity = 2.2976
Q2	-0.1328	-9.5279*	Max. of Log-likelihood =
Q3	-0.1191	-7.9107*	97.8894

*1 percent level of significance.

Table 5.4
McKinnon's Formulation of Money Demand (M2PP), 1981Q1–1989Q4
(36 Observations)

Explanatory Variable	Coefficients	T-Ratios	Diagnostic Tests
Const	0.7883	0.9748	R-Squared = 0.9929
GNPPP	0.1901	1.6520	F-Statistics = 559.0388*
M2PP(-1)	0.7578	9.9262*	D-h Statistics = 0.7479
IPGNP(-4)	0.3926	2.8803*	LM Test (4) = 0.8347
DDI1YR	0.1657	1.7453†	Heteroscedasticity = 1.6153
Q1	0.5556	2.5015‡	Max. of Log-likelihood =
Q2	0.1811	1.6442	79.0955
Q3	0.1535	1.6687	

*1 percent level of significance.
†10 percent level of significance.
‡5 percent level of significance.

This λ statistic is asymptotically distributed as chi squared with $J = 2$ degrees of freedom. The maximum log-likelihood value of Table 5.2 (72.6120) is lower than that in Table 5.4 (79.0955). By fitting the two maximum log-likelihood values into equation 5.1, $\lambda = 12.967$. From the percentiles of the chi-squared distribution table, the 0.995 value of λ^2 is 10.967. The likelihood ratio test decisively rejects the hypothesis that the additional coefficient estimates in Table 5.4 are zero.

The novelty of the result shown in Table 5.4 is that McKinnon's (1973) hypothesis has for the first time been applied to a developing socialist economy, and the result is not different from studies of other developing countries cited in Chapter 1 (major examples include Galbis 1977, 1979a, 1982, 1986; Mathieson 1979, 1980; Fry 1978a, 1978b, 1980b, 1982, 1984, 1989; Molho 1986; Thornton and Poudyal 1990). China in her first decade of reform experienced financial repression. The result based on the financial repression framework shows a lower estimate of 0.1901 (see Table 5.4), implying that income has less impact on demand for money once investment and real return on holding money are considered. The estimate on DDI1YR (0.1657) has the correct sign and suggests that if the Chinese authorities increase the real interest rate, demand for money rises considerably. This is precisely the essense of McKinnon's (1973) argument of complementarity for money and capital. The estimates in Table 5.4 reflect that the other empirical works on the demand for money shown in Table 5.1 have overlooked McKinnon's (1973) complementarity aspect, and the inclusion of the investment-per-capita variable (IPGNP) improves the results.

The empirical results suggest that the Chinese experience is best explained by a demand-for-money model that incorporates the different elements of the financial sector. The demand-for-money model presented characterizes the Chinese data best.

Investment Equations

McKinnon's (1973) investment equation is

$$\text{IPGNP} = \text{Con}_1 + \alpha_1\text{DDI1YR} + \alpha_2\text{IPGNP}(-1) \qquad \text{(INV1)}$$

The impact of DDI1YR on IPGNP is indirect since the real interest rate influences demand for money before it changes the level of investment. A more direct construction is to replace DDI1YR with money, as follows:

$$\text{IPGNP} = \text{Con}_2 + \beta_1\text{M2PP} + \beta_2\text{IPGNP}(-1) \qquad \text{(INV2)}$$

Equations INV1 and INV2 represent two different implementations of the same theoretical model. Let's assume we have two general equations:

$$y = X\alpha \qquad (5.2)$$

and

$$y = Z\beta \qquad (5.3)$$

The motivation for using the J-test is that equations 5.2 and 5.3 are *non-nested* regression models. The way to test equation 5.2, or equation INV1, against equation 5.3, or equation INV2, is *artifical nesting* in which both equations are embedded in a more general equation (MacKinnon 1992). This more general equation is

$$y = (1 - \lambda)(X\alpha) + \lambda(Z\beta) \qquad (5.4)$$

where λ is the parameter that has been introduced so as to nest equations 5.2 and 5.3 within equation 5.4. In other words, equation 5.4 collapses to equation 5.2 when $\lambda = 0$ and to equation 5.3 when $\lambda = 1$. If the coefficients (α and β) are known, we can test whether λ is equal to zero or one.

One problem in implementing the J-test is the fact that α and β are unknown parameters. Suppose it is equation 5.2 that one wishes to test against equation 5.4. MacKinnon (1992) suggests that we replace

(βs) with their consistent estimates *(b)*, obtained by estimating equation 5.3 by using ordinary least squares (OLS). Thus equation 5.4 becomes

$$y = (1 - \lambda) (X\alpha) + \lambda(Zb) \qquad (5.5)$$

which allows one to test the null hypothesis that $\lambda = 0$ using a t-test.

Similarly, if equation 5.3 is to be tested against equation 5.4, we replace (α) with their consistent estimates ($\hat{a}$s) obtained from estimating equation 5.2 using OLS. Thus, equation 5.4 becomes

$$y = (1 - \lambda) (X\hat{a}) + \lambda(Z\beta) \qquad (5.6)$$

which permits a t-test of the null hypothesis that $\lambda = 1$.

Table 5.5 shows the empirical results of a *non-nested* equation (INV1), and the *nested* equation when (INV2) is included. In the non-nested result, the coefficient estimate of the real return (DDI1YR) is positive (0.3427). This supports the earlier discussion that a reduction in the

Table 5.5
Real Interest Rate (DDI1YR) and Investment/Income (IPGNP), 1980Q3–1989Q4 (38 Observations)

Explanatory Variable	Coefficient	T-Ratios	Diagnostic Tests
Non-nested results:			
Const	0.1602	0.6979	R-Squared = 0.9948
DDI1YR	0.3427	2.5672*	F-Statistics = 1019.6†
IPGNP(-1)	0.7146	5.6485†	D-h Statistics = -0.6054
Time	0.0034	1.7136	LM Test (4) = 0.5250
Q1	-2.0332	-24.0536†	Heteroscedasticity = 3.8648
Q2	-0.0736	-0.6058	Max. of Log-likelihood =
Q3	-0.5268	-20.0858†	68.6315
Nested with INV2:			
Const	0.2701	0.9950	R-Squared = 0.9949
DDI1YR	0.2696	1.6482	F-Statistics = 835.5264†
IPGNP(-1)	0.7518	5.4590†	D-h Statistics = -1.6390
Time	0.0023	0.9822	LM Test (4) = 0.4839
Q1	-2.0243	-23.3303†	Heteroscedasticity = 4.3630
Q2	-0.0249	-0.1806	Max. Log-likelihood =
Q3	-0.5144	-16.5199†	66.8882
INV2	0.0292	0.7936	

*5 percent level of significance.
†1 percent level of significance.

negative real return can have a positive and large effect on investment per capita. In the nested equation result, however, the coefficient estimate of (INV2) is not significant (the probability value equals 0.434). The same exercise is carried out with equation INV2 as the *non-nested*, and the result is tested with a *nested* regression by including INV1. Table 5.6 shows that the nested results clearly cannot reject the hypothesis. The T-ratios of the nested equation all are insignificant, except for the coefficient estimate of INV1 (with a probability value of zero).

One other method is to treat the two investment equations (INV1 and INV2) as simultaneous equations and apply the generalized instrumental variable estimation method. The empirical results are shown in Table 5.7. For convenience then, the non-nested empirical results of the investment equation in Table 5.5 should be used as the most relevant findings. McKinnon's (1973) construction of the investment equation (INV1) is more appropriate than the more direct money/investment relationship (INV2), and the results in Table 5.5 should be used. The conclusion based on the empirical work on the demand for money and investment is that the first decade of China's economic reform shows a clear case of financial repression, and solutions should be centered around the efficient use of financial resources.

Table 5.6
Money (M2PP) and Investment/Income (IPGNP), 1980Q3–1989Q4
(38 Observations)

Explanatory Variable	Coefficient	T-Ratios	Diagnostic Tests
Non-nested results:			
Const	-11.7092	-8.1495*	R-Squared = 0.7420
M2PP	7.1731	8.0470*	F-Statistics = 23.7292*
M2PP(-1)	-6.0139	-7.1024*	DW Statistics = 2.0852
IPGNP(-1)	-0.8818	-7.9417*	TM Test (4) = 1.1005
IPGNP(-2)	-0.4951	-4.8980*	Heteroscedasticity = 0.0827
Nested with INV1			
Const	-0.1996	-0.5610	R-Squared = 0.9949
M2PP	0.1437	0.6579	F-Statistics = 1238.4*
M2PP(-1)	-0.1236	-0.6445	DW Statistics = 2.2058
IPGNP(-1)	-0.0166	-0.6132	LM Test (4) = 0.4155
IPGNP(-2)	-0.0078	-0.4103	Heteroscedasticity = 3.9811
INV1	0.9855	39.6694*	

*1 percent level of significance.

Table 5.7
Generalized Instrumental Variable Estimation

Explanatory Variable	Coefficient	T-Ratios	Diagnostic Tests
Dependent Variable: M2PP 1981Q1-1989Q4 36 observations List of Instruments: Const, GNPPP(-4), IPGNP(-1), IPGNP(-2), IPGNP(-4), DDI1YR, M2PP(-1), Q1, Q2, Q3.			
Const	1.1114	1.3911	R-Squared = 0.9926
GNPPP(-4)	0.1164	1.1371	F-Statistics = 532.7258†
IPGNP(-4)	0.3766	2.6959*	DW Statistics = 1.6963
I1YR	0.3501	4.3326†	Value of IV Minimand =
M2PP(-1)	0.7853	10.5495†	0.0020
Q1	0.5279	2.3197*	Sargan's Chi-Sq(5) = 2.0438
Q2	0.1679	1.4873	
Q3	0.1364	1.4524	
Dependent variable IPGNP 1981Q1-1989Q4 36 observations List of Instruments: Const, GPPPP(-4), IPGNP(-1), IPGNP(-2), IPGNP(-4), DDI1YR, M2PP(-1), Q1, Q2, Q3.			
Const	-13.2364	-8.4233†	R-Squared = 0.7280
M2PP	8.8478	8.3818†	F-Statistics = 20.7434†
M2PP(-1)	-7.5029	-7.5046†	DW Statistics = 1.6971
IPGNP(-1)	-0.9752	-8.1684†	Value of IV Minimand =
IPGNP(-2)	-0.5332	-4.8623†	1.4299
			Sargan's Chi-Sq(5) = 12.8632

*5 percent level of significance.
†1 percent level of significance.

Inflation

Different scholars have located different causes of inflation in China. Chen and Hou (1986) found the adjustment of official prices and the increase in the volume of currency in circulation are the major causes. Yunqi Li (1989) attributes China's inflation to the process of reform and excess demand, while Yining Li (1989) suggests that money circulation outside the monetary system was the major cause. Naughton (1991) also discusses two major causes: fiscal imbalances plus accommodating monetary policy and flaws in the sequencing of economic reform. The first question about inflation is to find the appropriate set of prices. By using Feltenstein and Ha's (1991) true price inflation, and incorporating price expectation (as used in Szapary 1989), the final regression equation derived shows that true price inflation in China depends on money supply in the last two periods and inflation in the previous period. Table 5.8 shows the empirical results.

Table 5.8

True Price Inflation (IYR), 1978Q2–1989Q4 (47 Observations, AR(4) Detected)

Explanatory Variables	Coefficients	T-Ratios	Diagnostic Tests
Const	-0.1289	-1.2799	R-Squared = 0.8192
M2PP(-1)	0.1015	1.5509	F-Statistics = 22.6602*
M2PP(-2)	-0.0801	-1.1928	DW Statistics = 1.7704
IYR(-1)	0.9248	6.2671*	

*1 percent level of significance.

Inflation in China is highly influenced by its lag and partly by the short-term impact of money supply. A negative estimate (-0.0801) for M2PP(-2) implies that its longer-term influence is weaker. A gradual reduction or a steady decline in money growth can lower China's true price inflation. The values of g, h, and k (respectively, the impact of money supply, expectation, and past expectation adjustment on inflation) in equations 4.8 and 4.9 can be worked out as follows:

$$g = 0.1015$$
$$kg - g = -0.0801, \text{ and}$$
$$hk + 1 - k = 0.9248$$

In solving these simultaneous equations, $h = 0.6433$ and $k = 0.2108$. Hence, $h > k > g$. The sum of the three values is 0.9556, which is close to one. The impact of expectation is three times greater than the adjustment impact and six times greater than the impact of money supply on inflation. This result is in line with the prediction. Expectation depends largely on past accumulated experience, and if past inflation has been high, expected inflation is high. Past experience has the greatest influence on China's inflation. Although the impact of money supply on inflation as measured by the estimate of g, equal to 0.1015, is the lowest, it nonetheless should not be overlooked, particularly if money supply expansion has been kept constantly high.

Autoregression of order four is detected and subsequently corrected. Neither quarterly dummies nor time trend are needed in the regression, but the T-ratios are not significant in the case of the constant and the two money supply aggregates. Given that the M2PP(-1) coefficient estimate is positive and the M2PP(-2) coefficient estimate is negative, the long-run trend is still positive. In fact, the insignificant T-ratios suggest that the growth rate of M2 might have been the more powerful explanatory variable.[1]

Consumption

The work on real consumption is really an extension of the financial repression framework. The purpose is to examine whether inflation has reduced real consumption, and the result can be compared with other recent studies. Table 5.9 shows the empirical results of consumption by Lorenzen (1989) and Portes and Santorum (1987). Lorenzen (1989) uses per capita income as the explanatory variable for both the urban and rural households and argues that the coefficient, the marginal propensity to consume, should be higher among the rural households than among urban households. Rather, the estimates have shown the "possibility" to consume, which should be lower in rural areas due to the presence of "forced" savings. Portes and Santorum (1987) regress households' desired expenditures on consumption goods and services on household savings of the previous period and changes in disposable income and disposable income in the previous period. Their second estimate is 0.6582.

Income is the variable common to both studies. The consumption equation in this analysis includes the yearly interest rate. The idea is to examine whether an improvement in interest rate leads to a rise in consumption. To see whether the inclusion of the second variable, *IYR*, increases the equation's explanatory power, the likelihood ratio test is

Table 5.9
Empirical Results for Consumption Compared

Lorenzen (1989, p. 6) 1986 Household Survey Dependent Variable: Per Capita Living Expenditure		
Urban Households		
Per Capita Income Available	0.959	
Rural Households		
Per Capita Net Income	0.775	

Portes and Santorum (1987, p. 366) 1955–1983 Dependent Variable: Households Desired Expenditures on Consumption Goods and Services		
Household Savings in Previous Period	Change in Disposable Income	Disposable Income in Previous Period
-0.6685	0.6582	1.0119

Sources: Lorenzen, G. 1989. *Income, Consumption, Saving and Hoarding of Private House-holds in China*, Discussion paper. Macau: China Economic Research Center, University of East Asia, p. 6; Portes, Richard R., and Anita Santorum. 1987. Money and the Consumption Goods Market in China, *Journal of Comparative Economics* 11, p. 366.

employed. Table 5.10 summarizes the results of the restricted equation (with GNPPP as the only explanatory variable) and the unrestricted equation (including IYR as the additional explanatory variable). The maximum log-likelihood value of the unrestricted equation is greater than that of the restricted equation. The λ^2 statistic is 5.4472, while the 0.950 value of λ^2 is 3.84. The likelihood ratio test result decisively rejects the hypothesis that the inclusion of the IYR variable will not improve the explanatory power of the unrestricted equation.

In the unrestricted equation, the coefficients of the two estimates have the correct signs, real GNP has a positive impact on real consumption, and a marginal propensity to consume of 0.6714 is acceptable. True price inflation has a considerable negative impact (-0.2010) on real consumption. Three quarterly dummies are employed, and all T-ratios except Q1 are significant.

Financial Productivity

The simple linear regression of the first two output equations examines the productivity of each financial resource in regard to output. A high-estimate coefficient implies that particular source of finance is ef-

Table 5.10
Real Consumption (CPP), 1978Q2–1989Q4 (47 Observations)

Explanatory Variable	Coefficient	T-Ratios	Diagnostic Tests
Restricted Equation			
Const	1.0637	2.2573*	R-Squared 0.8850
GNPPP(-1)	0.7785	11.2511†	F-Statistics = 80.8164†
Q1	-0.2581	-1.2387	DW Statistics = 1.2278
Q2	-0.2042	-10.3730†	LM Test (4) = 1.7002
Q3	-0.2444	-12.1391†	Heteroscedasticity = 0.5398
			Max. Log-likelihood = 80.4713
Unrestricted Equation			
Const	1.8285	3.2659†	R-Squared 0.8980
GNPPP(-1)	0.6714	8.3007†	F-Statistics = 72.2184†
IYR(-1)	-0.2010	-2.2879*	DW Statistics = 1.4985
Q1	-0.0184	-0.9160	LM Test (4) = 0.9806
Q2	-0.1977	-10.4219†	Heteroscedasticity = 2.4867
Q3	-0.2343	-11.8828†	Max. Log-likelihood = 83.2949

*5 percent level of significance.
†1 percent level of significance.

ficient, and vice versa if the coefficient estimate is low, or negative. The third output equation aims to show the effect of the loan rate on total output. Since the nominal loan rate has been held constant, the coefficient estimate actually measures the impact of a higher real loan rate (either by raising the nominal rate or reducing the true price inflation rate) on total output. Table 5.11 summarizes the empirical results.

In the case of agricultural output, both financial funds arising from state-budget expenditures, SBPP(−1), and bank loans, MLAPP(−1), have a weak impact on agricultural output, as the two estimates, 0.0745 and 0.0308, respectively, show. Between the two financial sources, state-budget expenditures have a greater impact on total output than bank loans. The coefficient for agricultural bank loans is not signifi-

Table 5.11
Empirical Results on Financial Productivity

Explanatory Variables	Coefficient	T-Ratios	Diagnostic Tests
Agricultural Output (YAPP) 1981Q2-1989Q4 35 observations			
Const	1.4705	2.1965*	R-Squared = 0.9804
SBPP(-1)	0.0745	2.5088*	F-Statistics = 233.1395†
MLAPP(-1)	0.0383	1.3354	D-h Statistics = 1.6630
YAPP(-1)	0.7481	5.8539†	LM Test (4) = 0.6593
Q1	-0.6606	-10.6848†	Heteroscedasticity = 0.1834
Q2	-0.6259	-11.1228†	
Q3	-0.4578	-25.9719†	
Industrial Output (YIPP) 1982Q1-1989Q4 32 observations AR(1) detected			
Const	1.3309	1.2221	R-Squared = 0.9023
SBPP(-1)	-0.0767	-4.0029†	F-Statistics = 36.9557†
MCFLPP(-1)	0.7651	4.8555†	DW Statistics = 2.0268
FDIPP(-4)	0.1286	1.9551‡	
MLFAPP(-4)	-0.0253	-0.6666	
SRFPP(-4)	0.0057	0.1227	
Total Output (YPP) 1978Q2-1989Q4 47 observations			
Const	2.2342	2.1171*	R-Squared = 0.9933
LDI1YR(-1)	0.1644	1.9067‡	F-Statistics = 982.0064†
YPP(-1)	0.9009	14.5075†	D-h Statistics = 0.9898
Time	0.0042	1.8716	LM Test (4) = 0.3235
Q1	-0.8131	-21.3160†	Heteroscedasticity = 1.3191
Q2	-0.6526	-28.3853†	
Q3	-0.5516	-27.7534†	

*5 percent level of significance.
†1 percent level of significance.
‡Marginally insignificant.

cant. Since these estimates are calculated in real terms, the results are acceptable. Moreover, a considerable portion of state-budget expenditures is made in the form of farm subsidies. Loan rates imposed on agricultural production have been extremely low, and their low impact on agricultural output is predictable.

In the case of industrial output, autoregression of order one is detected and corrected. The three variables, which are assumed to have a long-term impact on industrial output and the use of a one-year lag (-4), included foreign-direct investment (FDIPP), bank loans for fixed assets (MLFAPP), and self-raised funds (SRFPP). The sign and size of these three estimates are correct: foreign-direct investment is most efficient in expanding output and the coefficient is largest (the estimated coefficient is 0.1286); self-raised funds are mostly bonds issued by the enterprises and are self-managed, and the impact on output is also positive but weaker than foreign-direct investment (the estimate coefficient is 0.0057); bank loans for fixed assets have a negative estimate (-0.0253), reflecting the inefficiency of bank credits, since the nominal long-term loan rates in China were lower than short-term ones until the latter half of the 1980s. Despite these acceptable estimates, however, the T-ratio of FDIPP(-4) is marginally insignificant while the T-ratios of MLFAPP(-4) and SRFPP(-4) are insignificant. Neither quarterly dummies nor the time trend are needed in the regression.

For the other two variables, which are assumed to have a short-term impact, state-budget expenditures (SBPP) have a negative coefficient estimate (-0.0767), while bank loans for circulating funds (MCFLPP) have a large positive estimate of 0.7615. The T-ratios of both estimates are significant. State budget funds are used to maintain inefficient state enterprises, and their negative impact on industrial output is obvious. Although bank loans for circulating funds are relatively cheap, they are mostly short-term loans and a positive estimate is expected. Indeed, it has the biggest estimate among all financial resources. In the case of FDI, a relatively small estimate of 0.1286 might be due to the unavailability of foreign-direct investment data for industrial and service industries, because a large portion of foreign-direct investment has been geared to tourism and the hotel industry, as Table 2.25 illustrates.

The third output equation aims to see the efficiency of the real loan rate (LDI1YR) on total output (YPP). With high "true" price inflation and large state subsidies on loans, the low real loan rate will not function as an efficient financial instrument in output promotion, and the coefficient estimate of LDI1YR(-1) is expected to be low. The empirical result shows that an estimate of 0.1644 for the real loan rate is extremely low in promoting output (0.1644 can be regarded as the elasticity of the output curve). The T-ratio is marginally insignificant. A negative real loan rate has definitely encouraged unproductive investment projects. A higher real loan rate could have discriminated inefficient investment, and the number of rechanneled loans for more productive investment and output could have increased.

Two observations can be made. Nongovernment funds, such as foreign-direct investment and self-raised funds, presumably have a higher opportunity cost of capital resources. The empirical results show that they have a larger impact on industrial output, as funds are used more efficiently. Second, foreign investment is most efficient, and next are bank loans and self-raised funds, which require the payment of interest and repayment of principal; state budget funds are least efficient in output generation.

China's financially repressed economy, and her pursuit of a loose budgetary, banking, and financial policy is shown to be detrimental to her financial development. Financial funds are not in short supply, but their use has been inefficient. As such, the various problems, such as inflation, price reforms, shortage and hoarding of raw materials and consumption goods, and a falling export ratio are ultimately financial in nature. A correct financial policy can improve the performance of the economy tremendously. Scholars working on financial repression have argued repeatedly that a high real interest rate is the solution to many problems; it can attract more savings and it makes borrowing expensive, requiring borrowers to be efficient, thereby eliminating all inefficient investment activities. High real interest rates make money worth holding, since its purchasing power is high and reactivates money's store-of-value function. Efficient investments provide more output for the economy, which in turn eases the shortage problem. Inflation will further be discouraged as shortages diminish. Falling inflation makes money a more attractive asset, and large nominal wage demands fall. A higher purchasing power raises aggregate demand, which is matched by higher output from efficient investment activities.

Once the financial mechanism is functioning effectively, the improvement in investment efficiency will be matched by a parallel reduction in state budget funding of inefficient state enterprises. Over time, state enterprises have to improve their efficiency in order to repay interest and principal to banks. A reduction in state budget funding reduces state expenditures and money supply simultaneously, which in turn eases inflation and improves money holding as an asset. Furthermore, as output expands and shortages diminish, speculative activities decline. When speculation declines and prices are comparable to world prices, export will increase. Similarly, an efficient investment/output relationship can attract more foreign investment. In short, once the financial issue is handled effectively, it can eliminate many other problems that appeared in China's economic reform.

The financial repression framework can help to explain some major economic problems in China's reform. The analysis of the demand-for-money and investment equations originally constructed by McKinnon (1973) can be extended to explain the cause of inflation and financial productivity. The demand-for-money and investment equations basically show the complementarity of money and capital. The higher the return on capital, the greater the demand for money is, since money is the most popular nonphysical asset in China thus far. Inflation is seen as a crucial factor in the determination of the interest rate. The high inflation in China has been explained by the money and expectation factors. The empirical results also show that inflation has led to a decline in real consumption. The work on financial productivity is an extension of McKinnon's (1973) framework. It examines directly the efficiency of various financial resources. If the economy is financially repressed, financial resources tend to be wasted, since their price is distorted and unproductive investment activities have equal access. Financial productivity tends to be low as a consequence.

COST-OF-PRODUCTION INPUTS

The correct pricing of inputs is important in establishing a proper pattern of relative prices. The following relationship shows a typical pattern in any form of production:

Use of Inputs → Production Process → Outputs

The price of the final output very often depends on the cost of inputs, plus an element of value added. Inputs include different factors of production: raw materials, labor, capital and machinery, natural resources, and so on. The price of industrial products in most socialist countries is based on the cost-plus formula. The price of a product, p, is the sum of indirect labor cost, c, direct labor cost, v, and an element of economic surplus, s. The ex-factory price of an industrial output equals

$$p = c + v + s \qquad (5.7)$$

Both c and v relate to the use of factors of production. The prices of these factors of production are reflected in the values of c and v, which in turn determine the value of p, the price of the final product.

If the price of the final product is suppressed or controlled by the state with the use of subsidies, it is possible that $c + v + s > p$. If cost of production is restricted and the price of production inputs is distorted, it is possible that $c + v + s < p$. In the extreme case, both the factor and output prices are not related to each other. For simplicity, assume the authorities aim to "reform" the price of output, p, without corresponding changes in c and v. The question is, how can the new price, say p', be determined? Should it be doubled, 10 percent higher, or let market forces determine it? A price so determined must be related to its cost of production. There is no other way to determine the new price, p', meaningfully and systematically.

Price distortion arises when the price of the final product is set arbitrarily and has no relevance to its own cost of production. If there is no distortion in the price of factors of production, the value of p in equation 5.7 can be determined automatically. Factor price distortions can be eliminated when the factor is valued in such a way that it cannot achieve a price higher than its current value. If the authorities want to reform the price of output, the correct step would be to reform the price of factors or resources rather than arbitrarily setting the price to a particular level. If the prices of all production factors are reformed appropriately, the price of final outputs will be determined accordingly. An output which requires a high cost of production will have a high price and vice versa. Price reform should take place at the factor, or resource, end and not at the product end.

Consider a typical case in which the price of a major staple food — say, milk — is set at an arbitrarily low level. At the same time, factor prices — say, the wages of farm laborers — are kept low. If the authority wants to reform the price of milk, the first question is how to set the price of milk so as to reflect its cost of production as well as its price relative to all other goods. On the other hand, if the authority chooses to reform the wages of farm workers, or the prices of other inputs, the price of milk can be adjusted accordingly. The concern is the wages of farm workers and the cost of other inputs.

There are four types of production factors or resources: land and natural rsources, labor and professionals, raw materials, and financial capital. In the socialist system, the use of all these factors is decided by the state, their prices set arbitrarily. The so-called cost of production is not related to the factor's scarcity, nor to its alternative uses. If subsidies are given to finance production, output prices are also distorted. A typical example was found in the early 1980s when university professors at major universities had to look for a second job because their wages were even lower than those for many manual jobs.

In a monetarized economy, financial capital can mobilize the use of land, raw materials, and the employment of labor. As a factor of production, financial capital is "the first among the equals." Price reform must begin with financial prices, typically the rate of interest. In any investment, the availability of financial capital is the first necessary condition. Once financial capital is available, the employment of land, raw materials, and labor will follow. Whether the investment is economically sound depends on the alternative usage of capital, measured by the size of the interest rate. A positive real interest rate can be set by imposing a nominal rate higher than the inflation rate. A positive loan rate encourages the investor to employ other inputs competitively, and the price of the final product can be set accordingly. The revenue generated from the sale of the final product has to be high enough to reward all factors, including the payment of the principal borrowed and the interest charged. If the prices at the resource level are taken care of, price reform at the product level is not needed.

RELAXING INTEREST RATE CEILINGS

Attention to economic problems in the first decade of reform in China has focused on price reform. The point is that price distortion in consumption goods has its root in the price distortion of resources, especially financial resources that are being channeled to investment activities. It is therefore more appropriate to consider pricing the financial resources correctly. In China, the loan rate ceiling has been kept low for a long time. The argument is that a low interest rate stimulates investment, and output and income would therefore expand. Empirical economists (Galbis 1979a, 1982; Fry 1979, 1982a, 1982b; Mathieson 1979, 1980) working on financial liberalization have suggested that a low interest rate ceiling encourages unproductive investment and penalizes efficient investment. The relaxation of the interest rate ceiling can discourage unproductive investment and at the same time free more resources for efficient investment. Output will expand eventually, given an upward sloping supply of investment fund curve (as Fry 1979, 1982a, 1982b, assumed). The supply of investment funds increases, eventually bringing the twin advantages of lower interest and expanded output.

In the case of China, since state banks are the major financial institutions granting loans and the interest rates are decided centrally, the supply of investment funds is horizontal. The horizontal axis in Figure 5.1 represents two types of industrial investments; unproductive investments (UI) are grouped on the left-hand side of the axis, while productive investments (PI) are grouped on the right-hand side. Several criteria can be constructed to measure the productivity of investment. For example, the incremental investment/output ratio is the simplest measure. The upper portion of the vertical axis represents the real interest rate *(r)* on loans, while the lower portion indicates the level of total output *(Y)*. The downward sloping *DD* line is the demand curve for investment funds. A low interest rate, say $r1$, implies that credits are cheap, and unproductive investment activities will have equal

Figure 5.1
Real Interest Rate and Output

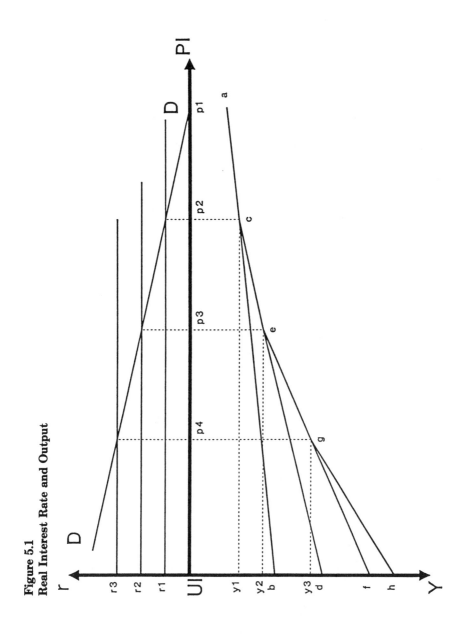

access to credit; total unproductive investment equals *UI–p2*, while productive investment is low with *p2–p1* only. Conversely, at a high interest rate, say *r3*, unproductive investment activities will not be able to repay the loans and subsequently will be reduced to *UI–p4*; more funds are available for productive investments, which increase to *p4–p1*.

The lower portion of Figure 5.1 shows the level of output that corresponds to each level of interest rate. When a low interest rate ceiling is imposed, say *r1*, the corresponding output schedule is indicated by the most elastic output line, *ab*. Given the demand curve, *DD*, output at *r1* is *y1*. The output is low because with a low interest rate ceiling, cheap credits cannot deter unproductive investment. This is exactly what the empirical result in Table 5.11 has illustrated; since the Chinese authorities have kept the real loan rate low (LDI1YR), an estimate of 0.1644 in the third-output equation represents a very elastic output line, *ab*, in Figure 5.1.

If the central authority relaxes the low interest ceiling and raises it to *r2*, the output schedule becomes more inelastic and moves out to a new output line, *cd*. The output line shifts because some unproductive investments are being discouraged by high interest rates, and at the same time more resources are freed for productive investment activities. Given the same level of investment demand, *DD*, output now increases to *y2*. Similarly, at even a higher interest rate, *r3*, the corresponding output schedule is *ef*, and the level of output is *y3*. Given a constant demand for investment funds, a lower interest ceiling cannot discriminate against unproductive investment, while a higher interest ceiling can free more resources for productive investments. The final output curve is the envelope line, *acegh*, in Figure 5.1. With the amount of domestic and foreign financial resources injected into the Chinese economy, the problem does not rest on the supply of resources but on correct pricing and efficient utilization. There is, of course, a limit to the rise in the real rate; a rate higher than that point discourages all investments, including the productive ones.

The division between unproductive and productive enterprises represented on the horizontal axis of Figure 5.1 needs some elaboration. Let's assume a general production function *(F)*, composed of capital *(K)*, interest rate *(r)*, and labor *(L)*. The interest rate measures the cost of capital, while *(K)* shows the quantity of capital. Further assume that the capital is represented by the amount of secured bank loans. The general production function can be written as

$$F\ (K,\ r,\ L) \tag{5.8}$$

Assume we have two enterprises. One is unproductive and can survive only when the cost of investment *(r)* is low. This enterprise engages in low-return investment activities, and its production function is

$$F_u \ (K_u, \ r, \ L) \tag{5.9}$$

On the other hand, the productive enterprise invests in high-return activities and can support a high cost of capital *(r)*. The production function accordingly is

$$F_p \ (K_p, \ r, \ L) \tag{5.10}$$

If the interest rate is low, the banks give equal access to both enterprises. Given that the quantity of bank loans *(K)* is limited, low-return investment activities cannot be screened out. Since K_u is spent inefficiently, output is low. In aggregate, the output schedule of all enterprises is low (as indicated by line *ab* in Figure 5.1). If the interest rate is set at a high level, however, the unproductive enterprise will find it difficult to secure bank loans. At the same time, more bank credits will be made available to the productive enterprise. Capital funds will then be channeled from the production function indicated by equation 5.9 to the productive enterprise in equation 5.10. Since the productive enterprises have more capital funds, output will rise, and in aggregate the output schedule becomes more inelastic.

The same idea is shown more briefly in Figure 5.2. The horizontal axis shows the investment returns: high, average, and low. The upper vertical axis is the level of interest rate, *r*, and the lower vertical axis is the level of output, *Y*. When *r* is low—say, at r_1 in Figure 5.2—low-return investment can have access to capital funds, so output is low at Y_1. At a higher interest rate, say r_2, however, low-return investment activities cannot survive, and capital funds will be given to efficient investment projects; output rises to Y_2, accordingly.

The socialist wisdom that a low interest rate makes investment cheaper for industrial enterprises has to be reexamined and replaced by an economic rationale that a high interest rate correctly reflects resource scarcity. Since state banks in China are the biggest group of financial institutions, they should initiate a more appropriate policy that can correctly reflect scarcity of resources. First, both the short-term and long-term loan rates must be made higher than deposit rates. This is the only assurance that the banks make a "profit" in the process of financial intermediation. Although it is impossible for any individual in China to borrow and deposit at the same time, a loan rate set lower than the deposit rate is unacceptable. Second, the loan rate must be raised gradually to, for example, twice the annual loan rate (at 8.28 percent in 1989), and held for a period of time in order for the policy to

Figure 5.2
Investment Returns and Output

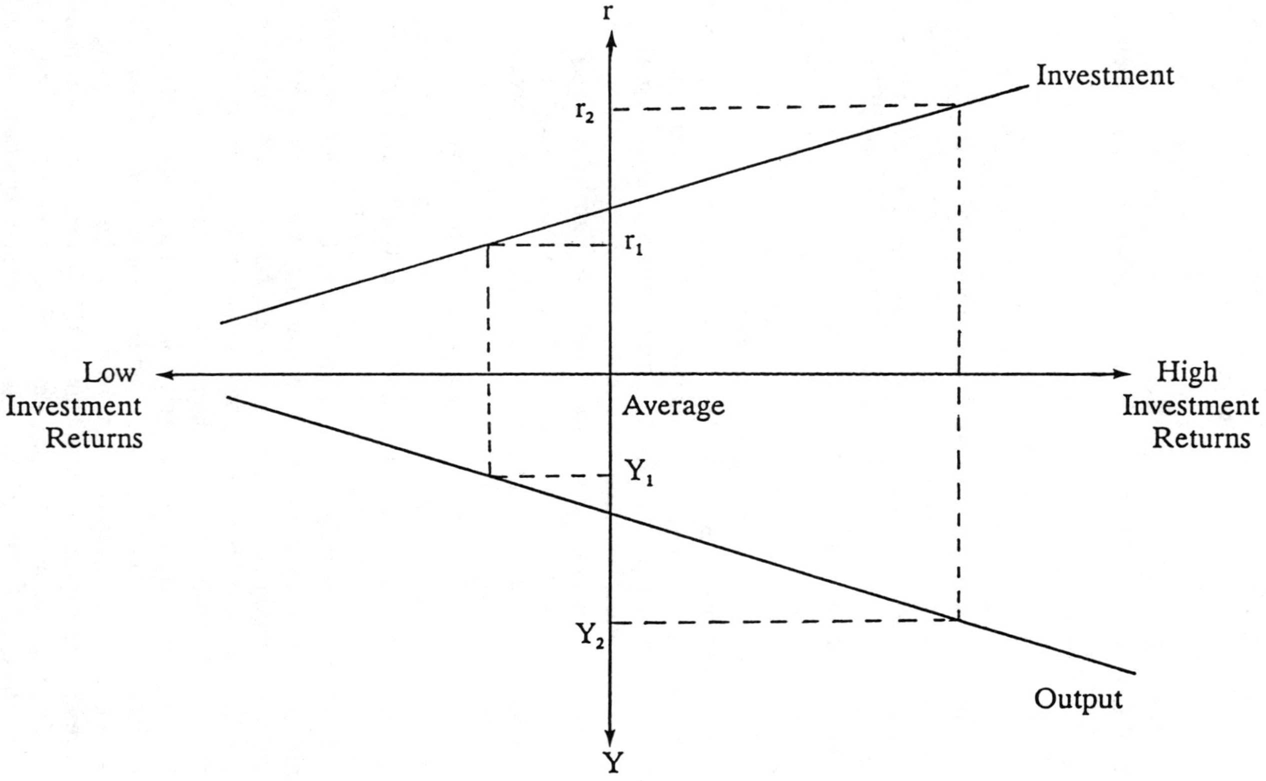

be effective. The high loan rate can be lowered once inflation has fallen to a more acceptable level. The banks' credit policy should be monitored closely. Increase in the output/loan ratio can be used as a measure of credit efficiency.

LINKAGE EFFECTS

There are basically two ways to solve China's problem of financial repression. One is through the institutional structure by removing the interest rate ceiling, and the other is to speed up the development of the private capital market. The benefits derived from removing the interest rate ceiling have positive linkage effects to the development of the capital market and vice versa. The removal of a low interest rate ceiling has wide ramifications for money supply, output creation, inflation reduction and a revised trend in expectation, reduction in subsidies and a falling reliance in budgetary assistance, the removal of industrial bottlenecks, and an expansion of exports.

Four positive linkage effects in regard to the economy can be identified. The first argues that a high interest rate ceiling that reallocates loans from less efficient to more efficient investments leads to a fall in cheap credits and checks the growth of money. As more loans are allocated to efficient investments, overall output expands. This has a cooling effect on shortages and bottlenecks and further eases inflationary pressure. A more stable output situation can be established once speculative and hoarding activities are discouraged. As inflation falls, money once again becomes a store of value.

Second, a rise in deposit rate, coupled with falling inflation resulting from increased output, improves the real return of holding money and raises bank deposits. Deposit expansion permits more loans to be made. Furthermore, once banks closely monitor enterprises' investment and output performance, subsidies and state budget assistance will have to be reduced. As output and demand rise, the state is able to improve its tax collection. Budgetary revenues increase while expenditures fall, the pressure of running a constant budget deficit is eliminated, and a "soft" budget gives way to the establishment of a sound fiscal framework.

The rise in interest rate has further impact on regulating other prices. In order to repay the loans, outputs have to be properly priced. The rise in final output price is a reflection of the cost and value added in production rather than a decision by some arbitrary mechanism. Similarly, for output to increase, workers' wages will be set at a new level so as to reflect their skill in and contribution to production. This has a positive multiplying effect – if one industry does it, all other industries will follow; if one enterprise does it, all other enterprises will imitate. Price reform in China has concentrated entirely on the end-product side, while proper pricing of financial resources so far has been ignored. The recommendation here is that if financial resources, which largely reflect the cost side of production, are properly priced, reform on the final output price becomes automatic, because the value added in the production process yields an appropriate price. Ultimately, all prices will be reformed, or adjusted, according to the cost of production. Price reform so far has been unsuccessful exactly because of past distortion in resource use, and relative commodity prices cannot be established. The first step in correcting price distortions in the financial sector is to properly price financial resources by raising the interest rate on loans and deposits gradually. As interest rates rise, they will have an inverse effect on price inflation. In the longer prospective, inflation revises downward to restore the real return on deposits, and the interest rate no longer needs to rise further. It is only then that price distortions are eliminated.

In addition, improvements in the real interest rate and financial productivity have spill-over effects on the capital market; increases in financial productivity will typically increase the return on financial resources raised in the capital market. And as the capital market develops and becomes more mature, more financial resources will be made available for investment.

The various positive effects can be grouped into the

1. Monetary Effect – As the real rate of interest rises, bank loans are given to productive investment, money supply through credit creation is lowered, and inflation is brought under control, while the value of money rises, thereby making money an attractive asset to hold.
2. Output Effect – As the real rate of interest rises, financial resources geared to productive investments increase output, thereby easing the shortage problem, and price speculation is reduced.
3. Budgetary Effect – As the real rate of interest rises, real return on bank deposits rises and total deposits expand, thereby giving banks the opportunity to make more loans to productive investments, reducing enterprises' need for subsidies, which is replaced by bank loans, and the budget deficit can be revised downward.
4. Price Regulation Effect – As the real rate of interest rises, both productive investment and total output increase, regulating the price of final products and wages in the process.
5. Equity Market Effect – Improvements in the performance of financial institutions, in terms of eliminating the negative interest rate, make productive investment more attractive. Financial resources raised in the capital market will then be used more productively, which in turn raises earnings on

capital. The equities issued and held become an important financial instrument. As more financial resources are absorbed in the efficient equity market, expansion in output further limits the inflationary pressures.

These five effects definitely will be exercising their impact jointly. All the positive consequences can be achieved gradually by first eliminating the low interest rate ceiling, which results in the effective pricing of financial resources, and second, by developing a more mature equity market in China. In addition, once the formal financial mechanism performs effectively, activities in the informal financial sector, typically the curb market, will be reduced. It is only through such activities that financial deepening starts to generate positive results for the economy as a whole.

POLICY RECOMMENDATIONS

Price reform in China has been concentrated on intermediate and end products, and price has been simply increased without due consideration of the relativity of prices. It certainly is an easier task to change prices of final products in order to respond to excess demand or to respond to the introduction of a market economy. Prices in China have been severely distorted and have often been set arbitrarily, due basically to a lack of relativity in the process of price determination. Relative prices cannot be properly set if price reform has not been carried out first at the resource end. If resources of production are priced to reflect their scarcity, prices of final products can be set to reflect their production costs accordingly.

Among all resources of production, the correct pricing of financial resources is most fundamental. Investment activities require financial resources, and the price of final output depends on the cost of financing the investment. The scarcity of investment resources is reflected in the rate of interest. Outputs increase only when investment resources are being allocated to efficient investments. Price reform should start from the resource end by setting a high interest rate to give a positive return on assets held. Enterprises that have remained inefficient are forced to reexamine their investment activities. More important, the price of final output should be related to the price of resources. Reform in the financial sector, and in particular the fixing of a positive real interest rate, is the first requirement, and all state banks should have a tighter policy on bank loans. Loan monitoring should be given an equally high priority. Strict economic principles should be adhered to so that investment efficiency can be assured and waste minimized. At the same time, channels for low-cost financial resources should be eliminated. State banks remain the most important source of loans. The state should at the same time abandon the use of subsidies on prices and on bank loans so that there is no alternative.

Furthermore, once bank loans and state subsidies are under control, other components of financial repression can be regulated. Typically, money supply will be regulated almost automatically. Gradually, the level of inflation and inflation expectation will fall, which in turn has other positive effects. The situation of financial repression will be replaced by a process of financial deepening as the money supply, subsidies, and inflation fall, while bank loans become more efficient at generating output. The state can improve the budget by eliminating subsidies and by providing inexpensive loans to enterprises. Public enterprises will have to improve their production efficiency to reflect more accurately the financial scarcity. Reform of commodities and other price factors will then be taken care of. Last, the role of the equity market should be made more explicit by active improvements in stock trading and issuing practices and regulatory frameworks.

Naughton (1991) points out that the sequencing of reform has created inflationary problems. Indeed, in the case of bank reforms shown in Table 2.3, for example, the objectives of banking practice reform are correct, but the pace of achievement has been weak. Reforms have mostly been conducted on an ad hoc basis; there should be a more cohesive strategy for financial reform in China. Pricing of financial resources has been argued to be the most fundamental issue in the process of economic reform in socialist economies. Second, money supply through credit creation and budget deficits should be tied to output expansion. Last, with output expansion on the one hand and a steady money growth on the other, price inflation could be controlled.

CONCLUSION

The empirical results show that China in her first decade of reform is a financially repressed economy. In particular, China is not short of financial resources, but their efficient use has been overlooked. Consequently, the various economic problems have their roots in the misuse of financial resources. Inflation is caused by significant money growth and fueled by high expectation and has reduced real consumption considerably. Various financial resources have different effects on output. State-budget expenditures have performed most poorly, basically because they were given out freely to state enterprises. Foreign-direct investment and self-raised funds performed positively, while bank loans for short-term circulation funds did better than bank loans for fixed assets. Nonetheless, subsidies to bank loans have reduced enterprises' frugal use of financial resources.

Given that price distortion is severe in China, price reform should begin from the resource end. The removal of a low interest rate ceiling is the thin end of a wedge that yields at least five positive linkage effects for the economy. Relaxing the low rate of interest first encourages more productive investments, as they are the ones that generate enough output to repay the loans. Output expansion can ease shortages and check inflation, while a sound credit policy can check money growth. As money becomes attractive to hold, the increase in deposits further permits loans for productive investment, which in turn conveys positive signals to the equity market. Once loan performance is monitored effectively, financial intermediaries can be the most important and effective source of finance. Ultimately, policy reforms in the financial sector can assist other price reforms positively, because relative prices are set for different intermediate and final products.

QUARTERLY DATA TABLES

Table 5.12 shows the quarterly data for the regression exercise. Table 4.4 determines whether the particular quarterly data are proxy.

The use of the "true" price is a theoretically sound concept. One concern is whether the real values of the variables so derived make any empirical sense. The true price of inflation is generally higher than other price indicators. It would be unacceptable and worrying, however, if the real values show a declining trend. Table 5.13 shows that this concern is unnecessary. Both the industrial and agricultural outputs fluctuated over the years; the gap of fluctuation has become narrower when compared to the nominal figures.

NOTE

1. Indeed, this author used the growth of M2 as an explanatory variable in the same equation by using yearly data for the period 1953–1989. The coefficient estimate for the growth of M2 is 0.4046, and the value of the T-ratios is significant at 3.9861.

Table 5.12
Quarterly Data*

Year/Quarter	Consumption	GNP	FixInv	M2	State Budget
1977 1	450.3			299.7	
1977 2	384.9			305.2	
1977 3	411.0			331.3	
1977 4	494.8			377.0	
1978 1	488.3	826.7		336.5	
1978 2	417.4	891.9		343.1	
1978 3	445.7	881.5		372.1	
1978 4	536.6	987.9		422.9	
1979 1	567.7	921.2		439.3	
1979 2	485.2	993.8		452.1	
1979 3	518.2	982.2		487.9	
1979 4	623.9	1100.8		551.8	
1980 1	654.6	1030.0	63.5	569.9	
1980 2	559.5	1111.1	170.6	574.2	
1980 3	597.5	1098.2	208.1	630.4	
1980 4	719.4	1230.8	468.6	746.2	
1981 1	723.9	1099.8	67.0	759.5	26.7
1981 2	618.8	1186.4	180.0	761.2	58.2
1981 3	660.8	1172.6	219.6	813.2	78.1
1981 4	795.5	1314.2	494.4	924.9	106.7
1982 1	789.9	1196.6	85.8	945.8	27.7
1982 2	675.1	1290.8	230.4	945.0	60.3
1982 3	721.0	1275.8	281.1	998.9	80.9
1982 4	868.0	1429.8	633.0	1120.6	110.5
1983 1	868.5	1338.5	99.7	1162.8	33.7
1983 2	742.3	1443.9	267.8	1194.3	73.3
1983 3	792.7	1427.1	326.7	1292.2	98.4

Year	Q				
1983	4	954.4	1599.4	735.8	1438.4	134.4
1984	1	1010.0	1604.2	127.8	1470.8	41.7
1984	2	863.3	1730.5	343.3	1499.8	90.9
1984	3	921.9	1710.4	418.8	1676.4	121.9
1984	4	1109.9	1916.9	943.0	2015.8	166.5
1985	1	1261.9	1971.9	177.4	2141.3	40.4
1985	2	1078.6	2127.2	476.3	2174.3	88.0
1985	3	1151.8	2102.5	581.0	2333.3	118.1
1985	4	1386.7	2356.4	1308.5	2622.5	161.3
1986	1	1436.0	2234.2	210.6	2680.6	43.7
1986	2	1227.3	2410.1	565.5	2809.7	95.1
1986	3	1310.7	2382.1	689.9	3034.3	127.6
1986	4	1578.0	2669.7	1553.6	3472.4	174.3
1987	1	1651.7	2626.3	253.9	3659.9	47.1
1987	2	1411.7	2833.1	681.9	3814.3	102.6
1987	3	1507.6	2800.2	831.8	4142.2	137.7
1987	4	1815.0	3138.3	1873.2	4529.8	188.1
1988	1	2079.0	3222.2	313.6	4796.3	39.9
1988	2	1776.9	3475.9	842.1	5035.9	86.9
1988	3	1897.6	3435.5	1027.3	5399.2	116.6
1988	4	2284.6	3850.4	2313.5	5931.9	159.3
1989	1	2302.7	3638.1	288.6	6218.3	33.9
1989	2	1968.1	3924.6	774.9	6526.8	73.7
1989	3	2101.8	3878.9	945.3	6883.4	98.9
1989	4	2530.4	4347.3	2128.9	7487.0	135.1
1990	1				7920.6	
1990	2				8314.6	
1990	3				8947.3	
1990	4				9678.6	

Source: Ministry of Foreign Economic Relations and Trade. 1977–1990. *Monthly Bulletin of Statistics.* Beijing: State Statistical Bureau.
*Except for interest rates and true prices, all figures are in Rmb 100 million.

Table 5.12 (continued)

Year/Quarter	Indus. Output	Agri. Output	True Price 1979=100	Interest Rate	Loan Rate
1977 1	887.0		68.11	3.24	5.04
1977 2	978.9		71.41	3.24	5.04
1977 3	943.9		78.44	3.24	5.04
1977 4	1007.8		80.44	3.24	5.04
1978 1	1007.2	334.0	71.10	3.24	5.04
1978 2	1111.5	270.2	74.62	3.24	5.04
1978 3	1071.8	300.2	81.92	3.24	5.04
1978 4	1144.4	492.6	83.91	3.24	5.04
1979 1	1088.7	405.9	82.30	3.24	5.04
1979 2	1150.6	328.4	86.13	3.96	5.04
1979 3	1151.3	364.9	96.05	3.96	5.04
1979 4	1237.0	598.8	100.00	3.96	5.04
1980 1	1157.0	459.7	93.40	3.96	5.04
1980 2	1339.0	371.9	99.49	5.40	5.04
1980 3	1259.2	413.3	111.19	5.40	5.04
1980 4	1258.7	678.1	123.03	5.40	5.04
1981 1	1155.3	521.4	118.88	5.40	5.04
1981 2	1325.1	421.8	124.13	5.40	5.04
1981 3	1286.6	468.7	136.37	5.40	5.04
1981 4	1398.4	769.1	137.32	5.40	5.04
1982 1	1291.6	593.6	137.31	5.40	5.04
1982 2	1432.3	480.2	141.21	5.40	7.20
1982 3	1361.0	533.6	155.26	5.76	7.20
1982 4	1454.1	875.6	155.17	5.76	7.20
1983 1	1382.4	657.4	152.78	5.76	7.20
1983 2	1584.2	531.8	161.80	5.76	7.20

Year	Q					
1983	3	1533.7	591.0	182.22	5.76	7.20
1983	4	1631.0	969.7	177.18	5.76	7.20
1984	1	1545.6	768.3	179.00	5.76	7.20
1984	2	1758.9	621.6	181.67	5.76	7.20
1984	3	1770.1	690.7	197.26	5.76	7.20
1984	4	1912.8	1133.4	196.38	5.76	7.20
1985	1	1904.2	865.1	187.26	5.76	7.20
1985	2	2178.3	699.9	201.57	6.84	7.20
1985	3	2057.9	777.8	221.73	7.20	7.80
1985	4	2111.5	1276.2	220.50	7.20	9.00
1986	1	1987.2	959.3	231.04	7.20	9.00
1986	2	2294.0	776.1	243.90	7.20	9.00
1986	3	2230.1	862.5	258.91	7.20	9.00
1986	4	2446.6	1415.1	258.71	7.20	9.00
1987	1	2265.5	1117.8	277.72	7.20	9.00
1987	2	2654.6	904.3	293.69	7.20	9.00
1987	3	2598.9	1004.9	315.87	7.20	9.00
1987	4	2791.8	1648.9	305.38	7.20	9.00
1988	1	2645.0	1402.1	312.60	7.20	9.00
1988	2	3122.4	1134.3	330.93	7.20	9.00
1988	3	3055.3	1260.5	344.87	7.92	9.00
1988	4	3312.5	2068.2	380.15	8.64	9.00
1989	1	2922.2	1562.2	416.61	9.99	9.00
1989	2	3474.0	1263.9	471.96	11.03	9.00
1989	3	3221.1	1404.5	525.93	11.34	9.00
1989	4	3337.8	2304.5	552.28	11.34	9.00
1990	1	2921.2		586.53	11.34	9.00
1990	2	3615.7		616.94	10.64	9.00
1990	3	3383.2		664.58	9.36	9.00
1990	4	3814.5		643.03	8.64	9.00

Table 5.12 (continued)

Year/Quarter	FDI	SRF	Loan for Circul. Fund	Loan for Fixed Asset	Agriculture Loan
1977 1					
1977 2					
1977 3					
1977 4					
1978 1					
1978 2					
1978 3					
1978 4					
1979 1					
1979 2					
1979 3					
1979 4			1808.5	11.2	193.1
1980 1			1827.7	20.8	222.8
1980 2			1922.1	32.3	225.0
1980 3			2172.9	55.5	192.6
1980 4			2091.0	53.6	217.3
1981 1	4.6	41.2	2113.1	58.6	243.4
1981 2	6.7	109.2	2189.6	65.1	243.2
1981 3	7.8	121.0	2488.3	83.7	212.5
1981 4	17.3	261.4	2351.2	94.1	246.2
1982 1	7.6	55.3	2330.9	106.9	289.5
1982 2	11.1	146.4	2402.1	121.4	
1982 3	12.9	162.2	2687.9	152.0	
1982 4	28.8	350.6	2539.4	151.4	
1983 1	8.4	65.6	2526.4	157.9	
1983 2	12.2	173.9			

1983	3	14.2	192.6	2656.6	167.4	290.2
1983	4	31.7	416.2	3003.9	192.1	231.2
1984	1	8.9	83.8	2833.9	195.3	262.6
1984	2	13.0	221.9	2813.6	206.5	300.9
1984	3	15.1	245.8	3016.7	227.5	333.4
1984	4	33.7	531.2	3763.0	294.0	366.5
1985	1	11.5	118.7	3689.8	290.3	427.1
1985	2	16.8	314.3	3700.1	319.3	442.5
1985	3	19.6	348.2	3908.2	355.1	429.9
1985	4	43.6	752.4	4553.5	529.1	409.2
1986	1	16.7	139.9	4377.0	531.7	446.3
1986	2	24.3	370.7	4554.6	757.2	496.4
1986	3	28.3	410.6	4791.6	831.6	529.7
1986	4	62.9	887.3	5631.5	976.0	570.1
1987	1	22.1	166.7	5452.9	966.3	621.0
1987	2	32.2	441.5	5592.2	1028.7	688.1
1987	3	37.5	489.1	5977.5	1101.2	731.4
1987	4	83.5	1056.8	6606.7	1286.3	691.1
1988	1	32.1	222.4	6637.2	1226.3	757.5
1988	2	46.8	589.2	7167.9	1333.2	434.0
1988	3	54.4	652.7	7485.3	1462.3	449.6
1988	4	121.2	1410.4	8026.0	1555.1	398.5
1989	1	34.6	217.1	8023.8	1545.1	422.5
1989	2	50.4	575.0	8166.5	1576.3	461.6
1989	3	58.6	637.0	8456.4	1629.9	471.5
1989	4	130.6	1376.5	9498.1	1780.2	471.2
1990	1			9623.9	1781.8	498.4
1990	2			9923.8	1850.6	553.3
1990	3			10597.9	1953.4	573.6
1990	4			11594.3	2214.9	571.9

Table 5.13
Output Deflated by True Price

Year	Industrial Output		Agricultural Output	
	Year Total	Quarter Average	Year Total	Quarter Average
1977	4502	1125		
1978	4969	1242	1785	446
1979	4633	1158	1853	463
1980	4613	1153	1789	447
1981	4064	1016	1682	421
1982	5665	1416	1680	420
1983	3832	958	1631	408
1984	3972	993	1699	425
1985	4538	1135	1739	435
1986	4438	1109	1614	403
1987	4526	1132	1568	392
1988	5173	1293	1701	425
1989	4823	1206	1327	332

Source: Macroeconomics Applications System Software Package. Department of Data Base and Programme Bank Management. 1981–1991. Beijing: State Information Centre.

6

Conclusion

ECONOMIC REFORM AND FINANCIAL PROBLEMS

It certainly was a historic breakthrough for Deng Xiaoping to declare the policy of economic reform in 1978. Nonconventional socialist economic concepts and practice were applied first with the "responsibility system" in the rural sector, and soon private households in the urban areas were allowed to trade and run small-scale businesses. Economic reform began gradually in the late 1970s, with both institutions and party officials "searching" for an unprecedented path. Success was "fast coming" and although real GNP still remained at single-digit growth rate until 1982, growth of real consumption was higher. For three consecutive years between 1983 and 1985, the growth of real GNP exceeded 10 percent. With the exception of 1989, real GNP grew by an average of 8.4 percent between 1979 and 1988, while nominal GNP grew by an average of nearly 15 percent in the same period.

However, economic structural changes were slow to come. Despite continuous increases in money supply, total investment in fixed assets, and domestic deposits, the Chinese economy was soon overheated and supply bottlenecks emerged. Inflation measured in retail sales at current prices became severe beginning in 1983. The overheating of the economy got worse despite periodic attempts by the central authorities to cool it down. By the late 1980s, industrial and material shortages had given rise to speculative and hoarding activities, which further restricted improvement in output. Statistical data review shows that financial resources were in good supply. Domestic financial resources included bank loans, state borrowing, state subsidies, and self-raised funds. Foreign financial resources consisted mainly of foreign-direct investment, foreign borrowing, and exports. With the exception of exports, all other domestic and foreign sources of finance expanded rapidly. For example, between 1979 and 1989, state borrowing (domestic and foreign) had increased by 676.8 percent, and total bank loans had expanded by 491.4 percent.

In China's first decade of economic reform, the efficient use of financial resources was the constraining factor. The various problems that emerged in the latter half of the 1980s can be solved through a process of sound financial development. The large money supply that authorities maintained for a number of years no doubt promoted inflation, while an easy bank credit policy encouraged unproductive investments at the expense of more productive ones. The cumulative effects were detrimental. A high expectation rate of inflation eroded the store-of-value function of money, and money circulation was so large that money transactions were made outside the financial system. Price inflation led to speculative and hoarding activities. Coupled with bottlenecks in industrial supply and household commodities, hoarding of commodities and materials was the more secure form of protection against inflation. Supplies of raw materials and commodities were further restricted. In the end, both enterprises and retailers could make their "profit" out of sheer price speculation.

The private capital market was slow to develop. Despite the issue of shares by enterprises beginning in the mid-1980s, share trading was restricted. In the first decade of economic reform in China, the equity market was not able to assist the reform process. However, the significance of the equity market came to light in 1989 when stock returns were higher than the interest rate. With the establishment of the two stock markets in Shanghai and Shenzhen in the early 1990s, these markets would develop further and assist in the raising of financial resources.

THEORETICAL FRAMEWORK AND EMPIRICAL FINDINGS

Financial development can be promoted through two channels. One is the development of an equity market wherein funds are accumulated through privatized institutions. The state is involved only in ensuring that legislation and regulations are proper and that trading in financial markets is standardized. The other channel is through the development of financial institutions and their financial policies. In China, although nonstate and semistate banking institutions emerged in the 1980s, state banks were still the biggest group of institutions involved in loans and deposits. The policies of these state banking institutions had considerable impact on the economy.

The McKinnon-Shaw theory of financial repression offers a direct approach to the Chinese situation. Although the theory did not include socialist economies originally, the relaxation of various conventional socialist practices in economic reform should have qualified China as a developing economy. The essential feature in the theory of financial repression is the complementarity of money and capital. An increase in the demand for money implies an increase in the availability of capital. However, an increase in the demand for money depends on the value of money. The other components of a financially repressed economy include a high inflation rate, which erodes the value of money rapidly, and a low interest rate ceiling, supposedly to encourage investment at lower cost. In the case of China, a particularly "soft" budget, an excessive amount of imports resulting in overall trade deficits, and a declining marginal productivity of loans were the additional features.

The demand-for-money equation and the investment equation specified in McKinnon's (1973) work were tested with Chinese data. In addition, empirical work included the cause of inflation and its impact on consumption. The productivity of various financial resources was fitted into a linear regression, and their coefficient estimates represent efficiency measures. Empirical work on financial productivity is an extension of the original financial repression framework. The point is that one also has to look at the output picture when considering whether an economy is financially repressed. The efficiency of financial resources reiterates the argument that the availability of financial resources is important, but equally important is the efficient use of these resources. If financial prices are distorted—say, in the rate of interest—they will have further implications for output, productivity, and inflation.

There are various limitations with Chinese data, in particular the availability of quarterly data and the specification of a price index. In the former, some proxy quarterly data are constructed for empirical work, while the yearly data are used to examine the trend. There are various indicators of the price index in China, such as the retail price index, the free market price index, and Chen and Hou's (1986) suppressed inflation. Feltenstein and Ha (1991) constructed a formula for the "true" price, which took into account a stable velocity of circulation. The true price is used as the more accurate price index to derive real variables. Eight linear equations are constructed to examine whether China is a financially repressed economy, whether inflation has a negative impact on real consumption, whether various financial resources exhibit different degrees of efficiency on output, and whether the real loan rate is ineffective for promoting efficient investment.

Empirical findings confirm that China's ineffective financial policy and structure are responsible for the experience of repression. Although there are some aspects which are beyond the control of the state or cannot be changed in a short time period, one crucial aspect, which is under the control of China's financial authorities, is the issue of the real loan rate. China has been keeping a low, and often negative, real loan rate ceiling. The socialist argument is that the rate ceiling will promote investment. In reality, such a financial policy jeopardizes productive investment. With an inexpensive loan supply, its frugal use is neglected. Investment projects need not be productive enough to pay for the cost of financial resources. Eventually, loans are given to unproductive investments. Such an easy credit policy is the direct cause of the twin evils of high inflation (through large money supply from credit creation and high expectation) and restricted output (due to unproductive investments).

A correct financial policy is to have a positive real loan rate so that financial resources are priced positively to discourage unproductive investments. It is only through a positive loan rate that total output can be expanded and at the same time free more resources that had been devoted to unproductive investment projects. Expansion of outputs gradually corrects the shortage problem, and as shortages are being eliminated, speculative activities will bring inflation down. The imposition of a positive real loan rate (either in the form of a higher nominal rate or a lower inflation) is considered the key to eliminating economic problems in China.

An alternative is to speed up the development of the equity market by introducing more standardized rules and regulations for healthy trading. Once the process of capital raising is privatized, efficient enterprises of different kinds can engage in productive investments. The private equity market can exert some degree of competitiveness on the official channel of investment fundings through bank loans and state borrowing. Financial policies will have to be changed once investment is more efficient in the privatized capital market. There is a dual strategy in China's financial development. One is to reinstate a sound financial and credit policy. This requires banking institutions to act as intermediaries, promoting investment positively and productively by pursuing a positive interest rate policy. The other is the privatized activities in the equity market. These two aspects reinforce each other: a sound financial policy will quicken development in the equity market, which in turn strengthens the financial policy.

REFORM LESSONS AND THE 1993 AUSTERITY PLAN

When Deng Xiaoping embarked on his courageous path of economic reform in 1978, the fundamental objective was to change the few major imbalances in the economy, such as that between heavy and light industries, consumption versus accumulation, and so on. To correct these imbalances and to improve the general living standards, the

Chinese economy requires a steady improvement in total output. The availability of financial resources is essential, but to use the financial resources inefficiently is equally detrimental to the reform process. Without improvement in total output, massive availability of financial resources will exert negative impacts on the economy, such as inflation. Low financial productivity in China is largely caused by the easy credit policy, which results in a low real interest that cannot reflect the scarcity of financial resources and the lack of development in the equity market.

Indeed, an inaccurate picture posed in the second half of the 1980s is that economic reform can be successful once the availability of financial resources is secured. Financial resources made available from various channels were thought to lead to economic reform. The end result, however, is a prolonged period of inflation and a low level of output. Such an inflation-led reform can only generate, at most, short-term effects, but the reform process cannot be sustained once industrial and consumption bottlenecks appear. The growth of financial resources must be in line with output growth. China is a politics-driven country; a massive injection of financial resources without a corresponding increase in output will simply not sustain the process of economic reform.

Looking at the economic and financial situations in the 1990s, one warning is that history may repeat itself. Despite the economic cooldown after the political unrest in China in 1989, financial resources were again forthcoming by the early 1990s. Enterprises and institutions once again looked to the availability of financial resources as indicators of growth and economic reform. There was a period of deflation in China after the political unrest in 1989, but by the early 1990s the wind of reform was blowing strong in southern China again, especially after Deng's visit to Guangdong and southern China in early 1992. There was a clear danger that economic overheating and shortages leading to speculative and hoarding activities would resurface in the mid-1990s when a massive injection of financial resources could push not output but inflation to yet another unprecedentedly high level. A major difference, however, is the rapid development of the equity market, if capital raised in the equity market is channeled to productive investment.

Executive Vice Premier Zhu Rongji was officially appointed on July 3, 1993, to replace Li Guixian, who had headed the People's Bank of China since 1988. A sixteen-point austerity plan aimed at controlling the dangerously overheated economy was announced on July 4, 1993. The plan consisted of

1. Calling in loans diverted to speculative schemes
2. Forcing workers within two weeks to buy all government bonds that had failed to sell

3. Raising interest rates

4. Forcing nonfinancial institutions to repay funds borrowed from financial institutions

5. Imposing a 20 percent cut in government spending and a ban on new imports of cars

6. Suspending price reform measures

7. Forbidding the issue of new IOUs to peasants

8. Ending dubious fund-raising schemes

9. Controlling real estate fever in development zones

10. Reducing the scale of infrastructure projects

11. Controlling how companies list shares on the stock market

12. Reforming the export financing system

13. Forcing banks to control the way they approve loans

14. Strengthening the central bank

15. Clearing transport bottlenecks that keep goods piling up

16. Sending inspection teams to ensure that provinces obey orders[1]

There are three general themes in the austerity plan. One is the use of monetary control and credit restriction as the major instruments for cooling off the economy. A 20 percent cut in the government budget is the only fiscal restriction. Investment priorities have to be changed, giving less emphasis to real estate development and more to projects that can ease bottleneck situations in China. On the whole, the Chinese authorities blame monetary disorder more than on the huge budget deficits over the years.

There are several economic and monetary factors leading to the austerity plan. The first half of 1993 showed a dangerously overheating economy.[2] The annualized GDP grew 13.9 percent in the first half of 1993, while GDP growth in 1992 was 12.8 percent. The year-on-year nationwide average inflation rate rose to 12.5 percent in the first half of 1993; inflation in major cities was 17.4 percent. In the month of June, the nationwide inflation rate was 14 percent, while major urban areas experienced 21.6 percent. Money supply increased by 10 percent in the first six months of 1993. In June alone, the year-on-year money supply increased by 50 percent. The state bank issued Rmb 140 billion in new loans during the first half of 1993.

Investment in fixed assets grew at a yearly rate of 61 percent in the first half, and state-owned enterprise investment rose 70.7 percent. Investment by state-owned enterprises in the eastern coastal areas grew by a yearly 81.2 percent, 28.7 points higher than the central region and 30 points higher than the western region. Investment in self-funded projects grew by 86 percent, equivalent to 49.3 percent of the total.

Total export rose by 4.4 percent as compared with the first six months in 1992, but imports were up by 23.2. The national industrial production rate was up by 25.1 percent, but state enterprises' industrial production had increased only by 10 percent, as compared to 45 percent in the case of collectively owned enterprises and 68.7 percent in the case of foreign-funded enterprises. Average retail sales were up by 21.6 percent, but in urban areas the rate was 31 percent. In real terms, urban income rose by 28 percent and rural income by 18 percent.

The two economic crises that emerged in the first half of 1993 were both monetary in nature. One was the exchange rate crisis. Three kinds of exchange rate existed in China: the official rate, the swap rate, and the black market rate. The official rate was set at 5.7 to the U.S. dollar. The swap rate was set at 8.2 before being liberalized on June 1, 1993, when it immediately jumped to around 10.8. The black market rate was most popular in Shenzhen, Guangzhou, Shanghai, and Beijing. It rose from HK$100 to HK$148 in the first six months of 1993. In early June, the yuan was devalued, and the decision to let the yuan float, imposed in February in Beijing, Tianjin, Qingdao, Shanghai, Xiamen, and Shenzhen, removed the exchange rate controls at swap centers. As of June 1993, China had US$50 billion in foreign reserve. Lack of proper trading regulations caused concerns in swap trading centers. Although only foreign and mainland businesspeople are allowed to trade at swap centers, in practice many individuals were permitted to enter the market through informal channels. These individual traders were involved mostly in the speculation of currency.[3] The value of the yuan bounced back on July 2 when Zhu Rongji was appointed to head the People's Bank of China.

Several aspects of the crisis were reflected in the rural economy. Grain prices had failed to keep up with inflation; real income for peasants in the last few years had stagnated or declined. Corruption among greedy party officials who were supposed to pay peasants for their produce was the immediate spark in the riot in Sichuan.[4] Another major aspect of unrest was the huge amount of credit remittance from the coastal to the interior regions that could not be cashed by rural households. The *China Daily* newspaper reported that eleven provinces were badly affected by the local governments' failure to cash postal orders sent by relatives making money in the cities.[5] Unrest in the countryside, where 80 percent of China's population lives, is one of the worst fears of the Chinese authorities.

The interest rate was raised twice in the first half of 1993.[6] In July, the People's Bank of China for the second time raised the rate for private and institutional fixed-term bank savings by an average of 1.72 percent, bringing the average interest for fixed deposits to 10.42 percent. The average rise for the rate on demand deposits was 0.99 percent, bringing the rate up to 3.15 percent. Such a mild increase and adjustment in interest rates, however, can have only a marginal impact on savings and investment. The real interest rate remains negative, given an inflation rate of over 15 percent. The cost of capital is still set below market price. In addition, although it is important to impose monetary restriction in the austerity plan, large budget deficits since the mid-1980s in China have generated a lot of "fiscal" capital to state-owned enterprises. The fiscal capital in some ways is more damaging than bank credits because the former is usually given out free as subsidies. The increase in money supply through fiscal deficit should not be overlooked. The low cost of capital is seen as the major cause of large expansion of credits.

The austerity plan still focuses on the "quantity" of monetary capital. The Chinese authorities believe that quantity restriction is the most effective means of cooling the economy. In the short run, "quantity" restriction can be effective because the amount of available financial capital is cut, and aggregate demand will fall, thereby restricting the rise in inflation. The "quality" issue, namely, the efficiency of financial capital, has still not been given enough attention. The availability and the spending of investment funds is the *major* concern of the Chinese authorities. How much output and wealth created through investment activities have not been given adequate attention? A Chinese economist has rightly remarked that "In the West, when a company raises funds, it invests them and creates more wealth. In China, funds are raised and then simply spent, there is no investment, no wealth created."[7]

Insofar as the austerity plan can temporarily cool off the economy and avoid a further deterioration in economic and political terms, the Chinese authorities must in the longer perspective accept the argument that the "quality" of investment activities is equally important if economic reform in China is to be deepened. To improve the quality of investment, capital must be priced properly. The distortion in pricing capital can be removed by keeping a positive interest rate, cutting budget subsidies, and imposing strict banking discipline.

POLITICAL REALITIES

Deng Xiaoping definitely set China in the right direction with the reform process in 1978. However, if output expansion is the major objective in economic reform, there should be a new interpretation of the interest rate as an economic mechanism and the equity market as a source of capital accumulation. If economic concepts are reformulated politically, the role of the interest rate ceiling should likewise be given a new economic assessment. Indeed, looking at the early period of reform in 1978–1979, banking institutions met and had set a number of suggestions on the reform of banking practices, pricing of financial resources, and the role of the interest rate (see, for example, Table 2.3), but these reform suggestions were not taken.

In the case of the equity market, a new political interpretation has been made. Development of the equity markets in the 1990s will definitely be more vigorous than in the 1980s. Capital raised in the equity market will be seen as more productive, and output growth will be higher. One problem is that the capital raised from the two stock markets in Shanghai and Shenzhen will be regional, and it will take some time before their effects are felt at the national level.

One crucial dimension of economic reform is the separation of political and economic decisions. There is no doubt that the People's Republic of China is a one-party state, and the Communist party rules the political future of the country. When it comes to economic matters, however, economic decisions should be related to improvements in the economic well being of the citizens. Political decisions should not interfere with economic decisions. All resources are state owned, but the efficient use and deployment of resources could be left to individuals interested in producing sound economic results. Economic achievements should not be hindered by the political system. Ordinary citizens are interested in improving their economic welfare.

Revising the role of the real interest rate as an economic instrument in regulating investment activities should be politically acceptable if the Chinese authorities want to deepen the process of economic reform positively. In the final analysis, it is output that could improve the livelihoods of ordinary citizens. The availability of financial resources is just the instrument and one condition upon which a rise in output could be achieved; it certainly is not an end in itself.

NOTES

1. *South China Morning Post,* July 4, 1993, Hong Kong.
2. Ibid., July 20, 1993, Hong Kong.
3. Ibid., June 6, 1993, Hong Kong.
4. Ibid., June 13, 1993, Hong Kong.
5. Ibid., July 4, 1993, Hong Kong.
6. Ibid., July 11, 1993, Hong Kong.
7. Ibid., July 4, 1993, Hong Kong.

Bibliography

Abbott, Graham J. 1985. A Survey on Savings and Financial Development in Asian Developing Countries. *Savings and Development* 9(4):395–419.

Adekanye, Femi A. 1991. Commercial Bank Performance in a Developing Country: A Case Study of Nigeria. Ph.D. Thesis. Department of Banking and Finance, City University Business School, London.

Aghevli, Bijan B. 1977. Inflationary Finance and Growth. *Journal of Political Economy* 85(6):1295–1307.

Aghevli, Bijan B., and Mohsin Khan. 1978. Government Deficits and the Inflationary Process in Developing Countries. *IMF Staff Papers* 25 (September):383–416.

Aho, C. Michael. 1973. The Use of Export Projections in Allocating Foreign Aid among and Domestic Resources within Developing Countries. *Journal of Development Studies* 10:403–429.

Akaike, H. 1969. Statistical Predictor Identification. *Annuals of the Institute of Statistical Mathematics* 21:203–217.

Anand, Ritu, and Sweder van Wijnbergen. 1989. Inflation and the Financing of Government Expenditure: An Introductory Analysis with an Application to Turkey. *The World Bank Economic Review* 3(1):17–38.

Arndt, H. W. 1983. Financial Development in Asia. *Asian Development Review* 1(1):86–100.

Asian Development Bank. 1984. *Domestic Resource Mobilization through Financial Development*. Manila: Economics Office.

———. 1985. *Improving Domestic Resource Mobilization through Financial Development*. Manila: Economics Office.

Bacha, Edmar L. 1972. Foreign Capital Inflow and the Output Growth Rate of the Recipient Country: One-Sector Models Compared. *Journal of Development Studies* 10:374–381.

Bachman, David. 1987. Implementing Chinese Tax Policy. In *Policy Implementary in Post-Mao China,* ed. David M. Lampton. Berkeley and Los Angeles: University of California Press.

Bade, Robin. 1972. Optimal Growth and Foreign Borrowing with Restricted Mobility of Foreign Capital. *International Economic Review* 13(3): 544–554.

Bahl, Roy W. 1971. A Regression Approach to Tax Effort and Tax Ratio Analysis. *IMF Staff Papers* 17(3):570–612.

Baiman, Stanley. 1982. Agency Research in Managerial Accounting: A Survey. *Journal of Accounting Literature* 1:154–213.

Balassa, Bela. 1982. *Development Strategies in Semi-Industrial Economies.* Baltimore: Johns Hopkins University Press.

Barnea, Amir, Robert A. Haugen, and Lemma W. Senbet. 1981. An Equilibrium Analysis of Debt Financing under Costly Tax Arbitrage and Agency Problems. *Journal of Finance* 36(3):569–581.

Basu, Kaushik. 1984. *The Less Developed Economy: A Critique of Contemporary Theory.* London: Basil Blackwell.

Baum, Richard, ed. 1980. *China's Four Modernizations: The New Technological Revolution.* Boulder, Colo.: Westview Press.

Baumol, William J., John C. Panzar, and Robert D. Willig. 1982. *Contestable Markets and the Theory of Industry Structure.* New York: Harcourt Brace Jovanovich.

Ben-Shahar, Haim. 1967. Capital Formation and Government Capital Policy in Developing Economies. *Journal of Development Studies* 4:86–96.

Berry, Albert. 1974. Static Effects of Technological Borrowing on National Income: A Taxonomy of Cases. *Weltwirtschaftliches Arch* 4.

Bhatt, Vinayak V., and Jacob Meerman. 1978. Resource Mobilization in Developing Countries: Financial Institutions and Policies. *World Development* 6(1):45–64.

Bhatt, Vinayak V., and Alan R. Roe. 1979. Capital Market Imperfections and Economic Development. *World Bank Staff Working Papers,* No. 38. Washington, D.C.: World Bank.

Blejer, Mario I., David Burton, Steven Dundaway, and Gyorgy Szapary. 1991. *China: Economic Reform and Macroeconomic Management.* Occasional Paper 76. Washington, D.C.: International Monetary Fund.

Blejer, Mario I., and Silvia B. Sagari. 1991. *Hungary: Financial Sector Reform in a Socialist Economy.* Country Economics Department, Working Paper WPS 595. Washington, D.C.: World Bank.

Blejer, Mario I., and Gyorgy Szapary. 1990a. The Changing Role of Macroeconomic Policies in China. *Finance and Development* 27(2):32–35.

——. 1990b. The Evolving Role of Tax Policy in China. *Journal of Comparative Economics* 14(3):452–472.

Blinder, Alan S., and Joseph E. Stiglitz. 1983. Money, Credit Constraints, and Economic Activity. *American Economic Review* 73(2):297–302.

Blitzer, Charles R., Peter B. Clark, and Lance Taylor. 1975. *Economy-Wide Models and Development Planning.* London: Oxford University Press.

Blomqvist, A. G. 1976. Empirical Evidence on the Two-Gap Hypothesis – A Revised Analysis. *Journal of Development Economics* 3:181–193.

Boudreaux, Donald J., and William F. Shugart II. 1989. The Effects of Monetary Instability on the Extent of Vertical Integration. *Atlantic Economic Journal* 17(2):1–10.

Breusch, T. S., and L. G. Godfrey. 1981. A Review of Recent Work on Testing for Autocorrelation in Dynamic Simultaneous Models. In *Macroeconomic Analysis: Essays in Macroeconomics and Econometrics*, ed. D. Currie, R. Nobay, and D. Peel. London: Croom Helm.

Breusch, T. S., and A. R. Pagan. 1980. The Lagrange Multiplier Test and Its Applications to Model Specification in Econometrics. *Review of Economic Studies* 47:239–253.

Brock, Philip L. 1984. Inflationary Finance in an Open Economy. *Journal of Monetary Economics* 14:37–53.

Buffie, Edward F. 1984. Financial Repression, the New Structuralists and the Stabilization Policy in Semi-Industrialized Economies. *Journal of Development Economics* 14:305–322.

Burki, Shahid Javed. 1988. Reform and Growth in China. *Finance and Development* 25(4):46–49.

Burton, David, and Jiming Ha. 1990. *Economic Reform and the Demand for Money in China.* Asian Department, WP/90/42. Washington, D.C.: International Monetary Fund.

Buxbaum, David C., Joseph E. Cassandra, and Paul D. Reynolds. 1982. *China Trade: Prospects and Perspectives.* New York: Praeger Press.

Byrd, William. 1983. *China's Financial System.* Boulder, Colo.: Westview Press.

———. 1987a. The Impact of the Two-Tier Plan/Market System in Chinese Industry. *Journal of Comparative Economics* 11:295–308.

———. 1987b. Plan and Market in the Chinese Economy: A Simple General Equilibrium Model. *Journal of Comparative Economics* 13(2):177–204.

———. 1992. *China Industrial Firms under Reform.* Washington, D.C.: World Bank.

Byrd, William, Gene Tidrick, Chen Jiyuan, Xu Lu, Tang Zongkun, and Chen Lantung. 1984. Recent Chinese Economic Reforms – Studies of Two Industrial Enterprises. *World Bank Staff Working Papers,* No. 652. Washington, D.C.: World Bank.

Chai, Joseph C. H. 1981. Domestic Money and Banking Reforms in China. *Hong Kong Economic Papers* 14:37–52.

———. 1983. *Changes in Property Rights and Income Distribution under China's Baogan Daohu System.* Discussion Paper No. 18. Department of Economics, University of Hong Kong.

———. 1987. Reform of China's Industrial Prices 1979–1985. In *China's Economic Reforms,* ed. Joseph C. H. Chai and Chi K. Leung, pp. 584–609. Hong Kong: Centre of Asian Studies, University of Hong Kong.

Chandavarkar, Anand G. 1985. The Non-Institutional Financial Sector in Developing Countries: Macroeconomic Implications for Savings Policies. *Savings and Development* 9(2):129–140.

Chang, Doug, and S. Jung Woo. 1984. Unorganized Money Markets in LDCs: The McKinnon-Shaw Hypothesis versus the van Wijnbergen Hypothesis. *Working Paper.* Nashville: Vanderbilt University, Department of Economics.

Chen, Chien Hsun. 1989. Monetary Aggregate and Macroeconomic Perform-ance. *Journal of Comparative Economics* 13:314–324.

Chen, Nai-Ruenn, and Chi-ming Hou. 1986. China's Inflation, 1979–1983: Measurement and Analysis. *Economic Development and Cultural Change* 34(4):811–835.

Chenery, Hollis. 1981. *Structural Change and Development Policy.* New York: Oxford University Press.

Chenery, Hollis B., and Michael Bruno. 1962. Development Alternatives in an Open Economy: The Case of Israel. *Economic Journal* 72(March):79–103.

Chenery, Hollis B., and Nicholas G. Carter. 1973. Foreign Assistance and De-velopment Performance, 1960–1970. *American Economic Review* 63(2): 459–468.

Chenery, Hollis B., and Arthur MacEwan. 1966. Optimal Patterns of Growth and Aid: The Case of Pakistan. In *The Theory and Design of Economic Development,* ed. Irma Adelman and Erik Thorbecke. Baltimore: Johns Hopkins University Press.

Chenery, Hollis B., Sherman Robin, and Moshe Syrquin. 1986. *Industrializa-tion and Growth: A Comparative Study.* New York: Oxford University Press.

Chenery, Hollis B., and Alan M. Strout. 1966. Foreign Assistance and Economic Development. *American Economic Review* 56(4):679–733.

Chenery, Hollis B., et al., eds. 1971. *Studies in Development Planning.* New York: Harvard University Press.

Cheng, Chu Yuan. 1982. *China's Economic Development —Growth and Struc-tural Change.* Boulder, Colo.: Westview Press.

Cheung, Steven N. S. 1989. Privatization vs. Special Interests: The Experience of China's Economic Reform. *Hong Kong Economic Papers* 19:1–8.

China Handbook. 1980. Hong Kong: Ta Kung Pao.

——. 1982. Hong Kong: Ta Kung Pao.

——. 1984. Hong Kong: Ta Kung Pao.

China Official Annual Report. 1982. Hong Kong: Kingsway International Publications.

Cho, Yoon Je. 1984. On the Liberalization of the Financial System and Effi-ciency of Capital Accumulation under Uncertainty. Ph.D. Thesis, Stan-ford University, Stanford, Calif.

Chow, Gregory C. 1985. A Model of Chinese National Income Determination. *Journal of Political Economy* 93(4):782–792.

——. 1986a. *The Chinese Economy.* Chinese University of Hong Kong Press, Hong Kong.

——. 1986b. Development of a More Market-Oriented Economy in China. Paper presented at the symposium, Economic Development in Chinese Societies. Hong Kong Economic Association, Hong Kong, December.

——. 1987. Money and Price Level Determination in China. *Journal of Com-parative Economics* 11(September):319–333.

Cochrane, Susan H. 1972. Structural Inflation and the Two-Gap Model of Eco-nomic Development. *Oxford Economic Papers* 24:385–398.

Cody, John, Helen Hughes, and David Wall, eds. 1980. *Policies for Industrial Progress in Developing Countries.* New York: Oxford University Press.

Cole, David C. 1987. Financial Development in Asia. *Asia-Pacific Economic Literature* 2(2):26–47.

Cole, David C., and H. T. Patrick. 1986. Financial Development in the Pacific Basin Market. In *Pacific Growth and Financial Interdependence*, ed. A. H. H. Tan and B. Kapur. Sydney: Allen & Unwin.

Conlisk, J., and D. Huddle. 1968. Allocating Foreign Aid: An Apprasial of a Self-Help Model. *Journal of Development Studies* 5:245–251.

Courakis, Anthony S. 1984. Constraints on Bank Choices and Financial Repression in Less Developed Countries. *Oxford Bulletin of Economics and Statistics* 46(4):341–370.

Dacy, Douglas C. 1975. Foreign Aid, Government Consumption, Saving and Growth in Less-Developed Countries. *Economic Journal* 85(September): 548–561.

Database of Chinese Economic Statistics. 1986. Guangzhou, People's Republic of China: Guangdong International Data Company.

Davidson, Paul. 1968. Money, Portfolio Balance, Capital Accumulation and Economic Growth. *Econometrica* 36(2):291–320.

de Vries, Jos. 1975. Compensatory Financing: A Quantitative Analysis. *World Bank Staff Working Papers*, No. 228. Washington, D.C.: World Bank.

de Wulf, Luc. 1985. Financial Reform in China. *Finance and Development* 22(4):19–22.

——. 1986. International Experience in Budgetary Trends during Economic Development and Its Relevance for China. *World Bank Staff Working Papers*, No. 760. Washington, D.C.: World Bank.

de Wulf, Luc, and David Goldsbrough. 1986. The Evolving Role of Monetary Policy in China. *IMF Staff Papers*, June:209.

Deaton, Angus. 1989. Saving in Developing Countries: Theory and Review. In *Proceedings of the World Bank Annual Conference on Development Economics*, pp. 61–108. Washington, D.C.: World Bank.

Dernberger, Robert F., and Richard S. Eckaus. 1988. *Financing Asian Development, China and India.* New York: University Press of America.

Desai, Padma, and Ricardo Martin. 1983. Measuring Resource-Allocational Efficiency in Centrally Planned Economies – A Theoretical Analysis. In *Marxism, Central Planning and the Soviet Economy*, ed. Padama Desai. Cambridge: MIT Press.

Diaz-Alejandro, Carlos. 1985. Goodbye Financial Repression, Hello Financial Crash. *Journal of Development Economics* 19(1-2):1–24.

Dickey, David A., and Wayne A. Fuller. 1979. Distribution of the Estimators for Autoregressive Time Series with a Unit Root. *Journal of the American Statistical Association* 74:427–431.

——. 1981. The Likelihood Ratio Statistics for Autoregressive Time Series with a Unit Root. *Econometrica* 49:1057–1072.

Dickie, Robert B. 1981. Development of Third World Securities Markets. *Law and Policy in International Business* 13:177–222.

Diwan, Romesh K. 1967. A Test of the Two-Gap Theory of Economic Development. *Journal of Development Studies* 4:529–537.

Dong, Fureng. 1982. The Relationship between Accumulation and Consumption in China's Economic Development. In *Economic Reform in the*

PRC, ed. George C. Wang, pp. 53–68. Boulder, Colo.: Westview Press.
——. 1990. Reform of the Economic Operating Mechanism and Reform of Ownership. In *The Chinese Economy and Its Future,* ed. Peter Nolan and Fureng Dong, pp. 63–71. Cambridge, Mass.: Polity Press.

Donnithorne, Audrey. 1986. Banking and Fiscal Changes in China since Mao. In *Conference on China's System Reforms,* Paper No. 31. Hong Kong: Centre of Asian Studies, University of Hong Kong.

Dooley, Michael, Jeffrey Frankel, and Donald J. Mathieson. 1987. International Capital Mobility: What Do Saving-Investment Correlations Tell Us? *IMF Staff Papers,* September:503–530.

Dooley, Michael P., and Donald Mathieson. 1987. Financial Liberalization in Developing Countries. *Finance and Development* 23(3):31–34.

Dornbusch, Rudiger, Stanley Fisher, and John Bossons. 1987. *Macroeconomics and Finance: Essays in Honor of Franco Modigliani.* Cambridge: MIT Press.

Dornbusch, Rudiger, and Alejandro Reynoso. 1989. Financial Factors in Economic Development. *American Economic Review,* Papers and Proceedings, 79(2):204–209.

Drake, Peter J. 1980. *Money, Finance and Development.* London: John Wiley & Sons.

Drazen, Allan. 1981. Inflation and Capital Accumulation under a Finite Horizon. *Journal of Monetary Economics* 8:247–260.

Eaton, Jonathan, and Lance Taylor. 1986. Developing Country Finance and Debt. *Journal of Development Economics* 22:209–265.

Eatwell, John, Murray Milgate, and Peter Newman, eds. 1987. *The New Palgrave Dictionary of Economics, Vol. 1.* London: Macmillan Press.

Edwards, Sebastian. 1988. *Real Exchange Rates, Devaluation and Adjustments: Exchange Rate Policy in Developing Countries.* Cambridge: MIT Press.

Ellis, Christopher J., and Barry J. Naughton. 1990. On the Theory of Household Saving in the Presence of Rationing. *Journal of Comparative Economics* 14(2):269–285.

Fama, Eugene F. 1970. Efficient Capital Markets: A Review of Theory and Empirical Work. *Journal of Finance* 25(2):383–417.
——. 1980a. Agency Problems and the Theory of the Firm. *Journal of Political Economy* 88(2):288–307.
——. 1980b. Banking in the Theory of Finance. *Journal of Monetary Economics* 6:39–57.
——. 1981. Stock Returns, Real Activity, Inflation, and Money. *American Economic Review* 71(4):545–565.
——. 1985. What's Different about Banks? *Journal of Monetary Economics* 15:29–39.
——. 1990. Stock Returns, Expected Returns, and Real Activity. *Journal of Finance* 45(4):1089–1108.

Fama, Eugene F., and Michael C. Jensen. 1983a. Agency Problems and Residual Claims. *Journal of Law and Economics* 26(June):327–349.
——. 1983b. Separation of Ownership and Control. *Journal of Law and Economics* 26(June):301–325.

Feder, Gershon. 1979. Economic Growth, Foreign Loans and Debt Servicing Capacity of Developing Countries. *Journal of Development Studies* 16:352–368.

——. 1982. On Exports and Economic Growth. *Journal of Development Economics* 12:59–73.

Fei, John, and Bruce Reynolds. 1987. A Tentative Plan for the Rational Sequencing of Overall Reform in China's Economic System. *Journal of Comparative Economics* 11:490–502.

Feinberg, Richard E., and Contributors. 1986. *Between Two Worlds: The World Bank's Next Decade.* New York: Transaction Books.

Feldstein, Martin, and Charles Horioka. 1980. Domestic Saving and International Capital Flows. *Economic Journal* 90(June):314–329.

Feltenstein, Andrew, and Ziba Farhadian. 1987. Fiscal Policy, Monetary Targets and the Price Level in a Centrally Planned Economy: An Application to the Case of China. *Journal of Money, Credit and Banking* 19(2): 137–156.

Feltenstein, Andrew, and Jiming Ha. 1991. Measurement of Repressed Inflation in China. *Journal of Development Economics* 36:279–294.

Feltenstein, Andrew, David Lebow, and Sweder van Wijnbergen. 1990. Savings, Commodity Market Rationing and the Real Rate of Interest in China. *Journal of Money, Credit and Banking* 22(2):231–252.

Fisher, Bernhard. 1981. Interest Rate Ceilings, Inflation and Economic Growth in Developing Countries. *Economics* 23:75–93.

FitzGerald, E. V. K., and Rob Vos. 1989. *Financing Economic Development: A Structural Approach to Monetary Policy.* Aldershot, England: Gower.

Friedman, Benjamin M. 1983. The Role of Money and Credit in Macroeconomic Analysis. In *Macroeconomics, Prices and Quantities,* ed. James Tobin, pp. 161–200. Washington, D.C.: Brookings Institution.

Friedman, Irving S. 1981. The Role of Private Banks in Stabilization Programs. In *Economic Stabilization in Developing Countries,* ed. William R. Cline and Sidney Weintraub. Washington, D.C.: Brookings Institution.

Fry, Maxwell J. 1978a. Monetary Policy and Domestic Saving in Developing ESCAP Countries. *Economic Bulletin for Asia and the Pacific* 29(1): 79–99.

——. 1978b. Money and Capital or Financial Deepening in Economic Development. *Journal of Money, Credit and Banking* 10(4):464–475.

——. 1979. The Cost of Financial Repression in Turkey. *Savings and Development* 3(2):127–135.

——. 1980a. Money, Interest, Inflation and Growth in Turkey. *Journal of Monetary Economics* 6:535–545.

——. 1980b. Saving, Investment, Growth and the Cost of Financial Repression. *World Development* 8:317–327.

——. 1982a. Models of Financially Repressed Developing Economies. *World Development* 10(9):731–750.

——. 1982b. Analyzing Disequilibrium Interest-Rate Systems in Developing Countries. *World Development* 10(2):1049–1057.

——. 1984. Saving, Financial Intermediation and Economic Growth in Asia. *Asian Development Review* 2(1):82–91.

——. 1988. *Money, Interest and Banking in Economic Development.* Baltimore: Johns Hopkins University Press.

——. 1989a. Financial Development Models for and Recent Financial Developments in Developing Countries. *Oxford Review of Economic Policy* 5(4):1–16.

——. 1989b. Foreign Debt Instability: An Analysis of National Saving and Domestic Investment Reponses to Foreign Debt Accumulation in 28 Developing Countries. *Journal of International Money and Finance* 8:315–344.

——. 1989c. Taiwan's Current Account Surplus: Embarras de Richesses? Tamkang Chair Lecture, Tamkang University, Taiwan.

——. 1991. Domestic Resource Mobilization in Developing Asia: Four Policy Issues. *Asian Development Review* 9(1):15–39.

Fukuchi, Takao. 1971. The One-Gap versus the Two-Gap Approach. *The Developing Economies* 9:3–15.

Fuller, Wayne A. 1976. *Introduction to Statistical Time Series.* New York: John Wiley.

Galbis, Vincente. 1976. Structuralism and Financial Liberalization. *Finance and Development* 13(2):33–37.

——. 1977. Financial Intermediation and Economic Growth in Less-Developed Countries: A Theoretical Approach. *Journal of Development Studies* 13: 58–72.

——. 1979a. Inflation and Interest Rate Policies in Latin America, 1967–76. *IMF Staff Papers* 26(2):334–366.

——. 1979b. Money, Investment, and Growth in Latin America, 1961–1973. *Economic Development and Cultural Change* 27(3):423–443.

——. 1982. Analytical Aspects of Interest Rate Policies in Less Developed Countries. *Savings and Development* 6(2):111–165.

——. 1986. Financial Sector Liberalization under Oligopolistic Conditions and a Bank Holding Company Structure. *Savings and Development* 10(2): 117–141.

Gallagher, Mark A. 1992. Bank Capital: Definition, Adequacy and Issue Announcement Effects. Ph.D. Thesis. Department of Banking and Finance, City University Business School, London.

Gelb, Alan H. 1989. *Financial Policies, Growth and Efficiency.* Country Economics Department, Working Paper WSP 202. Washington, D.C.: World Bank.

Georgescu-Roegen, Nicholas. 1970. Structural Inflation-Lock and Balanced Growth. *Economies et Sociétés* 4:557–605.

Germidis, Dimitri, and Rachel Meghir. 1989. *The Role of Financial Intermediation in the Mobilization of Household Savings in Developing Countries.* Paris: OECD Development Centre.

Gersovitz, Mark. 1982. The Estimation of the Two-Gap Model. *Journal of International Economics* 12(1):111–124.

Gilbert, R. Alton. 1984. Bank Market Structure and Competition: A Survey. *Journal of Money, Credit and Banking* 16(4):617–645.

Giovannini, Alberto. 1983. The Interest Elasticity of Savings in Developing

Countries: The Existing Evidence. *World Development* 11(7):601–607.

———. 1985. Savings and the Real Interest Rate in LDCs. *Journal of Development Economics* 18:197–217.

Glezakos, Constantine. 1978. Inflation and Growth: A Reconsideration of the Evidence from the LDCs. *Journal of Developing Areas* 12(January): 171–182.

Godfrey, L. G. 1978a. A Note on the Use of Durbin's h-Test When the Equation Is Estimated by Instrumental Variables. *Econometrica* 46:225–228.

———. 1978b. Testing against General Autoregressive and Moving Average Error Models When the Regressors Include Lagged Dependent Variables. *Econometrica* 46:1293–1302.

Goldfeld, Stephen M., and Daniel S. Sichel. 1990. The Demand for Money. In *Handbook of Monetary Economics,* vol. 1, ed. Benjamin M. Friedman and Frank H. Hahn, pp. 300–356. Amsterdam: Elsevier Science Publishers.

Goldsmith, Raymond W. 1969. *Financial Structure and Development.* New Haven, Conn.: Yale University Press.

Gonzales Arrieta, Gerardo M. 1988. Interest Rates, Savings and Growth in LDCs: An Assessment of Recent Empirical Research. *World Development* 16:589–605.

Goode, Richard. 1984. *Government Finance in Developing Countries.* Washington, D.C.: Brookings Institution.

Granger, Clive W. J. 1969. Investigating Causal Relations by Econometrical Models and Cross Spectral Methods. *Econometrica* 37(July):424–438.

Granger, Clive W. J., and Paul Newbold. 1986. *Forecasting Economic Time Series.* San Diego: Academic Press.

Gray, Jack, and Gordon White, eds. 1982. *China's New Development Strategy.* London: Academic Press.

Greene, William H. 1991. *Econometric Analysis.* New York: Macmillan.

Greer, Charles E., ed. 1988. *China Facts and Figures Annual,* vol. 11. Gulf Breeze, Fla.: Academic International Press.

———. 1989. *China Facts and Figures Annual,* vol. 12. Gulf Breeze, Fla.: Academic International Press.

Griffin, Keith B., and John L. Enos. 1969. Foreign Assistance: Objectives and Consequences. *Economic Development and Cultural Change* 18:313–327.

Grub, Phillip, and Bryan L. Sudweeks. 1988. Securities Markets and the People's Republic of China. *China Newsletter* 74(May/June):11–16.

Gunning, John W. 1983. Rationing in an Open Economy: Fix Price Equilibrium and Two-Gap Models. *European Economic Review* 23:71–98.

Gupta, Kanhaya L. 1984. *Financial and Economic Growth.* London: Croom Helm.

———. 1987. Aggregate Savings, Financial Intermediation, and Interest Rate. *Review of Economics and Statistics* 69(2):303–311.

Gupta, L. C. 1983. *Growth Theory and Strategy: New Direction.* London: Oxford University Press.

Gurley, John G., and Edward S. Shaw. 1955. Financial Aspects of Economic Development. *American Economic Review* 45(4):515–538.

———. 1960. *Money in a Theory of Finance.* Washington, D.C.: Brookings

Institution.

Harding, Harry. 1987. *China's Secondary Revolution.* Washington, D.C.: Brookings Institution.

Harris, Donald J. 1977. *Capital Accumulation and Income Distribution.* London: Routledge & Kegan Paul.

Harris, James W. 1979. Financial Deepening as a Prerequisite to Investment Growth: Empirical Evidence from Five East Asian Economies. *The Developing Economies* 17(3):295–308.

Harvey, Andrew. 1990. *The Economic Analysis of Time Series,* 2nd ed. London: Philip Allan.

Hax, Herbert. 1989. Ownership and Management in the Chinese Firm – The Agency Problem. In *Trends of Economic Development in East Asia,* ed. W. Klenner, pp. 393–402. Berlin: Springer-Verlag.

Hazari, Bharat. 1976. Foreign Aid, Conspicious Consumption and Domestic Savings: Some Theoretical Observations. *Journal of Development Studies* 12:197–207.

Heller, Peter S. 1975. A Model of Public Fiscal Behavior in Developing Countries: Aid, Investment and Taxation. *American Economic Review* 65: 429–444.

Helpman, Elhanan, and Efraim Sadka. 1979. Optimal Financing of the Government's Budget: Taxes, Bonds or Money? *American Economic Review* 69(1):152–160.

Hemming, Richard, and Ali M. Mansoor. 1988. *Privatization and Public Enterprises.* Occasional Paper No. 56. Washington, D.C.: International Monetary Fund.

Hiroyuki, Imai. 1987. *Estimation of Inflationary Pressure in China's Consumption Goods Market.* Discussion Paper. Department of Economics, Johns Hopkins University, Baltimore.

Ho, Henry C. Y. 1984. *Income Taxation and Direct Foreign Investment in China.* Discussion Paper No. 32. Department of Economics, University of Hong Kong.

——. 1985. *Distribution of Profits and the Change from Profit Remission to Tax Payments for State Enterprise in China.* Discussion Paper No. 57. Department of Economics, University of Hong Kong.

Ho, Yan-ki. 1986. China's Stock Issues – A Descriptive Note. Discussion Paper No. 8. Department of Economics, University of Hong Kong.

Ho, Yan-ki, and Joseph S. K. Wan. 1988. China's "Stock" Market. Working Paper No. 2. School of Business, Hong Kong Baptist College.

Holden, K., and A. Broomhead. 1990. An Examination of Vector Autoregressive Forecasts for the U.K. Economy. *International Journal of Forecasting* 6:11–23.

Hsiao, Cheng. 1981. Autoregressive Modelling and Money-Income Causality Detection. *Journal of Monetary Economics* 7(1):85–106.

Hsu, John C. 1990. *China's Foreign Trade Reform.* Cambridge, U.K.: Cambridge University Press.

Hsueh, Tien-tung, and Koon-lam Shea. 1981. Trade Stability, Balance and Trading Partner of the PRC. *The Developing Economies* 19:242–254.

Hsueh, Tien T., and Tun O. Woo. 1983. China's Foreign Trade since Deng

Xiaoping's Rise to Power. In *China in Readjustment,* ed. Chi K. Leung and Stephen Chin. Hong Kong: Centre of Asian Studies, University of Hong Kong.

Hu, Yebi. 1993. *China's Capital Market.* Hong Kong: Chinese University Press.

Huang Hsiao, Katharine. 1971. *Money and Monetary Policy in Communist China.* New York: Columbia University Press.

——. 1982. Money and Banking in the PRC: Recent Developments. *China Quarterly* September:462–477.

——. 1984. *Money and Banking in the Chinese Mainland.* Taipei: Chung-Hua Institute for Economic Research.

——. 1987. *The Government Budget and Fiscal Policy in Mainland China.* Taipei: Chung-Hua Institute for Economic Research.

Hussain, Athar, and Nicholas Stern. 1991. Economic Reform in China. *Economic Policy* April:141–186.

Igarashi, Masaki. 1989. Chinese Bonds in the Introduction of Foreign Capital. *China Newsletter,* Japan External Trade Organization (JETRO) 82(September):9–15.

Imai, Satoshi. 1991. China's Foreign Debt – Where It Stands Today. *China Newsletter,* Japan External Trade Organization (JETRO) 93(July/August):16–23.

Intriligator, Michael D., ed. 1971. *Frontiers of Quantitative Economics,* vol. 1. Amsterdam: North Holland Publishing Company.

——. 1974. *Frontiers of Quantitative Economics,* vol. 2. Amsterdam: North Holland Publishing Company.

Ishikawa, S. 1983. China's Economic Growth since 1949 – An Assessment. *China Quarterly* 94(June):242–281.

——. 1984. China's Economic System Reform: Underlying Factors and Prospects. In *China's Changed Road to Development,* ed. Neville Maxwell and Bruce McFarlane, pp. 9–20. Oxford: Pergamon Press.

Ito, Kazuhisa. 1984. Development Finance and Commercial Banks in Korea. *The Developing Economies* 22(4):453–475.

Ize, Alain, and Guillermo Ortiz. 1987. Fiscal Rigidities, Public Debt, and Capital Flight. *IMF Staff Papers* 34(2):311–332.

Jansen, Karel. 1989a. Financial Development and the Intersectoral Transfer of Resources: The Case of Thailand. *Development and Change* 20(1):5–34.

——. 1989b. Monetary Policy and Financial Development. In *Financing Economic Development: A Structural Approach to Monetary Policy,* ed. E. V. K. FitzGerald and Rob Vos, pp. 55–82. Aldershot, England: Gower.

Jao, Yu C. 1976. Financial Deepening and Economic Growth: A Cross Section Analysis. *Malaysia Economic Review* 21(1):47–58.

——. 1980. Hong Kong as a Regional Financial Centre: Evolution and Prospects. In *Hong Kong: Dilemmas of Growth,* ed. Chi K. Leung, J. W. Cushman, and Gungwu Wang, pp. 161–194. Canberra: Australian National University Press.

——. 1985. Financial Deepening and Economic Growth: Theory, Evidence and Policy. *Greek Economic Review* 7(3):187–225.

——. 1990. Financial Reform in China 1978-1989: Retrospect and Reappraisal. *Journal of Economics and International Relations* 3(4):279-309.

Jao, Yu C., and C. K. Leung. 1986. *China's Special Economic Zones.* New York: Oxford University Press.

Jao, Yu C., Victor Mok, and Lok S. Ho, eds. 1989. *Economic Development in Chinese Societies: Models and Experiences.* Hong Kong: Hong Kong University Press.

Jao, Yu C., et al. 1985. *Hong Kong and 1997: Strategies for the Future.* Hong Kong: Centre of Asian Studies, University of Hong Kong.

Jensen, Michael C. 1986. Agency Costs of Free Cash Flow, Corporate Finance and Takeovers. *American Economic Review,* Papers and Proceedings 76(May):323-329.

Jensen, Michael C., and William H. Meckling. 1976. Theory of the Firm: Managerial Behavior, Agency Costs and Ownership Structure. *Journal of Financial Economics* 3:305-360.

——. 1979. Rights and Production Functions: An Application to Labor Managed Firms and Codetermination. *Journal of Business* 52(4):469-506.

Joint Economic Committee, Congress of the United States. 1978. *Chinese Economy Post-Mao, Vol. 1 – Policy and Performance.* Washington, D.C.: U.S. Government Printing Office.

Junker, Louis J. 1967. Capital Accumulation, Savings-Centered Theory and Economic Development. *Journal of Economic Issues* 1:25-43.

Kaen, Fred R., and George A. Hachey. 1983. Eurocurrency and National Money Market Interest Rates: An Empirical Investigation of Causality. *Journal of Money, Credit and Banking* 15(3):327-338.

Kahkonen, Juha. 1987. Liberalization Policies and Welfare in a Financially Repressed Economy. *IMF Staff Papers* 34(3):531-547.

Kalecki, Michal. 1969a. *Introduction to the Theory of Growth in a Socialist Economy.* Oxford: Basil Blackwell.

——. 1969b. *Theory of Economic Dynamics: An Essay on Cyclical and Long Run Changes in Capitalist Economy.* New York: Augustus M. Kelly.

——. 1970. Problems of Financing Economic Development in a Mixed Economy. In *Induction, Growth and Trade: Essays in Honour of Sir Roy Harrod,* ed. W. A. Eltis, M. Fg. Scott, and J. N. Wolfe. Oxford: Claredon Press.

——. 1972. *Selected Essays on the Economic Growth of the Socialist and the Mixed Economy.* London: Cambridge University Press.

——. 1976. *Essays on Developing Economies.* Sussex: Harvester Press.

Kapur, Basant K. 1976a. Alternative Stabilization Policies for Less Developed Economies. *Journal of Political Economy* 84(4):777-796.

——. 1976b. Two Approaches to Ending Inflation. In *Money and Finance in Economic Growth and Development,* ed. Ronald I. McKinnon, pp. 199-226. New York: Marcel Dekker.

——. 1986. *Studies in Inflationary Dynamics: Financial Repression and Financial Liberalization in Less Developed Countries.* Singapore: Singapore University Press.

Kato, Hiroyuki. 1988. China's Economy at the Crossroads – Rapid Growth or Stable Growth. *China Newsletter,* Japan External Trade Organization (JETRO) 75(July/August):8-15.

Kessides, Christine, Timothy King, Mario Nuti, and Catherine Sokil. 1989.

Financial Reform in Socialist Economies. Economic Development Institute Seminar Series. Washington, D.C.: World Bank.

Khan, Zafar S. 1991. *Patterns of Direct Foreign Investment in China.* Washington, D.C.: World Bank.

Kincaid, G. Russell. 1988. Policy Implications of Structural Changes in Financial Markets. *Finance and Development* 25(1):2–5.

Kindleberger, Charles P. 1987. Financial Deregulation and Economic Performance. *Journal of Development Economics* 27(1):339–353.

Kitchen, Richard L. 1986. *Finance for the Developing Countries.* Chichester: John Wiley & Sons.

Koh, Sung S. 1989. *The Korean Stock Market: Structure, Behavior and Test of Market Efficiency.* Ph.D. Thesis. Department of Banking and Finance, City University Business School, London.

Kohsaka, Akira. 1984. The High Interest Rate Policy under Financial Repression. *The Developing Economies* 22(4):419–452.

———. 1987. Financial Liberalization in Asian NICs: A Comparative Study of Korea and Taiwan in the 1980s. *The Developing Economies* 25(4): 325–345.

Komiya, Ryutaro. 1989. Macroeconomics Development of China: Overheating in 1984–87 and Problems of Reform. *Journal of Japanese and International Economics* 3:64–121.

Kornai, Janos. 1982. *Growth, Shortage and Efficiency.* Oxford: Basil Blackwell.

———. 1986. *Contradictions and Dilemmas: Studies on the Soviet Economy and Society.* Cambridge: MIT Press.

Koutsoyiannis, A. 1977. *Theory of Econometric,* 2nd ed. London: Macmillan Press.

Krueger, Anne O. 1981. Interactions between Inflation and Trade Regime Objectives in Stabilization Programs. In *Economic Stabilization in Developing Countries,* ed. William R. Cline and Sidney Weintraub. Washington, D.C.: Brookings Institution.

Kumar, Ramesh C. 1983. Money in Development: A Monetary Growth Model à la McKinnon. *Southern Economic Journal* 50(1):18–36.

Kwok, Raymond H. F., and Kui-Wai Li. 1992. The Inter-relationship between Macroecnomics Variables and Stock Prices in the Newly Industrialized Economies of Asia. In *Rising Capital Market: Empirical Studies,* ed. Thomas Fetherston and Theodore Bos. Greenwich, Conn.: JAI Press.

Lal, Deepak. 1971. The Foreign Exchange Bottleneck Revisited: A Geometric Note. *Economic Development and Cultural Change* 20:722–730.

Lal, Deepak, and Sweder van Wijnbergen. 1985. Government Deficits, the Real Interest Rate and LDC Debt. *European Economic Review* 29(2):157–191.

Lam, N. V. 1989. The Interrelationship between Domestic Finance and External Finance. Seminar on the Mobilization of ASEAN Domestic Resources through Financial Institutions, ASEAN Committee on Finance and Banking, Kuala Lumpur, Malaysia.

Laumas, Prem S. 1982. Exports and the Propensity to Save. *Economic Development and Cultural Change* 4(July):831–841.

Lee Travers, S. 1982. Bias in Chinese Economic Statistics: The Case of the

Typical Example Investigation. *China Quarterly* 91(September):478–485.

Leff, Nathaniel H. 1976. Capital Markets in the Less Developed Countries: The Group Principle. In *Money and Finance in Economic Growth and Development*, ed. Ronald I. McKinnon, pp. 97–122. New York: Marcel Dekker.

Leff, Nathaniel H., and Kazuo Sato. 1975. A Simultaneous-Equations Model of Savings in Developing Countries. *Journal of Political Economy* 83(6): 1217–1228.

——. 1980. Macroeconomic Adjustment in Developing Countries: Instability, Short-Run Growth and External Dependency. *Review of Economics and Statistics* 62(2):170–179.

Levhari, David, and Don Patinkin. 1968. The Role of Money in a Simple Growth Model. *American Economic Review* 58(3):713–753.

Li, Chengrui. 1981. The Balance of Finance and Credit. *Jingji Yanjiu [Economic Research]* March(3):3–12.

Li, Kui-Wai. 1984. *Financing Economic Development in China 1978–1984.* Discussion Paper No. 41. Department of Economics, University of Hong Kong.

——. 1988a. The Reform and Management of Economic Finance in the PRC. Working Paper No. 28. Department of Business and Management, City Polytechnic of Hong Kong.

——. 1988b. The Reform of Some Economic Concepts in the PRC. In *Proceedings of the Tenth International Symposium on Asian Studies, Vol. 1,* pp. 263–274. Hong Kong: Asian Research Service.

——. 1988c. Sources of Secondary Data for Research on the Chinese Economy. Working Paper No. 22. Department of Business and Management, City Polytechnic of Hong Kong.

——. 1989a. The Chinese Version of Development Finance. *Atlantic Economic Journal* 17(1):63.

——. 1989b. Macro-Approaches to Development Finance: A Preliminary Survey. Research Paper No. 4. Department of Economics and Finance, City Polytechnic of Hong Kong.

——. 1991. Money, Inflation and Financial Repression in China. In *Proceedings of the Second International Conference on Asia-Pacific Financial Markets,* pp. 244–253. City Polytechnic of Hong Kong.

——. 1992a. Financial Inter-relationships in China's Economic Reform. Western Economic Association, 67th Annual International Conference, San Francisco.

——. 1992b. Savings, Foreign Resource and Monetary Aggregates in China, 1954–1989. *China Economic Review* 3(2):126–133.

Li, Kui-Wai, and Michael T. Skully. 1991. Financial Deepening and Institutional Development: Some Asian Experiences. *Savings and Development* 15(2):147–165.

——. 1992. Accumulation of Financial Resources in Asian Economies. *Savings and Development* 16(3):225–241.

Li, Yining. 1989. *The China Economy: Where Is She Heading?* Hong Kong: Commercial Press Publisher.

Li, Yunqi. 1989. China's Inflation: Causes, Effects, and Solutions. *Asian Survey* 29(7):655–668.

——. 1991. Changes in China's Monetary Policy. *Asian Survey* 31(5):422-433.

Lim, David. 1982. Fiscal Incentives and Direct Foreign Investment in Less Developed Countries. *Journal of Development Studies* 19:207-212.

Lin, Cyril Chiren. 1981. The Reinstatement of Economics in China Today. *China Quarterly* 85(March):1-48.

Liu, Guoguang. 1979. Some Issues Concerning the National Economic Overall Balance. *Jingji Yanjiu [Economic Research]* 3:36-44.

Liu, Guoguang, and Renwei Zhao. 1982. Relationship between Planning and the Market under Socialism. In *Economic Reform in the PRC*, ed. George C. Wang, pp. 89-104. Boulder, Colo.: Westview Press.

Liu, Zhiqiang. 1988. China's National Debt. *Beijing Review* 31(33):28-29, 40.

Lorenzen, G. 1989. *Income, Consumption, Saving and Hoarding of Private Households in China.* Discussion Paper. China Economic Research Center, University of East Asia, Macau.

Lundberg, Erik, ed. 1977. *Inflation Theory and Anti-Inflation Policy.* London: Macmillan Press.

MacKinnon, James G. 1992. Model Specification Tests and Artificial Regression. *Journal of Economic Literature* 30(March):102-146.

Mao, Yushi, and Paul Hare. 1989. Chinese Experience in the Introduction of a Market Mechanism into a Planned Economy: The Role of Pricing. *Journal of Economic Survey* 3(2):137-158.

Marquez, Jaime. 1985. Foreign Exchange Constraints and Growth Possibilities in the LDCs. *Journal of Development Economics* 19:39-57.

Marty, Alvin L. 1967. Growth and the Welfare Cost of Inflationary Finance. *Journal of Political Economy* 75(1):71-76.

Mason, Edwards. 1960. The Role of Government in Economic Development. *American Economic Review* 50:636-641.

Mathieson, Donald J. 1979. Financial Reform and Capital Flows in a Developing Economy. *IMF Staff Papers* September:450-489.

——. 1980. Financial Reform and Stabilization Policy in a Developing Economy. *Journal of Development Economics* 7:359-395.

——. 1986. International Capital Flows, Capital Control and Financial Control. In *Financial Policy and Reform in Pacific Basin Countries*, ed. H. S. Cheng. Lexington, Mass.: Lexington Books.

McKinnon, Ronald I. 1964. Foreign Exchange Constraints in Economic Development and Efficient Aid Allocation. *The Economic Journal* 74(June): 389-409.

——. 1973. *Money and Capital in Economic Development.* Washington, D.C.: Brookings Institution.

——. 1976. *Money and Finance in Economic Growth and Development.* New York: Marcel Dekker.

——. 1981. Financial Repression and the Liberalization Problem within Less-Developed Countries. In *The World Economic Order: Past and Prospects*, ed. Sven Grassman and Erik Lundberg. London: Macmillan.

——. 1984. The International Market and Economic Liberalization in LDCs. *The Developing Economies* 22:476-481.

——. 1986. Financial Liberalization and Economic Development. In *Financial Policy and Reform in Pacific Basin Countries*, ed. H. S. Cheng. Lexington, Mass.: Lexington Books.

——. 1988a. Financial Liberalization and Economic Development. Occasional Paper No. 6. International Centre for Economic Growth, Stanford, Calif., Stanford University.

——. 1988b. Financial Liberalization in Retrospect: Interest Rate Policies in LDCs. In *The State of Development Economics,* ed. Gustav Ranis and T. Paul Schultz. Oxford: Basil Blackwell.

——. 1989. The Order of Liberalization for Opening the Soviet Economy. Prepared for the International Task Force on Foreign Economic Relations, New York.

——. 1990a. *Financial Repression and the Productivity of Capital: Empirical Findings on Interest Rates and Exchange Rates.* Distinguished Speakers Program. Asian Development Bank, Manila.

——. 1990b. *Stabilizing the Rubble: The Problem of Internal Currency Convertibility.* Presented to the OECD Development Center, Paris.

——. 1991a. *Liberalizing Foreign Trade in a Socialist Economy: The Problem of Negative Value Added.* Memorandum Series No. 293. Center for Research in Economic Growth, Stanford, Calif., Stanford University.

——. 1991b. *The Order of Economic Liberalization.* Baltimore: Johns Hopkins University Press.

——. 1991c. *Taxation, Money and Credit in a Liberalizing Socialist Economy.* Memorandum Series No. 300. Center for Research in Economic Growth, Stanford, Calif., Stanford University.

——. 1992. *Macroeconomic Control in Liberalizing Socialist Economies: Asian and European Parallels.* Working Paper No. PB92-05. Centre for Pacific Basin Monetary and Economic Studies, Federal Reserve Bank of San Francisco.

McKinnon, Ronald I., and Donald J. Mathieson. 1981. How to Manage a Repressed Economy. In *Essays in International Finance,* vol. 145. Department of Economics, Princeton University, Princeton, N.J.

Michalopoulos, Constantine. 1975. Production and Substitution in Two-Gap Models. *Journal of Development Studies* 11(4):343–356.

Ministry of Foreign Economic Relations and Trade. Various years. *Monthly Bulletin of Statistics.* Beijing: State Statistical Bureau.

Modigliani, Franco. 1970. The Life Cycle Hypothesis of Saving and Intercountry Differences in the Saving Ratio. In *Induction, Growth and Trade: Essays in Honour of Sir Roy Harrod,* ed. W. A. Eltis, M. Fg. Scott, and J. N. Wolfe. Oxford: Claredon Press.

——. 1986. Life Cycle, Individual Thrift, and the Wealth of Nations. *American Economic Review* 76(3):297–313.

Molho, Lazaros E. 1986. Interest Rates, Savings, and Investment in Developing Countries: A Re-examination of the McKinnon-Shaw Hypotheses. *IMF Staff Papers* 33(1):90–116.

Moore, B. J. 1986. Inflation and Financial Deepening. *Journal of Development Economics* 20:125–133.

Muellbauer, John, and Richard Portes. 1978. Macroeconomic Models with Quantity Rationing. *The Economic Journal* 88(December):788–821.

Mundell, Robert. 1963. Inflation and Real Interest. *Journal of Political Economy* June:280–283.

Nakajima, Seiichi. 1983. The Prospects for Achievement of China's Long-Term Economic Target: An Investment Perspective. *China Newsletter,* Japan External Trade Organization (JETRO) 42(January/February):15-21.

Nambu, Minoru. 1988. Recent Trends in China's National Finance and Taxation System. *China Newsletter,* Japan External Trade Organization (JETRO) 72(January/February):2-9.

———. 1991. Problems in China's Financial Reforms. *China Newsletter,* Japan External Trade Organization (JETRO) 92(May/June):2-10, 18.

Naughton, Barry. 1985. False Starts and Second Wind: Financial Reforms in China's Industrial System. In *The Political Economy of Reform in Post-Mao China,* ed. Elizabeth J. Perry and Christine Wong, pp. 223-252. Cambridge: Harvard University Press.

———. 1987a. The Decline of Central Control Over Investment in Post-Mao China. In *Policy Implementation in Post-Mao China,* ed. David M. Lampton. Berkeley and Los Angeles: University of California Press.

———. 1987b. Macroeconomic Policy and Response in the Chinese Economy: The Impact of the Reform Process. *Journal of Comparative Economics* 11:334-353.

———. 1991. Why Has Economic Reform Led to Inflation? *American Economic Review,* Papers and Proceedings 81(2):207-211.

Neher, Philip A. 1971. *Economic Growth and Development: A Mathematical Introduction.* London: John Wiley & Sons.

Newlyn, Walter T. 1977. The Inflation Tax in Developing Countries. *Journal of Development Studies* 13(1):8-21.

———. 1985. Measuring Tax Effort in Developing Countries. *Journal of Development Studies* 21:390-405.

———. ed. 1977. *The Financing of Economic Development.* Oxford: Claredon Press.

Nichols, Donald A. 1974. Some Principles of Inflationary Finance. *Journal of Political Economy* 82(2):423-430.

Nolan, Peter, and Fureng Dong, eds. 1990. *The Chinese Economy and Its Future.* Cambridge, Mass.: Polity Press.

North, Douglass C. 1987. Institutions, Transaction Costs and Economic Growth. *Economic Inquiry* 25(3):419-428.

Oborne, Michael. 1986. *China Special Economic Zones.* Paris: OECD Development Centre.

Okubo, Isao. 1990. Financial Difficulties and Prospects for the Future. *China Newsletter,* Japan External Trade Organization (JETRO) 86(May/June): 12-18.

Patrick, Hugh T. 1966. Financial Development and Economic Growth in Underdeveloped Countries. *Economic Development and Cultural Change* January:174-189.

Peebles, Gavin. 1982. *The Interpretation of Monetary Events in China: A Preliminary Analysis from a Comparative Socialist Perspective.* Discussion Paper No. 8. Department of Economics, University of Hong Kong.

———. 1984. Money under Modern Socialism: A Review with Tested Applications to the People's Republic of China. Discussion Paper No. 33. Department of Economics, University of Hong Kong.

——. 1987. Chinese Monetary Management 1953-1982. In *China's Economic Reforms*, ed. Joseph Chai and Chi K. Leung, pp. 503-550. Centre of Asian Studies, University of Hong Kong.

——. 1991. *Money in the People's Republic of China*. Sydney: Allen & Unwin.

Perkins, Dwight H. 1986. *China—Asia's Next Economic Giant?* New York: University of Washington Press.

——. 1988. Reforming China's Economic System. *Journal of Economic Literature* 26(June):601-645.

Pesaran, M. Hashem, and Bahram Pesaran. 1987. *Microfit: An Interactive Econometric Software Package User Manual*. London: Oxford University Press.

Phelps, Edmund S. 1965. Second Essay on the Golden Rule of Accumulation. *American Economic Review* 55(4):793-813.

Polak, Jacques J. 1989. *Financial Policies and Development*. Paris: Development Centre of the Organization for Economic Cooperation and Development.

Porter, Richard C., and Susan I. Ranney. 1982. An Eclectic Model of Recent LDC Macroeconomic Policy Analysis. *World Development* 10(9):751-756.

Portes, Richard R. 1977. The Control of Inflation: Lessons from East European Experience. *Economica* 44(May):109-130.

——. 1983. Central Planning and Monetarism: Fellow Travellers? In *Marxism, Central Planning and the Soviet Economy*, ed. Padma Desai. Cambridge: MIT Press.

Portes, Richard R., and Anita Santorum. 1987. Money and the Consumption Goods Market in China. *Journal of Comparative Economics* 11:354-371.

Portes, Richard R., and David Winter. 1977. The Supply of Consumption Goods in Centrally Planned Economies. *Journal of Comparative Economics* 1(December):351-365.

——. 1980. Disequilibrium Estimates for Consumption Goods Markets in Centrally Planned Economies. *Review of Economic Studies* 47(146): 137-159.

Prybyla, Jan S. 1981. Key Issues in the Chinese Economy. *Asian Survey* 21(9): 925-946.

——. 1986. China's Economic Experiment: From Mao to Market. *Problems of Communism* 35(1):21-38.

Qian, Yingyi. 1988. Urban and Rural Household Savings in China. *IMF Staff Papers* 35(December):592-627.

Rajaram, Anand. 1991. *Reforming Prices: The Experience of China, Hungary and Poland*. Washington, D.C.: World Bank.

Rawski, Thomas G. 1979. *Economic Growth and Employment in China*. London: Oxford University Press.

Reynolds, Bruce L. 1983. Economic Reform and External Imbalance in China, 1978-81. *American Economic Review*, Papers and Proceedings 73: 325-328.

——. 1986. Monetary Control, Over-Investment and Inflationary Pressure during Decentralization. In *China's System Reforms Conference*, Conference Paper No. 33. Hong Kong: Centre of Asian Studies, University of Hong Kong.

——. 1987a. Towards a Macro Model of the Chinese Economy. In *China's*

Economic Reforms, ed. Joseph Chai and C. K. Leung, pp. 49–63. Hong Kong: Centre of Asian Studies, University of Hong Kong.

——. 1987b. Trade, Employment and Inequality in Post-Reform China. *Journal of Comparative Economics* 11:479–489.

Reynolds, Paul D. 1982. *China's International Banking and Financial System.* New York: Praeger.

Riskin, Carl. 1987. *China's Political Economy: The Quest for Development since 1949.* London: Oxford University Press.

Roy, Durgadas. 1986. Financial Structure and Development in Some Third World Asian Countries: A Cross-Country Review. *Economic Bulletin for Asia and the Pacific* 37(1):55–66.

Santomero, Anthony M. 1984. Modeling the Banking Firm: A Survey. *Journal of Money, Credit and Banking* 16(4, Part 2):576–616.

Scherer, John, ed. 1978–1987. *China Facts and Figures Annual.* Gulf Breeze, Fla.: Academic International Press.

Schumpeter, Joseph A. [1934] 1983. *The Theory of Economic Development.* New York: Transaction Books, Harvard University Press.

Schwert, G. W. 1990. Stock Returns and Real Activity: A Century of Evidence. *Journal of Finance* 45(4):1237–1257.

Schworm, William E. 1980. Financial Constraints and Capital Accumulation. *International Economic Review* 21(3):643–660.

Shahadan, Faridah, and Nor A. H. Idris. 1987. *Financing for Development: With Special Reference to ASEAN.* Singapore: Oxford University Press.

Shaw, Edward S. 1973. *Financial Deepening in Economic Development.* New York: Oxford University Press.

Shaw, G. K. 1967. Monetary-Fiscal Policy for Growth and the Balance of Payments Constraints. *Econometrica* 35(May):198–202.

Shen, Gensheng. 1993. The Emerging Securities Market in China. International Conference on the Asia-Pacific Economy, Economic Modelling Bureau of Australia, Cairns, Australia.

Shen, Xiaofang. 1990. A Decade of Direct Foreign Investment in China. *Problems of Communism* 39(2):61–74.

Sheng, Hong, and Zou Gang. 1990. On the Money Supply in the Course of Economic Development: The So-Called Loss of Control Over Money in 1984. *Chinese Economic Studies* 23(3):75–90.

Shionoya, Tsukumo. 1970. Economic Growth and the Price Level. In *Induction, Growth and Trade: Essays in Honour of Sir Roy Harrod*, ed. W. A. Eltis, M. Fg. Scott, and J. N. Wolfe. Oxford: Claredon Press.

Shoup, Carl S. 1962. Debt Financing and Future Generations. *Economic Journal* December:887–897.

Sims, Christopher A. 1972. Money, Income and Causality. *American Economic Review* 62(September):540–552.

Sines, Richard H. 1979. Financial Deepening and Industrial Production: A Microeconomic Analysis of the Venezuelan Food Processing Sector. *Social and Economic Studies* 28(2):450–474.

Skully, Michael T., and George J. Viksnins. 1987. *Financing East Asia's Success.* London: Macmillan.

Snowden, P. N. 1987. Financial Market Liberalization in LDCs: The Incidence of Risk Allocation Effects of Interest Rate Increases. *Journal of Development Studies* 24(1):83–93.

State Information Centre. 1992. *Macroeconomic Applications System Software Package.* Department of Data Base and Programme Bank Management, Beijing.

Stiglitz, Joseph E., and Andrew Weiss. 1981. Credit Rationing in Markets with Imperfect Information. *American Economic Review* 71(3):393–410.

Strong, Norman, and Martin Walker. 1987. *Information and Capital Markets.* Oxford: Basil Blackwell.

Sundararajan, Vasudevan. 1990. *Financial Sector Reform and Central Banking in Centrally Planned Economies.* Working Paper WP/90/120. Washington, D.C.: International Monetary Fund.

Szapary, Gyorgy. 1989. Monetary Policy and System Reforms in China. Ninth Latin American Meeting of the Econometric Society, Santiago, Chile.

Tallman, Ellis W. 1989. Financial Asset Pricing Theory: A Review of Recent Developments. *Economic Review,* Federal Reserve Bank of Atlanta, November/December:26–41.

Tam, On Kit. 1985. *China's Agricultural Modernization.* London: Croom Helm.

——. 1986. Reform of China's Banking System. *World Economy* 9(4):427–440.

——. 1987. The Development of China's Financial System. *Australian Journal of Chinese Affairs* 17(January):95–113.

——. 1988. Rural Finance in China. *China Quarterly* 113(March):60–76.

——. 1991. Capital Market Development in China. *World Development* 19(5): 511–532.

Tanzi, Vito. 1976. Fiscal Policy, Keynesian Economics and the Mobilization of Savings in Developing Countries. *World Development* 4(10):907–917.

——. 1978. Inflation, Real Tax Revenue and the Case for Inflationary Finance: Theory with an Application to Argentina. *IMF Staff Papers* 25(September):417–451.

——. 1982. Fiscal Disequilibrium in Developing Countries. *World Development* 10(12):1069–1082.

——. 1989. The Impact of Macroeconomic Policies on the Level of Taxation and the Fiscal Balance in Developing Countries. *IMF Staff Papers* 36(3): 633–656.

Tanzi, Vito, and Mario I. Blejer. 1982. Inflation, Interest Rate Policy, and Currency Substitutions in Developing Economies: A Discussion of Some Major Issues. *World Development* 10(9):781–789.

Tanzi, Vito, Mario I. Blejer, and Mario O. Teijeiro. 1987. Inflation and the Measurement of Fiscal Deficits. *IMF Staff Papers* December:711–738.

Taylor, Lance. 1974. Book Reviews of *Money and Capital in Economic Development,* by Ronald I. McKinnon, and *Financial Deepening in Economic Development,* by Edward S. Shaw. *Journal of Development Economics* 1:81–84.

——. 1979. *Macro Models for Developing Countries.* New York: McGraw-Hill.

——. 1981. IS/LM in the Tropics: Diagrammatics of the New Structuralist Macro Critique. In *Economic Stabilization in Developing Countries,* ed. William R. Cline and Sidney Weintraub. Washington, D.C.: Brookings Institution.

——. 1983. *Structuralist Macroeconomics: Applicable Models for the Third World.* New York: Basic Books.

Thirlwall, A. P. 1978. *Growth and Development,* 2nd ed. London: Macmillan.

Thornton, Daniel, and Dallas S. Batten. 1985. Lag-Length Selection and Tests of Grange Causality between Money and Income. *Journal of Money, Credit and Banking* 17(2):164–178.

Thornton, John, and Sri Ram Poudyal. 1990. Money and Capital in Economic Development: A Test of the McKinnon Hypothesis for Nepal. *Journal of Money, Credit and Banking* 22(3):395–399.

Tinbergen, J. 1970. A Didactical Note on the Two-Gap Theory. In *Induction, Growth and Trade: Essays in Honour of Sir Roy Harrod,* ed. W. A. Eltis, M. Fg. Scott, and J. N. Wolfe. Oxford: Claredon Press.

Tobin, James. 1961. Money, Capital, and Other Stores of Value. *American Economic Review,* Papers and Proceedings 2(May):26–37.

——. 1965. Money and Economic Growth. *Econometrica* 33(4):671–684.

——. 1969. A General Equilibrium Approach to Monetary Theory. *Journal of Money, Credit and Banking* 7(1):15–29.

——. 1974. Monetary Policy in 1974 and Beyond. *Brookings Papers on Economic Activity* I:219–232.

——. 1978. Monetary Policies and the Economy: The Transmission Mechanism. *Southern Economic Journal* 44(3):421–431.

——. 1980. *Asset Accumulation and Economic Activity.* Oxford: Basil Blackwell.

——. 1982. *Essays in Economics: Vol. 3, Theory and Policy.* Cambridge: MIT Press.

——. 1984. On the Efficiency of the Financial System. *Lloyds Bank Review* July:1–15.

——. [1971] 1987a. *Essays in Economics: Vol. 1, Macroeconomics.* Cambridge: MIT Press, North Holland Publishing Company.

——. 1987b. *Policies for Prosperity – Essays in a Keynesian Mode.* New York: Wheatsheaf Books.

Tobin, James, and William C. Brainard. 1977. Asset Markets and the Cost of Capital. In *Economic Progress: Private Values and Public Policy,* ed. R. Nelson and B. Balassa. Amsterdam: North Holland.

Trzcinka, Charles. 1986. On the Number of Factors in the Arbitrage Pricing Model. *Journal of Finance* 41(2):347–368.

Tsang, Shu-ki. 1989a. Is the Quantity Theory of Money Relevant to China? School of Business Working Paper, Hong Kong Baptist College.

——. 1989b. Problem of Monetary Control for a Socialist Developing Economy under Reform: The Case of China. School of Business Working Paper, Hong Kong Baptist College.

Tso, Peter S. 1983. *A Model of Investment and Financing.* Discussion Paper No. 11. Department of Economics, University of Hong Kong.

U Tun Wai. 1980. The Role of Unorganized Financial Markets in Economic Development and in the Formulation of Monetary Policy. *Savings and Development* 4:259–265.

——. 1989. Public Sector Activities and the Mobilization of ASEAN Domestic Resources. Seminar on the Mobilization of ASEAN Domestic Resources through Financial Institutions. ASEAN Committee on Finance and

Banking, Kuala Lumpur, Malaysia.

van Brabant, Josef M. 1990. Socialist Economics: The Disequilibrium School and the Shortage School. *Journal of Economic Perspectives* 4(2):157–175.

van Wijnbergen, Sweder. 1982. Stagflationary Effects of Monetary Stabilization Policies – A Quantitative Analysis of South Korea. *Journal of Development Economics* 10(2):133–169.

———. 1983a. Credit Policy, Inflation and Growth in a Financially Repressed Economy. *Journal of Development Economics* 13:45–65.

———. 1983b. Interest Rate Management in LDCs. *Journal of Monetary Economics* 12(3):433–452.

———. 1985. Macroeconomic Effects on Change in Bank Interest Rates: Simulation Results for South Korea. *Journal of Development Economics* 18(2-3):541–554.

———. 1986a. *Fiscal Deficits, Exchange Rate Crises and Inflation.* Discussion Paper DRD198, Development Research Department. Washington, D.C.: World Bank.

———. 1986b. Macroeconomic Aspects of the Effectiveness of Foreign Aid: On the Two-Gap Model, Home Goods Disequilibrium and Real Exchange Rate Misalignment. *Journal of International Economics* 21:123–136.

———. 1988. Inflation, Balance of Payments Crisis and Public Sector Deficits. In *Economic Effects of the Government Budget,* ed. Elhanan Helpman, Assaf Razin, and Efraim Sadka. Cambridge: MIT Press.

———. 1989. External Debt, Inflation and the Public Sector: Towards Fiscal Policy for Sustainable Growth. *World Bank Economic Review* 3(3): 297–320.

van Wijnbergen, Sweder, Robert Rocha, and Ritu Anand. 1989. *Inflation, External Debt and Financial Sector Reform: A Quantitative Approach to Consistent Fiscal Policy.* Latin America and the Caribbean Country Department II, WPS 261. Washington, D.C.: World Bank.

Vegh, Carlos A. 1989. Government Spending and Inflationary Finance. *IMF Staff Papers* 36(3):657–676.

Viksnins, George J. 1980. *Financial Deepening in ASEAN Countries.* Honolulu: Pacific Forum, distributed by University of Hawaii Press.

Wang, George C. 1982. *Economic Reform in the PRC.* Boulder, Colo.: Westview Press.

Wang, N. T., ed. 1980. *Business with China: An International Reassessment.* New York: Pergamon Press.

Wang, Yan. 1988. Financial Reform: Decentralization and Liberalization. In *Planning and Finance in China's Economic Reforms,* ed. Thomas P. Lyons and Yan Wang. Cornell University East Asia Paper No. 46. New York: Cornell University.

Weisskopf, Thomas E. 1972a. An Econometric Test of Alternative Constraints on the Growth of Underdeveloped Countries. *Review of Economics and Statistics* 54:67–78.

———. 1972b. The Impact of Foreign Capital Inflow on Domestic Savings in Underdeveloped Countries. *Journal of International Economics* 2:25–38.

Williamson, Oliver E. 1975. *Markets and Hierarchies: Analysis and Anti-Trust Implications.* New York: Free Press.

——. 1986. *Economic Organization.* New York: New York University Press.
Williamson, Stephen D. 1986. Costly Monitoring, Financial Intermediation, and Equilibrium Credit Rationing. *Journal of Monetary Economics* 18:159–179.
Winston, Gordon C. 1971. Capital Utilization in Economic Development. *Economic Journal* 81(March):36–60.
Wong, Kar-Yiu. 1992. Inflation, Corruption, and Income Distribution: The Recent Price Reform in China. *Journal of Macroeconomics* 14(1):105–123.
Woo, S. Jung. 1986. Financial Development and Economic Growth: International Evidence. *Economic Development and Cultural Change* 34(2): 336–346.
World Bank. 1983. *China: Socialist Economic Development,* Vols. 1 and 2. Washington, D.C.: World Bank.
——. 1985. *China: Long Term Development Issues and Options.* Washington, D.C.: World Bank.
——. 1988a. *China: External Trade and Capital.* Washington, D.C.: World Bank.
——. 1988b. *China: Finance and Investment.* Washington, D.C.: World Bank.
——. 1989. *World Development Report 1989.* Washington, D.C.: World Bank.
——. 1990. *China: Macroeconomic Stability and Industrial Growth under Decentralized Socialism.* Washington, D.C.: World Bank.
Wu, Cuilan. 1989. China's Reform of the Financial and Tax System. In *Financial Reform in Socialist Economies,* ed. Christine Kessides et al., pp. 64–72. Economic Development Institute Seminar Series. Washington, D.C.: World Bank.
Wu, Jinglian, and Renwei Zhao. 1987. The Dual Pricing System in China's Industry. *Journal of Comparative Economics* 11:309–318.
Xia, Xiaoxun, and Jun Li. 1987. Consumption Expansion: A Grave Challenge to Reform and Development. In *Reform in China: Challenges and Choices,* ed. Bruce L. Reynolds, pp. 89–107. New York: M. E. Sharpe Publisher.
Xu, Jing'an. 1987. The Stock-Share System: A New Avenue for China's Economic Reform. *Journal of Comparative Economics* 11:509–514.
Xu, Meiheng. 1989. Structural Reform and Financial Reform in China. In *Financial Reform in Socialist Economies,* ed. Christine Kessides et al., pp. 126–146. Economic Development Institute Seminar Series. Washington, D.C.: World Bank.
Xue, Muqiao. 1982. Readjust the National Economy and Strike an Overall Balance. *Chinese Economic Studies* Winter:67–84.
Yamashita, Shoichi. 1968. Macroeconomic Effects on Foreign Aid. *The Developing Economies* 6:356–372.
Yang, Peixin. 1982. *China's Finance.* Beijing: People's Publisher.
——. 1989. Inflation and Monetary Crisis I, II, and III. *Hong Kong Economic Daily,* April 14, 21, and 28.
Yeats, Alexander J. 1991. *China Foreign Trade and Comparative Advantage: Prospects, Problems and Policy Implications.* Washington, D.C.: World Bank.
Yeh, K. C. 1984. Macroeconomic Changes in the Chinese Economy during the Readjustment. *China Quarterly* 100(December):691–716.

Yoo, Jang H. 1977. The Role of Money as a Conduct of Savings and Invest-
    ment in the UDCs. *KYKLOS* 30(3):520–525.
Yoon, Je Cho. 1986. Inefficiencies from Financial Liberalization in the Absence
    of Well-Functioning Equity Markets. *Journal of Money, Credit and
    Banking* 18(2):191–199.
Yueh, Yak Y., and Christopher Howe. 1984. China's International Trade: Policy
    and Organizational Change and Their Place in the Economic Readjust-
    ment. *China Quarterly* 100(December):813–848.
Zhou, Xiaochuan, and Li Zhu. 1987. China's Banking System: Current Status,
    Perspective on Reform. *Journal of Comparative Economics* 11:399–409.

Index

ABOUT THE AUTHOR

KUI-WAI LI is a University Senior Lecturer in the Department of Economics and Finance at City Polytechnic of Hong Kong. Doctor Li received his Ph.D. at the City University Business School in London, and he specializes in Asian finances and economics.